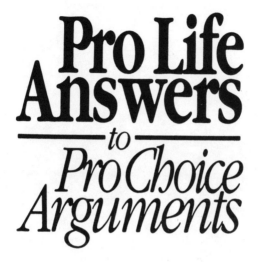

Pro Life Answers

to

Pro Choice Arguments

Pro Life Answers
to
Pro Choice
Arguments

Randy C. Alcorn

MULTNOMAH
Portland, Oregon

Front cover photo is of nineteen week unborn child. Cover photos by Dr. Rainer Jonas. Permission granted from Right to Life of Michigan, Grand Rapids.

Edited by Rodney L. Morris
Cover design by Bruce DeRoos

© 1992, 1994 Eternal Perspective Ministries
Published by Multnomah Publishers, Inc.

Printed in the United States of America.

Library of Congress Cataloging-in-Publication Data

Alcorn, Randy C.
Prolife answers to prochoice arguments / Randy C. Alcorn.
p.   cm.
Includes bibliographical references.
ISBN 0-88070-472-1
1. Pro-life movement—United States—Handbooks, manuals, etc.
2. Abortion—United States—Handbooks, manuals, etc. I. Title.
HQ767.5.U5A43 1992
363.4'6'0973—dc20   92-15392
                                                              CIP

00 01 02 03 — 18 17 16 15

To my parents,
Arthur Loren Alcorn and Lucille Vivian Alcorn,
who gave me the gift of life,
and never made me feel they regretted it.

ACKNOWLEDGMENTS

Some highly qualified people gave their valuable time to examine this manuscript and make insightful corrections and comments. Their expertise helped to ensure medical, scientific, and psychological accuracy, as well as clarity and logical consistency. My heartfelt thanks to:

David J. Sargent, M.D.

Jeannie Hill, R.N.

Kathy Rodriquez, Ph.D.

Randall L. Martin, M.D.

Cynthia L. Martin, R.N.

Rainy Takalo, R.N.

Gary Lovejoy, Ph.D.

Paul deParrie, writer

Carol Everett, former abortion clinic owner

Jennifer Eastberg, former abortion clinic counselor

Kathy Walker, president of Women Exploited by Abortion

Ron and Kathy Norquist, friends and coworkers

Rod Morris, friend and editor

Nanci, Karina, and Angela Alcorn, my best friends and most valued consultants

CONTENTS

2b. The child may die and the mother live, or the mother may die and the child live, proving they are two separate individuals.

2c. The unborn child takes an active role in his own development, controlling the course of the pregnancy and the time of birth.

2d. Being inside something is not the same as being part of something.

2e. Human beings should not be discriminated against because of their place of residence.

3. "The unborn is an embryo or a fetus—just a simple blob of tissue, a product of conception—not a baby. Abortion is terminating a pregnancy, not killing a child." 46

3a. Like *toddler* and *adolescent*, the terms *embryo* and *fetus* do not refer to nonhumans, but to humans at particular stages of development.

3b. Semantics affect perceptions, but they do not change realities; a baby is a baby no matter what we call her.

3c. From the moment of conception the unborn is not simple, but very complex.

3d. Prior to the earliest first trimester abortions, the unborn already has every body part she will ever have.

3e. Every abortion stops a beating heart and terminates measurable brain waves.

3f. Even in the earliest abortions, the unborn child is clearly human in appearance.

3g. Even before the unborn is obviously human in appearance, she is what she is—a human being.

3h. No matter how much better it sounds, "terminating a pregnancy" is still terminating a life.

4. "The fetus may be alive, but so are eggs and sperm. The fetus is a potential human being, not an actual one; it's like a blueprint not a house, an acorn not an oak tree." 53

4a. The ovum and sperm are each a product of another's body; unlike the fertilized egg, neither is an independent entity.

4b. The physical remains after an abortion indicate the end not of a potential life but of an actual life.

4c. Something nonhuman does not become human by getting older and bigger; whatever is human must be human from the beginning.

4d. Comparing preborns and adults to acorns and oaks is dehumanizing and misleading.

4e. Even if the analogy were valid, scientifically speaking an acorn is simply a little oak tree, just as an embryo is a little person.

5. **"The unborn isn't a person, with meaningful life. It's only inches in size, and can't even think; it's less advanced than an animal."   56**

5a. Personhood is properly defined by membership in the human species, not by stage of development within that species.

5b. Personhood is not a matter of size, skill, or degree of intelligence.

5c. The unborn's status should be determined on an objective basis, not on subjective or self-serving definitions of personhood.

5d. It is a scientific fact that there are thought processes at work in unborn babies.

5e. If the unborn's value can be compared to that of an animal, there is no reason not to also compare the value of born people to animals.

5f. It is dangerous when people in power are free to determine whether other, less powerful lives are meaningful.

6. **"A fetus isn't a person until quickening or viability."   62**

6a. Quickening is a gauge of personhood only if someone's reality or value is dependent upon being noticed by another.

6b. Viability is an arbitrary concept. Why not associate personhood with heartbeat, brain waves, or something else?

6c. The point of viability constantly changes because it depends on technology, not the unborn herself. Eventually babies may be viable from the point of conception.

6d. In a broad sense, many born people are not viable because they are incapable of surviving without depending on others.

6e. Someone's helplessness or dependency should motivate us to protect her, not to destroy her.

7. "Obviously life begins at birth. That's why we celebrate birthdays, not conception days, and why we don't have funerals following miscarriages." 66

7a. Our recognition of birthdays is cultural, not scientific.

7b. Some people *do* have funerals after a miscarriage.

7c. Funerals are an expression of our own subjective attachment to those who have died, not a measurement of their true worth.

7d. There is nothing about birth that makes a baby essentially different than he was before birth.

8. "No one can really know that human life begins before birth." 68

8a. Children know that human life begins before birth.

8b. Pregnant women know that human life begins before birth.

8c. Doctors know that human life begins before birth.

8d. Society knows that human life begins before birth.

8e. The media know that human life begins before birth.

8f. Prochoice advocates know that human life begins before birth.

Part Two: Arguments Concerning Rights and Fairness

9. "Even if the unborn are human beings, they have fewer rights than the woman. No one should be expected to donate her body as a life support system for someone else." 77

9a. Once we grant that the unborn are human beings, it should settle the question of their right to live.

9b. The right to live doesn't increase with age and size, otherwise toddlers and adolescents have less right to live than adults.

9c. The comparison between baby's rights and mother's rights is unequal. What is at stake in abortion is the mother's lifestyle, as opposed to the baby's life.

9d. It is reasonable for society to expect an adult to live temporarily with an inconvenience if the only alternative is killing a child.

10. "Every person has the right to choose. It would be unfair to restrict a woman's choice by prohibiting abortion." 82

10a. Any civilized society restricts the individual's freedom to choose whenever that choice would harm an innocent person.

10b. "Freedom to choose" is too vague for meaningful discussion; we must always ask, "Freedom to choose *what*?"

10c. People who are prochoice about abortion are often not pro-choice about other issues with less at stake.

10d. The one-time choice of abortion robs someone else of a life-time of choices and prevents him from ever exercising his rights.

10e. Everyone is prochoice when it comes to the choices prior to pregnancy and after birth.

10f. Nearly all violations of human rights have been defended on the grounds of the right to choose.

11. "Every woman should have control over her own body. Reproductive freedom is a basic right." 85

11a. Abortion assures that 750,000 females each year do *not* have control over their bodies.

11b. Not all things done with a person's body are right, nor should they all be legally protected.

11c. Prolifers consistently affirm true reproductive rights.

11d. Even prochoicers must acknowledge that the "right to control one's body" argument has no validity if the unborn is a human being.

11e. Too often "the right to control my life" becomes the right to hurt and oppress others for my own advantage.

11f. Control over the body can be exercised to prevent pregnancy in the first place.

11g. It is demeaning to a woman's body and self-esteem to regard pregnancy as an unnatural, negative, and "out of control" condition.

12. "Abortion is a decision between a woman and her doctor. It's no one else's business. Everyone has a constitutional right to privacy." 88

12a. The Constitution does not contain a right to privacy.

12b. Privacy is never an absolute right, but is always governed by other rights.

12c. The encouragement or assistance of a doctor does not change the nature, consequences, or morality of abortion.

12d. The father of the child is also responsible for the child and should have a part in this decision.

12e. The father will often face serious grief and guilt as a result of abortion. Since his life will be significantly affected, shouldn't he have something to say about it?

13. "It's unfair for an unmarried woman to have to face the embarrassment of pregnancy or the pain of giving up a child for adoption." 92

13a. Pregnancy is not a sin. Society should not condemn and pressure an unmarried mother into abortion, but should help and support her.

13b. The poor choice of premarital sex is never compensated for by the far worse choice of killing an innocent human being.

13c. One person's unfair or embarrassing circumstances do not justify violating the rights of another person.

13d. Adoption is a fine alternative that avoids the burden of child raising, while saving a life and making a family happy.

13e. The reason that adoption may be painful is the same reason that abortion is wrong—a human life is involved.

14. "Abortion-rights are fundamental for the advancement of women. They are essential to having equal rights with men." 94

14a. Early feminists were prolife, not prochoice.

14b. Some active feminists still vigorously oppose abortion.

14c. Women's rights are not inherently linked to the right to abortion.

14d. The basic premises of the abortion-rights movement are demeaning to women.

14e. Some of the abortion-rights strategies assume female incompetence and subject women to ignorance and exploitation.

14f. Abortion has become the most effective means of sexism ever devised, ridding the world of multitudes of unwanted females.

15. "The circumstances of many women leave them no choice but to have an abortion." 99

15a. Saying they have no choice is not being prochoice, but proabortion.

15b. Those who are truly prochoice must present a woman with a number of possible choices, rather than just selling the choice of abortion.

15c. "Abortion or misery" is a false portrayal of the options; it keeps women from pursuing—and society from providing—positive alternatives.

16. "I'm personally against abortion, but I'm still prochoice. It's a legal alternative and we don't have the right to keep it from anyone." 101

16a. To be prochoice about abortion is to be proabortion.

16b. The only good reason for being personally against abortion is a reason that demands we be against other people choosing to have abortions.

16c. What is legal is not always right.

Part Three: Arguments Concerning Social Issues

17. " 'Every child a wanted child.' It's unfair to children to bring them into a world where they're not wanted." 107

17a. Every child is wanted by someone—there is no such thing as an unwanted child.

17b. There is a difference between an unwanted pregnancy and an unwanted child.

17c. "Unwanted" describes not an actual condition of the child, but an attitude of adults.

17d. The problem of unwantedness is a good argument for wanting children, but a poor argument for aborting them.

17e. What is most unfair to "unwanted" children is to kill them.

18. "Having more unwanted children results in more child abuse." 111

18a. Most abused children were wanted by their parents.

18b. Child abuse has not decreased since abortion was legalized, but has dramatically increased.

18c. If children are viewed as expendable before birth, they will be viewed as expendable after birth.

18d. It is illogical to argue a child is protected from abuse through abortion since abortion *is* child abuse.

19. "Restricting abortion would be unfair to the poor and minorities, who need it most." 113

19a. It is not unfair for some people to have less opportunity than others to kill the innocent.

19b. The rich and white, not the poor and minorities, are most committed to unrestricted abortion.

19c. Prochoice advocates want the poor and minorities to have abortions, but oppose requirements that abortion risks and alternatives be explained to them.

19d. Planned Parenthood's abortion advocacy was rooted in the eugenics movement and its bias against the mentally and physically handicapped and minorities.

20. "Abortion helps solve the problem of overpopulation and raises the quality of life." 116

20a. The current birth rate in America is less than what is needed to maintain our population level.

20b. The dramatic decline in our birth rate will have a disturbing economic effect on America.

20c. Overpopulation is frequently blamed for problems with other causes.

20d. If there is a population problem that threatens our standard of living, the solution is not to kill off part of the population.

20e. Sterilization and abortion as cures to overpopulation could eventually lead to mandatory sterilization and abortion.

20f. The "quality of life" concept is breeding a sense of human expendability that has far-reaching social implications.

21. "Even if abortion were made illegal, there would still be many abortions."   120

21a. That harmful acts against the innocent will take place regardless of the law is a poor argument for having no law.

21b. The law can guide and educate people to choose better alternatives.

21c. History shows that laws concerning abortion have significantly influenced whether women choose to have abortions.

22. "The anti-abortion beliefs of the minority shouldn't be imposed on the majority."   121

22a. Major polls clearly indicate it is a majority, not a minority, who believe there should be greater restrictions on abortion.

22b. Many people's apparent agreement with abortion law stems from their ignorance of what the law really is.

22c. Beliefs that abortion should be restricted are embraced by a majority in each major political party.

22d. In 1973 the Supreme Court imposed a minority morality on the nation, ignoring the votes of citizens and the decisions of state legislatures.

23. "The anti-abortion position is a religious belief that threatens the vital separation of church and state."   128

23a. Many nonreligious people believe that abortion kills children and that it is wrong.

23b. Morality must not be rejected just because it is supported by religion.

23c. America was founded on a moral base dependent upon principles of the Bible and the Christian religion.

23d. Laws related to church and state were intended to assure freedom *for* religion, not freedom *from* religion.

23e. Religion's waning influence on our society directly accounts for the moral deterioration threatening our future.

Part Four: Arguments Concerning Health and Safety

24. "If abortion is made illegal, tens of thousands of women will again die from back-alley and clothes-hanger abortions." 137

24a. For decades prior to its legalization, 90 percent of abortions were done by physicians in their offices, not in back alleys.

24b. It is not true that tens of thousands of women were dying from illegal abortions before abortion was legalized.

24c. Women still die from *legal* abortions in America.

24d. If abortion became illegal, abortions would be done with medical equipment, not clothes hangers.

24e. We must not legalize procedures that kill the innocent just to make the killing process less hazardous.

24f. The central horror of illegal abortion remains the central horror of legal abortion.

25. "Abortion is a safe medical procedure, safer than full-term pregnancy and childbirth." 141

25a. Abortion is not safer than full-term pregnancy and childbirth.

25b. Though the chances of a woman's safe abortion are now greater, the number of suffering women is also greater because of the huge increase in abortions.

25c. Even if abortion were safer for the mother than childbirth, it would still remain fatal for the innocent child.

25d. Abortion can produce many serious medical problems.

25e. The statistics on abortion complications and risks are often understated due to the inadequate means of gathering data.

25f. The true risks of abortion are rarely explained to women by those who perform abortions.

26. "Abortion is an easy and painless procedure."   145

26a. The various abortion procedures are often both difficult and painful for women.

26b. Abortion is often difficult and painful for fathers, grandparents, and siblings of the aborted child.

26c. Abortion is often difficult and painful for clinic workers.

26d. Abortion is difficult and painful for the unborn child.

26e. Even if abortion were made easy or painless for everyone, it wouldn't change the bottom-line problem that abortion kills children.

27. "Abortion relieves women of stress and responsibility, and thereby enhances their psychological well-being."   151

27a. The many post-abortion therapy and support groups testify to the reality of abortion's potentially harmful psychological effects.

27b. The suicide rate is significantly higher among women who have had abortions than among those who haven't.

27c. Postabortion syndrome is a diagnosable psychological affliction.

27d. Many professional studies document the reality of abortion's adverse psychological consequences on a large number of women.

27e. Abortion can produce both short and longer term psychological damage, especially a sense of personal guilt.

27f. Most women have not been warned about and are completely unprepared for the psychological consequences of abortion.

30d. Handicapped children are often happy, always precious, and usually delighted to be alive.

30e. Handicapped children are not social liabilities, and bright and "normal" people are not always social assets.

30f. Using dehumanizing language may change our thinking, but not the child's nature or value.

30g. Our society is hypocritical in its attitude toward handicapped children.

30h. The adverse psychological effects of abortion are significantly more traumatic for those who abort because of deformity.

30i. The arguments for killing a handicapped unborn child are valid only if they also apply to killing born people who are handicapped.

30j. Abortions due to probable handicaps rob the world of unique human beings who would significantly contribute to society.

31. "What about a woman who is pregnant due to rape or incest?"   175

31a. Pregnancy due to rape is extremely rare, and with proper treatment can be prevented.

31b. Rape is never the fault of the child; the guilty party, not an innocent party, should be punished.

31c. The violence of abortion parallels the violence of rape.

31d. Abortion does not bring healing to a rape victim.

31e. A child is a child regardless of the circumstances of his conception.

31f. What about already-born people who are "products of rape"?

31g. All that is true of children conceived in rape is true of those conceived in incest.

Final Thoughts on the Hard Cases   *179*

1. No adverse circumstance for one human being changes the nature and worth of another human being.

2. Laws must not be built on exception cases.

Part Six: Arguments Against the Character of Prolifers

32. "Anti-abortionists are so cruel that they insist on showing hideous pictures of dead babies." 185

32a. What is hideous is not the pictures themselves, but the reality they depict.

32b. Pictures challenge our denial of the horrors of abortion. If something is too horrible to look at, perhaps it is too horrible to condone.

32c. Nothing could be more relevant to the discussion of something than that which shows what it really is.

32d. It is the prochoice position, not the prolife position, that is cruel.

33. "Prolifers don't care about women, and they don't care about babies once they're born." 189

33a. Prolifers are actively involved in caring for women in crisis pregnancies and difficult child-raising situations.

33b. Prolifers are actively involved in caring for "unwanted" children and the other "disposable people" in society.

33c. It is "abortion providers" who do not provide support for women choosing anything but abortion.

34. "The anti-abortionists are a bunch of men telling women what to do." 191

34a. More women than men oppose abortion.

34b. The great majority of prolife workers are women.

34c. If men are disqualified from the abortion issue, they should be disqualified on both sides.

34d. Men are entitled to take a position on abortion.

34e. Of women who have had abortions, far more are prolife activists than prochoice activists.

35. "Anti-abortionists talk about the sanctity of human life, yet they favor capital punishment." 193

35a. Not all prolifers favor capital punishment.

35b. Capital punishment is rooted in a respect for innocent human life.

35c. There is a vast difference between punishing a convicted murderer and an innocent child.

36. "Anti-abortion fanatics break the law, are violent, and bomb abortion clinics."   194

36a. Media coverage of prolife civil disobedience often bears little resemblance to what actually happens.

36b. Rescuing should not be condemned without understanding the reasons behind it.

36c. Peaceful civil disobedience is consistent with the belief that the unborn are human beings.

36d. Prolife protests have been remarkably nonviolent, and even when there has been violence it has usually been committed by clinic employees and escorts.

36e. Abortion clinic bombing and violence are rare, and are neither done nor endorsed by prolife organizations.

37. "The anti-abortionists distort the facts and resort to emotionalism to deceive the public."   199

37a. The facts themselves make abortion an emotional issue.

37b. It is not the prolife position but the prochoice position that relies on emotionalism more than truth and logic.

37c. The prolife position is based on documented facts and empirical evidence, which many prochoice advocates ignore or distort.

37d. The prochoice movement consistently caricatures and misrepresents prolifers and their agenda.

38. "Anti-abortion groups hide behind a profamily facade, while groups such as Planned Parenthood are truly profamily because they assist in family planning."   202

38a. The prochoice movement's imposition of "family planning" on teenagers has substantially contributed to the actual cause of teen pregnancy.

38b. Through its opposition to parental notification and consent, Planned Parenthood consistently undermines the value and authority of the family.

38c. As demonstrated in the case of Becky Bell, the prochoice movement is willing to distort and exploit family tragedies to promote its agenda.

38d. The prochoice movement and the media ignore family tragedies that do not support the prochoice agenda.

Summary Argument

39. "The last two decades of abortion rights have helped make our society a better place to live." 208

39a. Abortion has left terrible holes in our society.

39b. Abortion has made us a nation of schizophrenics about our children.

39c. Abortion is a modern holocaust in which we are accomplices.

39d. Abortion is taking us a direction from which we might never return.

39e. Abortion has ushered in the brave new world of human pesticides.

Final Appeals

WHY THIS BOOK IS NECESSARY

"Do we really need another book on abortion? What could possibly be said that hasn't been said already?"

Those are legitimate questions deserving a response. Given the number of books on abortion, why have I written yet another one, and why should you bother to read it?

This book is necessary because the stakes are so high in the abortion debate.

Abortion is the most frequently performed surgery on adults in America.[1] One out of three babies conceived in the United States is deliberately aborted.[2] Since about 40 percent of all pregnancies are unplanned,[3] this means that well over two out of three unplanned pregnancies are terminated by abortion. Abortions outnumber live births in fourteen major metropolitan areas.[4] There are nearly 1.6 million reported abortions in this country every year.[5] There have been twenty-eight million since abortion was legalized across America in 1973.

If the prochoice position is correct, the freedom to choose abortion is an expression of equal rights, fairness, and justice. Abortion is at best a healthy and at least a necessary part of making society a better place for all. If we ever go back to a time when abortion is not freely available, it will be the most gigantic step backward in the history of human rights.

If the prolife position is correct, the forty-four hundred abortions occurring every day represent forty-four hundred human casualties. And though none of these deaths is reported on the evening news, each aborted child is just as real and just as valuable as older children. If these unborn are really babies, then America has one of the highest infant mortality rates in the world.

If abortion does *not* kill children, the prolife mentality is at best a nuisance and at worst a serious threat to women's rights and personal liberty. If abortion *does* kill children, the prochoice mentality is responsible for the deaths of 1.6 million innocent people each year, more than the combined total of Americans who have died in all wars in our history. This is not one of those cases where "it doesn't make a difference who's right and who's wrong." No matter who is right, the stakes are enormously high.

This book is necessary because there is so much tension and uncertainty about abortion.

In their extensive surveys of Americans, James Patterson and Peter Kim discovered that among issues people feel strongly about, abortion was number one—even above such hot issues as anti-Semitism, alcohol abuse, homelessness, the death penalty, pornography, and flag burning. A full 75 percent felt strongly about abortion one way or another.[6]

That many Americans feel strongly about abortion does not mean they have solid reasons for their feelings. A *Newsweek* poll asked, "Do you ever wonder whether your own position on abortion is the right one or not?" Significantly, 38 percent said yes and 7 percent didn't know, which indicates uncertainty as well.[7] Isn't it remarkable that an issue which is so important, and which people feel so strongly about, is nonetheless so uncertain in the minds of so many? This book is written in part for that large number of uncertain people, in the hope that their uncertainty reflects openness to another point of view and to facts and logic which they may never have heard before.

This book is necessary because the educational system does not present both sides of the abortion issue.

A representative of the National Abortion Rights Action League spoke in a high school social science class on the merits of abortion. Afterward, a student in the class asked the teacher if she could invite me to present a different view. When I arrived, the instructor, himself firmly prochoice, informed me that he had polled the students the day before and they had voted 23-1 for the prochoice position. Of course, they had made up their minds based on the information they'd been given. Unfortunately, the information they'd been given was neither accurate nor complete.

I presented the scientific, logical, and common-sense case for the humanity, value, and rights of unborn children. I showed them intrauterine pictures demonstrating the development of the unborn at even the earliest stage that abortions occur. Some of the students were visibly shocked. Though these were objective and accessible scientific facts, no one had ever told them such things before. All they had ever heard were slogans and cliches about rights and privacy and choice, never tangible facts on which to build an accurate position.

After the presentation, the teacher said to me, "If we were to vote again, it would be different. Minds were changed today." Then he added something amazing: "You know, until now I had never heard the prolife position."

We must not miss this colossal irony. We live in what is supposed to be the most open-minded society in human history. We pride ourselves on giving our children an education that is broad, objective, and fact-oriented. Yet here we have an intelligent, well-read social science teacher with a master's degree and decades of experience in the classroom, *who had never once heard a presentation of the prolife position.* Having never heard an alternative, how could he believe other than what he did? The poll of his students showed that just as he had accepted the prochoice position uncritically from others, they had done the same from him.

I, too, have never heard an accurate representation of the prolife position from any of the sources this teacher has relied upon for information—public education and the media. Like most Americans, he has never studied the scientific evidence. He has never researched the nature and development of the unborn. He has not watched the movies of the unborn child in his mother's uterus. He has not looked thoughtfully at the pictures of aborted babies. He has not talked at length with women scarred by abortion.

Even the most educated people in America today have never really heard the prolife position. But some will object, "I've heard what the anti-abortionists think." No—the majority have heard merely a caricature of that position. What they have heard is not the prolife position but what prochoice advocates say is the prolife position.

Yet this violates a fundamental rule of objective research. It's like listening to the Republican candidate for president explain the Democratic candidate's views, then thinking you've given the Democrat a fair hearing. It's like having a Ford dealer tell you about the difference between Ford and Toyota trucks, then saying you know all about Toyota trucks. *You will never get an accurate view of any position until you hear an unedited version of it directly from a person who actually holds that position.*

31

I have listened at length to prochoice advocates. I have heard and understood their position. Have you ever listened at length to a prolife advocate and really heard his or her position? Heard it to the point of understanding, even if you disagree? If not, this book is your opportunity.

This book is necessary because the media are biased against the prolife position.

What most Americans know—or think we know—is what we have been told by the media. Few of us have arrived at our position on abortion after careful research. Rather, we have accepted whatever we have been told. For years the prochoice position has had a hotline to our brains. By reading newspapers and magazines and watching television, we have all earned the equivalent of a doctorate in prochoice thinking.

On some issues it is possible to get a fairly balanced view. Given the variety of positions reflected in different media sources, we can compare and sift through the information from both sides. But in the case of abortion, the two sides are not represented to most Americans. A person who reads the newspaper, subscribes to one of the newsweeklies, listens to the radio, and watches national and local news programs may appear to be well informed. But when it comes to the abortion issue, in most cases he receives input from only one side.

Interviews with 240 journalists and editors in the media elite indicate that a full 90 percent of them approve of abortion for almost any reason, a much higher percentage than in the general public.[8] Numbers of these are prochoice activists, whose means of activism is the news source for which they work. Because they approve of abortion rights—often with a passion—they want viewers and readers to approve, too. So they tell us things that make us approve, and don't tell us things that would make us disapprove. Bias is a fact of life. I have it and so do you. But most Americans don't get their information from me or you. Most get it from the popular media. Because of the extreme dominance of the prochoice position, the media is out of balance, and most Americans have not even begun to hear a fair representation of both sides in the abortion debate.

The *Los Angeles Times* has required its writers to use the terms *pro-choice* and *anti-abortion*.[9] This lets one group start with the crucial semantic edge of sounding positive and the other with the deadly disadvantage of sounding negative. The *Times* gives editors, reporters, and readers no choice but prochoice.

Consider the comparative coverage of two demonstrations, one pro-choice and one prolife, both in Washington, D.C., almost exactly one year apart. According to the park police, the prochoice rally in April 1989 had about 125,000 people. Nevertheless, the figure consistently used by the media was 300,000. The April 1990 prolife rally was attended by an estimated 300,000 people. It was at least twice as large as the prochoice event. (A major news network first reported the crowd at 60,000 until they were embarrassed into raising the figure.)

The day after the prochoice rally, the *Washington Post* gave it front page coverage. Every conceivable angle of the rally was featured in no less than a dozen separate stories, including the lead story that went more than fifteen columns. The *Post* had also printed a map and schedule for the march in its Sunday edition, which was the equivalent of tens of thousands of dollars in free advertising and recruiting.[10] Likewise, *USA Today* gave a front-page, full-color picture the Friday before.

A year later, the day after the much larger prolife rally, the *Washington Post* devoted to that event a grand total of one story and one photograph on page B3. *Time*, which gave a five-page cover story to the smaller rally, devoted no coverage whatsoever to the prolife rally.

The bias has been so blatant and people have begun to complain enough that, to their credit, some consciences in the media are being pricked. Lisa Myers of NBC said, "Some of the stories I have read or seen have almost seemed like cheerleading for the prochoice side."[11] Ethan Bronner of the *Boston Globe* said, "I think that when abortion opponents complain about a bias in newsrooms against their cause, they're absolutely right."[12] Richard Harwood of the *Washington Post* said his paper's coverage of a prolife event was "shabby," and admitted, "This affair has left a blot on the paper's professional reputation."[13] David Shaw of the *Los Angeles Times* gives many illustrations of media bias on abortion, including this: "Abortion opponents are often described as 'militant' or 'strident.' Such characterizations are seldom used to describe abortion-rights advocates, many of whom can be militant or strident—or both."[14]

What happens when a reporter goes against the grain of the pro-choice bias? Susan Okie of the *Washington Post* wrote a story that wasn't even about abortion, but about new procedures for saving premature babies. She was warned that this kind of story was not good for the abortion rights movement. That the story was true and accurate was beside the point. When corrected she said she felt like she was "being herded back into line."[15]

Susan Okie's experience is by no means unique. *Newsweek* warns us that the "thought police" are now everywhere, teaching us to be PC— "politically correct."[16] PC has been called the "New McCarthyism" because it labels and punishes people who use terminology or take positions out of line with the progressive liberal establishment of education (which is normally mirrored by the media). *Newsweek* included a photograph of forty buttons with politically correct slogans; nine were abortion-related, and every one was a prochoice slogan. As anyone in higher education and the media will tell you, it is PC to be prochoice and it isn't PC to be prolife.

This book is necessary because it is a comprehensive, documented, and accurate presentation of the prolife position.

Is this book biased? Of course it is. The question is not bias, the question is which bias is most solidly based on the facts. Which bias is the most reasonable and defensible?

I have tried to be fair. I have tried not to quote people out of context, and I have sought to accurately represent the prochoice position. I know many prochoice people whom I love and respect. I do not believe they are plotting to destroy society. I think they honestly but mistakenly believe that abortion is a necessary option that is ultimately best for women and for society.

Are the interactions between prochoicers and prolifers destined to be dialogues of the deaf? Or is there a common ground upon which they can meet? I believe there is at least a three-fold common ground.

First, there is the common ground of empirical data, of scientific and psychological evidence that we need not and should not deny. Second, we share the ability (though it is hard to hold to in the face of our prejudices) to be logical and rational in applying this truth. Third, though it is not as large or solid as it was even two decades ago, most people still share a common ground of morality and some sense of justice, fairness, and compassion.

Some readers will also share a confidence in the Bible as the Word of God, and see it as the basis upon which morality must be built. Yet I have found that even among those who do not accept the Bible's authority, there is often enough common ground to discuss the abortion issue and to arrive at similar conclusions because of a mutual respect for the social justice and compassion reflected in the Scriptures, embodied in Jesus Christ, and traditionally respected throughout our nation's history.

I do not ask anyone to accept the prolife position without thinking. On the contrary, I ask that readers look at the evidence and weigh it on its own merit. I ask that stereotypes of the prolife position be set aside. I further ask the reader to be intellectually honest and resist the temptation to be "politically correct" by holding to the prochoice position even if it turns out that the evidence contradicts it.

Do I encourage people to study the prochoice position as well as the prolife? Of course! Go to the prochoice sources and decide for yourself whether I'm stating their arguments accurately. I'm completely anti-censorship on the abortion issue. Let's put all the cards on the table. Let's not hold back any of the evidence. Let's bring out the statistics, study the intrauterine pictures, show pictures of aborted unborns, hear from women who have had abortions, both prochoicers and prolifers. Let's listen to geneticists and biologists, as well as abortionists who are prochoice and former abortionists who are now prolife. Let each side present its case, and may the best case win. Truth is always served by a full disclosure of the facts. Error has good reason to fear such disclosure.

This book is necessary because it is an organized, logical, and easily referenced resource offering answers to every major prochoice argument.

This book presents prolife answers to the most frequently used prochoice arguments. Most readers will recognize these arguments, but many readers will never have heard answers to them.

This book is written in a clear, concise, and easily referenced format. I have designed it to be user-friendly, with the busy reader in mind. I use an outline style, with highlighted features that allow the reader to scan major points and subpoints. It is meant to be used and reused as a ready-reference. The detailed table of contents allows you to quickly locate any argument and response. It is designed to help you find a quick answer to what the teacher, television personality, or secretary at work said earlier today.

If you are prochoice, I ask you to read this book with the open mind our society claims to value so highly. If the prolife side proves to be as senseless and irrational as you have been led to believe, fine. You can give it the first-hand rejection it deserves. But if the prolife position proves to be sensible and accurate, then you must rethink your position even if doing so is not politically correct or popular in your circles of influence. Fair enough?

If you are one of those "on the fence," I ask you to make this book part of a quest for truth. You can hear the prochoice position anywhere—just turn on a TV or read the paper. But this book may be your first opportunity to examine the prolife position. Please examine it carefully.

If you are prolife, I ask you to think through the foundations for the position you hold so that you will be able to hold to it more firmly in the face of continuous attack. It is not enough to say, "I know I'm right, though I'm not sure why." We must know how to intelligently defend our position, and to educate others about the truth. If you already know what you believe, look in these pages for documentation as well as fresh and readily understandable ways to communicate to others.

If the prolife position is wrong, we should abandon it. If it is right, then innocent human lives depend on our ability and willingness at every opportunity to persuade others of the truth about the value, dignity, and rights of unborn children. I hope this book will serve you well in the task of education and communication, as you speak up for those who cannot speak for themselves.

PART ONE

ARGUMENTS CONCERNING LIFE, HUMANITY, AND PERSONHOOD

ARGUMENTS CONCERNING LIFE, HUMANITY, AND PERSONHOOD

1. "It is uncertain when human life begins; that's a religious question that cannot be answered by science."

An article printed and distributed by the National Abortion Rights Action League (NARAL) describes as "anti-choice" the position that "human life begins at conception." It says the prochoice position is, "Personhood at conception is a religious belief, not a provable biological fact."[1]

1a. If there *is* uncertainty about when human life begins, the benefit of the doubt should go to preserving life.

Suppose there is uncertainty about when human life begins. If a hunter is uncertain whether a movement in the brush is caused by a person, does his uncertainty lead him to fire or not to fire? If you're driving at night and you think the dark figure ahead on the road may be a child, but it may just be the shadow of a tree, do you drive into it or do you put on the brakes? If we find someone who may be dead or alive, but we're not sure, what is the best policy? To assume he is alive and try to save him, or to assume he is dead and walk away?

Shouldn't we give the benefit of the doubt to life? Otherwise we are saying, "This may or may not be a child, therefore it's all right to destroy it."

1b. Medical textbooks and scientific reference works consistently agree that human life begins at conception.

Many people have been told that there is no medical or scientific consensus as to when human life begins. This is simply untrue. Among those scientists who have no vested interests in the abortion issue, there is an overwhelming consensus that human life begins at conception. (Conception is the moment when the egg is fertilized by the sperm, bringing into existence the zygote, which is a genetically distinct individual.)

Dr. Bradley M. Patten's textbook, *Human Embryology*, states, "It is the penetration of the ovum by a spermatozoan and the resultant mingling of the nuclear material each brings to the union that constitutes the culmination of the process of fertilization and *marks the initiation of the life of a new individual.*"[2] (Unless otherwise noted, quoted words in italics have been italicized by me, rather than the original author.)

Dr. Keith L. Moore's text on embryology, referring to the single-cell zygote, says, "The cell results from fertilization of an oocyte by a sperm and is *the beginning of a human being.*"[3] He also states, "Each of us started life as a cell called a zygote."[4]

Doctors J. P. Greenhill and E. A. Friedman, in their work on biology and obstetrics, state, "The zygote thus formed represents *the beginning of a new life.*"[5]

Dr. Louis Fridhanler, in the medical textbook *Biology of Gestation*, refers to fertilization as "that wondrous moment that marks the beginning of life for a new unique individual."[6]

Doctors E. L. Potter and J. M. Craig write in *Pathology of the Fetus and the Infant*, "Every time a sperm cell and ovum unite a new being is created which is alive and will continue to live unless its death is brought about by some specific condition."[7]

Popular scientific reference works reflect this same understanding of when human life begins. *Time* and Rand McNally's *Atlas of the Body* states, "In fusing together, the male and female gametes produce a fertilized single cell, the zygote, which is *the start of a new individual.*"[8] In an article on pregnancy, the *Encyclopedia Britannica* says, "*A new individual is created* when the elements of a potent sperm merge with those of a fertile ovum, or egg."[9]

These sources confidently affirm, with no hint of uncertainty, that life begins at conception. They state not a theory or hypothesis and certainly not a religious belief—every one is a secular source. Their conclusion is squarely based on the scientific and medical facts.

1c. Some of the world's most prominent scientists and physicians testified to a U.S. Senate committee that human life begins at conception.

In 1981, a United States Senate Judiciary Subcommittee invited experts to testify on the question of when life begins. All of the quotes from the following experts come directly from the official government record of their testimony.[10]

• Dr. Alfred M. Bongioanni, professor of pediatrics and obstetrics at the University of Pennsylvania, stated:

> I have learned from my earliest medical education that human life begins at the time of conception. . . . I submit that *human life is present throughout this entire sequence from conception to adulthood* and that any interruption at any point throughout this time constitutes a termination of human life. . . .
>
> I am no more prepared to say that these early stages [of development in the womb] represent an incomplete human being than I would be to say that the child prior to the dramatic effects of puberty . . . is not a human being. *This is human life at every stage. . . .*"

• Dr. Jerome LeJeune, professor of genetics at the University of Descartes in Paris, was the discoverer of the chromosome pattern of Down's syndrome. Dr. LeJeune testified to the Judiciary Subcommittee, "*after fertilization has taken place a new human being has come into being.*" He stated that this "is no longer a matter of taste or opinion," and "not a metaphysical contention, it is plain experimental evidence." He added, "*Each individual has a very neat beginning, at conception.*"

• Professor Hymie Gordon, Mayo Clinic: "By all the criteria of modern molecular biology, life is present from the moment of conception."

• Professor Micheline Matthews-Roth, Harvard University Medical School: "It is incorrect to say that biological data cannot be decisive. . . . *It is scientifically correct to say that an individual human life begins at conception.* . . . Our laws, one function of which is to help preserve the lives of our people, should be based on accurate scientific data."

• Dr. Watson A. Bowes, University of Colorado Medical School: "The beginning of a single human life is from a biological point of view a simple and straightforward matter—*the beginning is conception.* This straightforward biological fact should not be distorted to serve sociological, political, or economic goals."

A prominent physician points out that at these Senate hearings, "Pro-abortionists, though invited to do so, failed to produce even a single expert witness who would specifically testify that life begins at any point other than conception or implantation. Only one witness said no one can tell when life begins."[11]

1d. Many other prominent scientists and physicians have likewise affirmed with certainty that human life begins at conception.

• Ashley Montague, a geneticist and professor at Harvard and Rutgers, is unsympathetic to the prolife cause. Nevertheless, he affirms unequivocally, "The basic fact is simple: *life begins not at birth, but conception.*"[12]

• Dr. Bernard Nathanson, internationally known obstetrician and gynecologist, was a cofounder of what is now the National Abortion Rights Action League (NARAL). He owned and operated what was at the time the largest abortion clinic in the western hemisphere. He was directly involved in over sixty thousand abortions.

Dr. Nathanson's study of developments in the science of fetology and his use of ultrasound to observe the unborn child in the womb led him to the conclusion that he had made a horrible mistake. Resigning from his lucrative position, Nathanson wrote in the *New England Journal of Medicine* that he was deeply troubled by his "increasing certainty that I had in fact presided over 60,000 deaths."[13]

In his film, "The Silent Scream," Nathanson later stated, "Modern technologies have convinced us that *beyond question the unborn child is simply another human being*, another member of the human community, indistinguishable in every way from any of us." Dr. Nathanson wrote *Aborting America* to inform the public of the realities behind the abortion rights movement of which he had been a primary leader.[14] At the time Dr. Nathanson was an atheist. His conclusions were not even remotely religious, but squarely based on the biological facts.

• Dr. Landrum Shettles was for twenty-seven years attending obstetrician-gynecologist at Columbia-Presbyterian Medical Center in New York. Shettles was a pioneer in sperm biology, fertility, and sterility. He is internationally famous for being the discoverer of male- and female-producing sperm. His intrauterine photographs of preborn children appear in over fifty medical textbooks. Dr. Shettles states,

> I oppose abortion. I do so, first, because I accept what is biologically manifest—*that human life commences at the time of conception*—and, second, because I believe it is wrong to take innocent human life under any circumstances. My position is scientific, pragmatic, and humanitarian.[15]

• **The First International Symposium on Abortion** came to the following conclusion:

> The changes occurring between implantation, a six-week embryo, a six-month fetus, a one-week-old child, or a mature adult are merely stages of development and maturation. The majority of our group could find no point in time between the union of sperm and egg, or at least the blastocyst stage, and the birth of the infant at which point we could say that this was not a human life.[16]

• **The Official Senate report on Senate Bill 158**, the "Human Life Bill," summarized the issue this way:

> Physicians, biologists, and other scientists agree that *conception marks the beginning of the life of a human being*—a being that is alive and is a member of the human species. There is overwhelming agreement on this point in countless medical, biological, and scientific writings.[17]

2. "The fetus is just a part of the pregnant woman's body, like her tonsils or appendix."

2a. A body part is defined by the common genetic code it shares with the rest of its body; the unborn's genetic code differs from his mother's.

Every cell of the mother's tonsils, appendix, heart, and lungs shares the same genetic code. The unborn child also has a genetic code, distinctly different from his mother's. Every cell of his body is uniquely his, each different than every cell of his mother's body. Often his blood-type is also different, and half the time even his gender is different.

Half of the child's forty-six chromosomes come from his biological father, half from his mother. Except in the rare cases of identical twins, the combination of those chromosomes is unique, distinct even from that of a brother or sister coming from the same parents.

Just as no two people have identical fingerprints, no two people have identical genetic fingerprints. If one body is inside another, but each has its own unique genetic code, then there is not one person, but two separate people. John Jefferson Davis states:

It is a well-established fact that a genetically distinct human being is brought into existence at conception. Once fertilization takes place, the zygote is its own entity, genetically distinct from both mother and father. The newly conceived individual possesses all the necessary information for a self-directed development and will proceed to grow in the usual human fashion, given time and nourishment. It is simply untrue that the unborn child is merely "part of the mother's body." In addition to being genetically distinct from the time of conception, the unborn possesses separate circulatory, nervous, and endocrine systems.[1]

A Chinese zygote implanted in a Swedish woman will always be Chinese, not Swedish, because his identity is based on his genetic code, not that of the body in which he resides. If there were only one body involved in a pregnancy, then that body has two noses, four legs, two sets of fingerprints, two brains, two circulatory systems, and two skeletal systems. Half the time the child is male; clearly his sexual organs are not part of his mother's body, but his own. In reality, it is a scientific fact that the mother is one distinctive and self-contained person, and the child is another.

2b. The child may die and the mother live, or the mother may die and the child live, proving they are two separate individuals.

The child-guest is a temporary resident of the mother-host. He will leave on his own as long as he is not prematurely evicted. There are many cases where a mother has been fatally injured, after which a doctor has delivered her child safely. The mother's body dies, the baby lives. Unmistakably, the baby was not merely a part of his mother's body, or he would have died with her. In California, a child was born several months after her mother was declared "brain dead."[2] Obviously they were two distinct individuals prior to the child's birth.

2c. The unborn child takes an active role in his own development, controlling the course of the pregnancy and the time of birth.

New Zealand fetology professor A. W. Liley is known as the "father of fetology." Among his many pioneer achievements was the first intrauterine blood transfusion. Dr. Liley has stated:

Physiologically, we must accept that the conceptus is, in a very large measure, in charge of the pregnancy. . . . Biologically, at no stage can we subscribe to the view that the fetus is a mere appendage of the mother. . . . It is the embryo who stops his mother's periods and makes her womb habitable by developing a placenta and a protective capsule of fluid for himself. He regulates his own amniotic fluid volume and although women speak of their waters breaking or their membranes rupturing, these structures belong to the fetus. And finally, it is the fetus, not the mother, who decides when labor should be initiated.[3]

Dr. Peter Nathanielsz of Cornell University concurs. He says that the unborn's brain sends a message to his own pituitary gland which in turn stimulates the adrenal cortex to secrete a hormone which stimulates the mother's uterus to contract.[4] A woman goes into labor not because her body is ready to surrender the unborn child, but because the unborn child is ready to leave her body.

2d. Being inside something is not the same as being part of something.

One's body does not belong to another's body merely because of proximity. A car is not part of a garage because it is parked there. A loaf of bread is not part of the oven in which it is baked. Louise Brown, the first test-tube baby, was conceived when sperm and egg joined in a petri dish. She was no more a part of her mother's body when placed there than she had been part of the petri dish where her life began. A child is not part of the body in which she is carried. As a person inside a house is not part of the house, so a person inside another's body is not part of that person's body.

2e. Human beings should not be discriminated against because of their place of residence.

A person is a person whether she lives in a mansion or an apartment or on the street. She is a person whether she's trapped in a cave, lying dependently in a care center, or residing within her mother. We all believe a premature baby lying in a hospital incubator deserves to live. Would the exact same baby deserve to live any less simply because she was still in her mother?

Consider this true-to-life scenario. Two women become pregnant on the same day. Six months later Woman A has a premature baby, small but healthy. Woman B is still pregnant. One week later both women decide they don't want their babies anymore. Why should Woman B be allowed to kill her baby and Woman A not be allowed to kill hers?[5] Since there is no difference in the nature or development of the two babies, why would Woman B's action be exercising a legitimate right to choose, while Woman A's action would be a heinous crime subjecting her to prosecution for first degree murder? It is irrational to recognize the one child as a baby and pretend the other one isn't.

I know a former prochoice nurse who was converted to a prolife position after seeing premature babies being frantically saved by a medical team in one room, while down the hall, babies the same age were being aborted.

In 1974, the U.S. Congress voted unanimously to delay capital punishment of a pregnant woman until after her delivery. Every congressman—including those of the prochoice persuasion—knew in his heart that this unborn baby was a separate person not guilty of his mother's crime. No stay of execution was requested for the sake of her tonsils, heart, or kidneys. It was done only for the sake of her child, a separate human being with a life and rights of his own.

3. "The unborn is an embryo or a fetus—just a simple blob of tissue, a product of conception—not a baby. Abortion is terminating a pregnancy, not killing a child."

3a. Like *toddler* and *adolescent*, the terms *embryo* and *fetus* do not refer to nonhumans, but to humans at particular stages of development.

The word *embryo* is used of any living creature at an early stage of development. *Fetus* is a Latin word meaning "young one" or "little child."

It is scientifically inaccurate to say an embryo or a fetus is not a human being simply because he is at an earlier stage of development than a born infant. This is like saying that a toddler is not a human being—or is less of a human being—because he is not yet an adolescent. Or, that an adolescent is not a human being because he is not yet an adult.

Stage of development has nothing to do with human worth. One of my daughters is two years older than the other. Does this mean she is two years better? Is a two-year-old child more precious now than he was a year ago? Is a child more worthy to live after birth than before birth?

3b. Semantics affect perceptions, but they do not change realities; a baby is a baby no matter what we call her.

"A rose by any other name would smell as sweet." A baby by any other name is still a baby. Though *fetus* was once a good word that spoke of a young human being, it is now used with a subhuman connotation. Referring to the fetus allows us not to use the B-word (baby). The prochoice movement labors to avoid the B-word for it reminds us of the reality that abortion kills a child. This reality must be denied at all costs, because anyone who is understood to be arguing for the right to kill babies is fighting an uphill battle.

Product of conception, and its abbreviated form *POC*, goes a step further in depersonalizing the unborn child. In reality, the infant, the ten-year-old, and the adult are *all* "products of conception," no more or no less than the fetus. As the product of a horse's conception is always a horse, the product of human conception is always a human. Still, the use of impersonal terminology allows us to overlook this reality.

Sometimes the characterization of the unborn is overtly hostile. I heard one prochoice advocate refer to unwanted pregnancy as a "venereal disease," and abortion as the "cure." Abortion-rights advocates have referred to unborn babies as debris[1], garbage, and refuse[2] to justify abortion. Holocaust scholar Raul Hilberg argues that the key to the widespread destruction of the Jewish people was the use of degrading terminology such as "useless eaters" and "garbage" that blinded society to the fact that real people were being killed.[3]

3c. From the moment of conception the unborn is not simple, but very complex.

The newly fertilized egg contains a staggering amount of genetic information, sufficient to control the individual's growth and development for an entire lifetime. A single thread of DNA from a human cell contains information equivalent to a library of one thousand volumes, or six hundred thousand printed pages with five hundred words on a page. The genetic information stored in the new individual at conception is the equivalent of fifty times the amount of information contained in the *Encyclopedia Britannica*.[4]

3d. Prior to the earliest first-trimester abortions, the unborn already has every body part she will ever have.

At eighteen days after conception the heart is forming and the eyes start to develop. By twenty-one days the heart is not only beating but pumping blood throughout the body. By twenty-eight days the unborn has budding arms and legs. By thirty days she has multiplied in size ten thousand times. She has a brain and blood flows through her veins.

By thirty-five days, mouth, ears, and nose are taking shape. At forty days the preborn child's brain waves can be recorded. The child's heartbeat, which began three weeks earlier, can already be detected by an ultrasonic stethoscope. By forty-two days the skeleton is formed and the brain is controlling the movement of muscles and organs. The unborn reflexively responds to stimulus, and may already be capable of feeling pain (see Argument 26d). This is before the earliest abortions take place.

Famous intrauterine photographer Leonart Nilsson is best known for his photo essays in *Life* magazine and his best-selling book *A Child Is Born*. In his "Drama of Life Before Birth," he says this of the unborn at forty-five days after conception (this is just six-and-a-half weeks, when many women don't yet know they are pregnant): "Though the embryo now weighs only 1/30 of an ounce, it has all the internal organs of the adult in various stages of development. It already has a little mouth with lips, an early tongue and buds for 20 milk teeth. Its sex and reproductive organs have begun to sprout."[5] (See "tear drop" photograph of a miscarried child at this stage, on back cover of this book.)

By eight weeks hands and feet are almost perfectly formed, and fingerprints are developing. Already, "Mother's movements stimulate the fetus's balance and motion detectors."[6] (See photograph of living child at eight weeks, at top of back cover of this book.) By nine weeks a child will bend fingers around an object placed in the palm. Fingernails are forming and the child is sucking his thumb. The nine-week baby has "already perfected a somersault, backflip and scissor kick."[7]

By ten weeks the child squints, swallows, and frowns. (See black and white photographs #1 and #2 at the center of this book.) By eleven weeks he urinates, makes a wide variety of facial expressions, and even smiles. By twelve weeks the child is kicking, turning his feet, curling and fanning his toes, making a fist, moving thumbs, bending wrists, and opening his mouth.[8]

All this happens in the first trimester, the first three months of life. In the remaining six months in the womb *nothing new develops or begins functioning*. The child only grows and matures.

3e. Every abortion stops a beating heart and terminates measurable brain waves.

Using figures dependent on abortion clinic records, about half of all abortions occur at eight weeks or less, 90 percent happen within twelve weeks, and 9 percent from thirteen to twenty weeks. The other 1 percent (fifteen thousand per year) are reported at beyond twenty one weeks.[9]

However, abortion clinic workers say clinics underreport later abortions, and even *Newsweek* admits, "Statistics on abortion are notoriously suspect."[10] I have personally interviewed abortion clinic workers who say no abortions occur before six weeks, and most do not occur until the baby's eighth week of development. Even when pregnancies are detected earlier, operators want to make sure the unborn is large enough to do a proper inventory of his severed body parts. (A hand or leg inadvertently left in the mother will cause a dangerous infection.)

What this means is that every description of an unborn child prior to fifty-six days gestation is true of the majority of aborted unborns. Every description prior to forty-two days—including beating heart (twenty-one days) and measurable brain waves (forty days)—is true of every single aborted child. An actual audio tape of the clear, strong heartbeat of an infant at less than seven weeks was made by obstetrician-gynecologist Dr. Louis Hicks of Lexington, Kentucky.[11] It is sobering to listen to the beating heart of an unborn child who is at the *earliest* age abortions are performed.

What do we call it when a person no longer has a heartbeat or brain waves? Death. What should we call it when there *is* a heart beat and there *are* brain waves? Life. *It is an indisputable scientific fact that each and every legal abortion in America today stops a beating heart, and stops already measurable brain waves.*

3f. Even in the earliest abortions, the unborn child is clearly human in appearance.

The biggest disadvantage to the preborn child is that there is no window to the womb. His fate is in the hands of those who cannot see him. There are technologies, however, that have allowed us for almost thirty years to see into the womb. Both still and moving pictures show the startlingly clear humanity of the preborn. Watching obviously human unborn children through ultrasound convinced famous abortionist Bernard Nathanson that for years he had, unwittingly, been killing human beings.[12] A liberal Ivy League professor and his wife changed their minds on this issue when a sonogram of their amniocentesis showed their unborn child grabbing hold of the needle.

One of the color photos on the back cover of this book is of an unborn child at eight weeks of development. Notice the clearly discernible eyes, ears, mouth, nose, and hands. The tear-drop shaped picture below it is of an unruptured ectopic pregnancy six weeks after the mother's last menstrual period, taken after surgery by a medical photographer at the University of Minnesota. Notice again the clearly discernible features, especially eyes and hands. Remember that few abortions take place before this stage. This is the true appearance of one of the youngest of the forty-four hundred children killed in America every day. Sadly, few women getting abortions know this. Abortion clinics do not show them such pictures.

When I showed a picture of an eight-week developed unborn, a pro-choice advocate—an intelligent college graduate—looked at me with disdain and asked, "Do you really think you're going to fool anyone with this trick photography?" This woman, whom I'm convinced was sincere in her belief, had been taught the unborn was a blob of tissue. But when she looked at the actual picture she saw this was clearly a little human being. Therefore she was forced to conclude either that what she had been taught was wrong, or that this was a phony picture. It was easier to conclude the latter. Yet, as I pointed out to her, she could go to such secular sources as Harvard University Medical School textbooks, or the August 1990 *Life* magazine, or Nilsson's *A Child Is Born* and find exactly the same thing. I wonder if she ever investigated the scientific data.

Unfortunately, the problem is not just ignorance but misinformation. An abortion clinic spokesperson told the *Winnipeg Sun* that the unborn is "a frog-like thing . . . without a heartbeat, brain, eyes or internal organs."[13] A Kansas state representative, getting her information from a paid lobbyist of the abortion industry, stated that the unborn child at seven *months* "looks a lot like chopped liver."[14] (See photograph #3 at the center of this book, which shows the unborn at four months.) I often hear people who believe and pass on such utterly false information.

A prochoice video aired on a cable television network showed a little pool of blood with no visible tissue, much less body parts, and said, "This is the contents of an emptied uterus after an eight-week abortion. It is clearly not a baby, despite what anti-abortionists say in their propaganda."[15] Since the scientific facts of human development are indisputable, there are only two possible explanations. First, the video did not show the full remains of the abortion. Second, the child was so hopelessly torn apart in the abortion that his body parts were no longer discernible. In either case, it is an attempt at deception, as one look at the photograph of the eight week baby on the back cover of this book clearly shows.

Despite the widespread ignorance and misinformation on the subject, whenever we discuss abortion in this country we are always discussing the death of a preborn with clearly discernible human features. In no way is it, nor does it even appear to be, a "blob of tissue."

3g. Even before the unborn is obviously human in appearance, she is what she is—a human being.

The cells of the new individual divide and multiply rapidly, resulting in phenomenal growth. There is growth precisely because there is a new and distinct life. Long before a woman knows she's pregnant there is within her a living, growing human being. Between five and nine days the new person burrows into the wall of the womb for safety. Already his or her sex can be determined by scientific instruments. By fourteen days a hormone produced by the new child suppresses the mother's menstrual period. It will be two more weeks before his clearly human features are discernible, and three more before they are obvious. Still, he is what he is, regardless of his appearance. One need not look human to be human. At conception the unborn does not appear human to us who are used to judging humanity purely by appearance. Nevertheless, in the objective scientific sense he is every bit as human as any older child or adult.

Though I have emphasized the clearly human features of the unborn after six weeks of development, this does not mean babies are any less human before they look human. No matter how he or she looks, no matter which organs have developed and which haven't, *a child is a child, and abortion terminates that child's life*. The earliest means to cause abortion, including RU-486 and all abortion pills, are—and will always be—still too late to avoid taking a life.

Even if someone takes the scientifically untenable position that the unborn is not a human being until it looks human and its heart and brain are functioning, he is still acknowledging the humanity of the twenty-eight million unborns killed by abortion in America in the last two decades.

3h. No matter how much better it sounds, "terminating a pregnancy" is still terminating a life.

Two years before abortion was legalized in America, a prochoice advocate instructed nurses in a prominent journal, "Through public conditioning, use of language, concepts and laws, the idea of abortion can be separated from the idea of killing."[16] The same year a symposium on abortion in Los Angeles offered this training: "If you say, 'Suck out the baby,' you may easily generate or increase trauma; say instead, 'Empty the uterus,' or 'We will scrape the lining of the uterus,' but never 'We will scrape away the baby.' "[17] Interestingly, Hitler's command to take the Jews to their death in the camps was couched in the phrase "empty the ghettos."

Language is not just the expression of minds but the molder of minds. The ways words are used can tremendously influence someone's receptivity to an idea—even an idea which communicated in straightforward terms would be abhorrent.

Using words that focus on what happens to the pregnancy and the uterus takes attention away from the crux of the abortion issue—the individual residing in the uterus. But no matter how many words we use, and how we use them, "terminating a pregnancy" is terminating a human life. The one may sound better than the other, but the realities are one and the same.

We must cut through the semantic fog and always find our way back to the bottom-line realities. As one prolife feminist says, "Prolifers don't object to terminating pregnancies. Pregnancies are only supposed to last a short while. We favor terminating them at around nine months. The objection is to killing children."[18]

4. "The fetus may be alive, but so are eggs and sperm. The fetus is a potential human being, not an actual one; it's like a blueprint not a house, an acorn not an oak tree."

4a. The ovum and sperm are each a product of another's body; unlike the fertilized egg, neither is an independent entity.

Faye Wattleton, former president of Planned Parenthood, on a television panel countered the argument that an unborn baby is a living being by saying to a prolife congressman, "Your sperm are alive too."[1] Similarly, in a widely read article in *Parade* magazine, Carl Sagan attacked the position that abortion kills children by asking, "So is masturbation mass murder?" and, "Why isn't it murder to destroy a sperm or an egg?"[2] The answer, as every scientist should know, is that there is a vast and fundamental difference between sperm and unfertilized eggs on the one hand, and fertilized eggs on the other.

Neither egg nor sperm is complete. Like cells of one's hair or heart, neither egg nor sperm has the capacity to become other than what it is. Both are dead-ends, destined to remain what they are until they die within a matter of days.

In contrast, when egg and sperm are joined, a new, dynamic, and genetically distinct human life begins. *This life is neither sperm nor egg nor a simple combination of both. It is independent, with a life of its own, on a rapid pace of self-directed development.* From the first instant of fertilization that first single cell contains the entire genetic blueprint in all its complexity. This accounts for every detail of human development, including the child's sex, hair and eye color, height, and skin tone.[3] Take that single cell of the just conceived zygote, put it next to a chimpanzee cell and a gorilla cell, and "a geneticist could easily identify the human. Its humanity is already that strikingly apparent."[4]

4b. The physical remains after an abortion indicate the end not of a potential life but of an actual life.

A film called "The Gift of Choice," produced by the Religious

Coalition for Abortion Rights, claims that the unborn is "a probability of a future person," as opposed to the actuality of a present person. But what is left after an abortion are small but perfectly formed body parts—arms and legs, hands and feet, torso and head.

Photograph #4, at the center of this book, shows a hand taken from the discarded remains of an abortion, held in the hand of an adult. Look at it, then decide for yourself if this was a potential or actual human life.

In his how-to manual *Abortion Practice*, Colorado abortionist Dr. Warren Hern states, "A long curved Mayo scissors may be necessary to decapitate and dismember the fetus."[5] One must have a head in order to be decapitated and body parts in order to be dismembered.

Potential life cannot be ended because it hasn't begun. Human body parts are the product of actual human lives that have ended.

4c. Something nonhuman does not become human by getting older and bigger; whatever is human must be human from the beginning.

Dr. Thomas Hilgers states, "No individual living body can 'become' a person unless it already is a person. No living being can become anything other than what it already essentially is."[6]

Dr. Paul Ramsay says this:

> Thus it might be said that in all essential respects the individual is whoever he is going to become from the moment of impregnation. He already is this while not knowing this or anything else. Thereafter, his subsequent development cannot be described as becoming something he is not now. It can only be described as a process of achieving, a process of becoming the one he already is. Genetics teaches us that we were from the beginning what we essentially still are in every cell and in every generally human attribute and in every individual attribute.[7]

4d. Comparing preborns and adults to acorns and oaks is dehumanizing and misleading.

When an acorn is stepped on, the forest experiences no moral dilemma. When a "toddler" sapling or a "teenage" oak dies the "mother tree" does not weep, nor do the sapling's siblings. We naturally value oak trees more than acorns. Unfortunately, the comparison encourages us to make the quantum leap of concluding we should value bigger and older people more than smaller and younger ones (specifically, the unborn). But what are our reasons for valuing the oak tree over the acorn? They are not moral or humanitarian, but simply pragmatic. The oak tree serves us well, either aesthetically or for the lumber or fire wood it can provide. Acorns are plentiful and expendable. But *why* are they expendable? For the same reason the oak tree is also ultimately expendable—it isn't a person, only a thing.

A baby, however, isn't a thing, it's a person. The unborn are not more expendable because they haven't developed into infants, nor infants more expendable because they haven't developed into toddlers, nor teenagers more expendable because they haven't developed into adults.

4e. Even if the analogy were valid, scientifically speaking an acorn is simply a little oak tree, just as an embryo is a little person.

Despite the dehumanizing elements of the acorn-oak analogy, those who understand what an acorn is will realize that, ironically, the analogy serves the opposite purpose for which it is intended!

Blueprints are not houses, nor do they become houses no matter how long we care to wait, because by nature they are something else. But while the blueprint in no sense becomes the house, *the acorn does become the oak tree*. It can do so only because in the most basic sense it *is* the oak tree!

While no house was ever a blueprint, every oak tree was once an acorn. So it is with the person—a person doesn't simply come from an embryo or fetus. A person *was* an embryo, then a fetus. As every oak tree was an acorn, every person was once a fertilized egg.

All the oak tree is or ever will be was in the acorn. If the acorn were destroyed, there would be no oak tree. Likewise, all that the adult is or ever will be was in the embryo. If the embryo were destroyed, there would be no baby, no teenager, and no adult. When the baby dies the teenager dies. When the embryo dies, the baby dies. Abortion doesn't kill potential people. It kills actual people.

> 5. "The unborn isn't a person, with meaningful life. It's only inches in size, and can't even think; it's less advanced than an animal."

5a. Personhood is properly defined by membership in the human species, not by stage of development within that species.

> A living being's designation to a species is determined not by the stage of development but by the sum total of its biological characteristics—actual and potential—which are genetically determined. . . . If we say that [the fetus] is not human, e.g. a member of Homo Sapiens, we must say it is a member of another species. *But this cannot be.*[1]

Dictionaries define *person* as a "human being," "human individual," or "member of the human race." What makes a dog a dog is that he came from dogs. His father was a dog and his mother was a dog, and therefore he is a dog. What makes a human a human is that he came from humans. His father was a human person and his mother was a human person, so he can be nothing other than a human person.

We must not be confused by statements such as Carl Sagan's:

> Despite many claims to the contrary life does not begin at conception: It is an unbroken chain that stretches back nearly to the origin of the Earth, 4.6 billion years ago. Nor does *human* life begin at conception: It is an unbroken chain dating back to the origin of species, tens or hundreds of thousands of years ago.[2]

Sagan misses the point entirely. We aren't talking about a mystical connectedness to the history of the universe. We're talking about whether our unborn are human beings and whether they deserve to live or die. Carl Sagan notwithstanding, the beginning of each human life is not a process but an event—conception.

5b. Personhood is not a matter of size, skill, or degree of intelligence.

Prochoice advocates argue that a child aborted in the first trimester may be less than an inch or two in size, or less than an ounce or two in weight. But what measure of personhood is size? Is an NBA player more of a person than someone half his size? If a two-hundred-pound man loses fifty pounds does he lose one fourth of his personhood? Scales and rulers are no measurement of human nature or worth.

Joseph Fletcher maintains an "individual" is not a "person" unless he has an IQ of at least 40.[3] British anthropologist Ashley Montague says no one becomes human until he is molded by social and cultural influences. By this he means that more intelligent and educated people (such as himself) are more human than the inferior elements of society (such as some of the rest of us).[4]

If personhood is determined by one's current capacities, then someone who is unconscious or sick could be killed immediately because he is not demonstrating superior intellect and skills. "But give the man time and he'll be able to function as a person." Give the baby time and so will she.

Age, size, IQ, or stage of development are simply differences in degree, not in kind. Our kind is humanity. We are people, human beings. We possess certain skills to differing degrees at different stages of development. When we reach maturation there are many different degrees of skills and levels of IQ. But none of these make some people better or more human than others. None make some qualified to live, and others unqualified.

5c. The unborn's status should be determined on an objective basis, not on subjective or self-serving definitions of personhood.

The Fourteenth Amendment says the state shall not deprive any "person" of life without due process of law. Of course, when this was written the word *human* was a synonym for person and could just as easily have been used. The Supreme Court admitted in *Roe v. Wade*, "If the suggestion of personhood [of the unborn] is established, the appellant's [pro-abortion] case, of course, collapses, for the fetus' right to life is then guaranteed specifically by the [fourteenth] amendment."[5]

To solve this problem the court chose to abandon the historic meaning of personhood. In the years that have followed, artificial distinctions have been made by prochoice advocates to differentiate between humans and "persons." Part of the reason for this is that the scientific fact that life begins at conception paints the prochoice movement into a corner. The old and still popular argument, "this isn't human life," is privately known by many prochoice advocates to be erroneous. They realize it's only a matter of time before the public learns the truth. The newer strategy is to say "OK, this is human life, but it isn't really a person." (Once someone is committed to the prochoice position, rather than abandon it when the scientific facts contradict it, the tendency is to come up with another line of defense.)

We must not reduce issues of life and death and basic human rights to a semantic game in which we are free to redefine our terms. Changing the meaning of words doesn't change reality. The concept of personhood is now virtually worthless as an ethical guide in the matter of abortion. The only objective questions we can ask are:

1. "Is it human, that is, did it come from human beings?"

2. "Is it a genetically unique individual?"

3. "Is it alive and growing?"

If the answers are yes, then "it" is a "he" or "she," a living person, worthy of protection.

5d. It is a scientific fact that there are thought processes at work in unborn babies.

Associated Press reported a study showing that "babies start learning about their language-to-be before they are born." University of North Carolina psychology professor Dr. Anthony DeCasper was quoted as saying, "The implication is that fetuses heard, perceived, listened and learned something about the acoustic structure of American English."[6]

A *Newsweek* article states, "Life in the womb represents the next frontier for studies of human development, and the early explorations of the frontier—through ultrasound, fiber-optic cameras, miniature microphones—have yielded startling discoveries."[7] The same article says, "With no hype at all, *the fetus can rightly be called a marvel of cognition, consciousness and sentience*." It also says that scientists have already detected sentience (self-awareness) in the second trimester.[8] Indeed, the extraordinary capacities and responses of preborn children have been well documented by scientific studies for years.[9]

By early in the second trimester the baby moves his hands to shield his eyes to bright light coming in through his mother's body. "The fetus also responds to sounds in frequencies so high or low that they cannot be heard by the human adult ear."[10] He hears loud music and may even cover his ears at loud noises from the outside world. At seventeen weeks, when abortions are still commonly performed, the child experiences Rapid Eye Movement (REM) sleep, indicating that he is not only sleeping but dreaming.[11] Can we say that someone capable of dreaming is incapable of thinking?

There is no doubt whatsoever that later abortions kill a sentient, thinking human being. By the end of the second and the start of the third trimester (at twenty-four weeks) the "brain's neural circuits are as advanced as a newborn's."[12] It seems unthinkable that anyone aware of the facts could favor the current legality of abortions in the second and third trimesters. That such abortions are adamantly defended by pro-choice advocates should cause us to ask whether their position is based on facts at all or merely personal preference or wishful thinking.

But are earlier abortions any better than later ones? Since there is a functioning brain with measurable brain waves at forty days of development, who are we to say that these tiny brains can't do what brains do—think? Yet virtually all abortions legal in America occur after forty days. And even if an abortion process is made available that takes the life before there is the capacity for thought, does this destroy the life in a way that is any less real or significant? Does it change the fact that a child who would have had a name and a family and a life will now have none of these?

5e. If the unborn's value can be compared to that of an animal, there is no reason not to also compare the value of born people to animals.

Scientist and bioethicist Peter Singer denounces what he calls "speciesism"—valuing humans above animals. He stretches the conventional definition of *person* beyond recognition by saying that not only can humans be nonpersons, but nonhumans can be persons:

> We should reject the doctrine that places the lives of members of our species above the lives of members of other species. Some members of other species are persons; some members of our own species are not. No objective assessment can give greater value to the lives of members of our species. . . .[13]

Singer has also stated:

> If we compare a severely defective human infant with a nonhuman animal, a dog or a pig, for example, we will often find the nonhuman to have superior

59

capacities, both actual and potential, for rationality, self-consciousness, communication and anything else that can plausibly be considered morally significant.[14]

Once such logic is adopted there is no stopping place. One nuclear physicist says, "It should be recognized that not all men are human. . . . It would seem to be more inhumane to kill an adult chimpanzee than a newborn baby, since the chimpanzee has greater mental awareness."[15] Of course, if our concern is for mental awareness we could kill the chimpanzee or the baby or a teenager painlessly in his sleep, when he is not mentally aware. The real question is whether there is some reason to regard human life as inherently more valuable than nonhuman life. Our society has always acted on that premise. It is deeply rooted in the Judeo-Christian heritage of western civilization. Abortion is both a cause and effect of this new "sliding scale" view of human worth.

The problem is not whether animals should be treated humanely. Of course they should. The problem is whether *humans* should be treated humanely. Here our double standard becomes obvious. It is a serious and enforced crime in America to break an eagle egg. In many places goldfish are no longer given as prizes at fairs because they were being flushed down toilets, and this was considered cruel. Abigail Van Buren of "Dear Abby" has said people should not be allowed to put to death their pets for any reason. Yet she has repeatedly affirmed that she is prochoice about aborting babies.

When a Greenpeace activist came to a friend's house and asked for a donation to save the whales and seals, she responded, "I think your cause is worthy, but I give to one I think is even more worthy—saving the lives of baby humans." The activist, who was vocally prolife and anti-choice when it comes to killing baby seals, scowled and walked away. His attitude is increasingly common in our society. Save the whales; kill the children.

5f. It is dangerous when people in power are free to determine whether other, less powerful lives are meaningful.

In the 1973 *Roe v. Wade* decision the Supreme Court questioned whether the unborn had "meaningful" lives. But meaningful to whom, and when? Is the fact that your life was not taken from you as an unborn meaningful to you now? If a mother wants her baby, his life is highly meaningful, which is why she mourns if there is a miscarriage. If the mother doesn't want her baby, then his life is not meaningful to her. *But is the worth of a human being dependent upon whether others think his life is meaningful?* Does the unborn transform from person to nonperson with each of his mother's changes of mind? And doesn't every human being regard the life he had in the womb as meaningful, since had it been terminated he would not now be alive?

Black people, women, Indians, Jews, and many others have been declared nonpersons or persons whose lives are not meaningful. But for whose benefit? That of the people in power, who have declared for their own economic, political, or personal advantage who is meaningful and who isn't. It was whites deciding that blacks were less human. It was males deciding women had fewer rights. Now it is big people deciding little people don't have rights.

Personhood is not something to be bestowed on living human beings, large or small, by an intellectual elite with vested interests in ridding society of undesirables. Personhood has an inherent value, a value that comes from being a member of the human race. For those who believe the Bible, this is linked to being created in the image of God. But even those who are not Christians can hold to the position—though it is increasingly difficult to do so—that human life is valuable even when it is young or small or "less useful" to others.

This question is much broader than the issue of abortion. Exactly the same logic is being used with already born children. Dr. Charles Hartshorne of the University of Texas at Austin says, "Of course, an infant is not fully human. . . . I have little sympathy with the idea that infanticide is just another form of murder. Persons who are already functionally persons in the full sense have more important rights even than infants."[16]

Once it is acceptable to kill unborn children, no one who is weak or vulnerable can be safe. Is the handicapped fully human? Is his life meaningful? How about the elderly? If those who cannot think do not deserve to live, what about those who think the wrong way?

Are we ready for the brave new world into which the logic of abortion-rights has led us?

6. "A fetus isn't a person until quickening or viability."

6a. Quickening is a gauge of personhood only if someone's reality or value is dependent upon being noticed by another.

Quickening is an old term for when the mother first becomes aware of the movements of the child within her. Because the uterus is not highly sensitive to touch, quickening often happens in the second trimester, long after the child has started moving. Some women feel their children very early, others don't feel their presence until months later.

Surely we cannot believe that one child becomes human when his mother senses him at twelve weeks development, and another doesn't become human until his mother senses him at twenty. One person's ability or inability to recognize the presence of another has nothing whatsoever to do with the second person's reality. *Human life begins at conception, not at perception.*

6b. Viability is an arbitrary concept. Why not associate personhood with heartbeat, brain waves, or something else?

Viability is the point at which the fetus becomes capable of surviving without having to depend on his mother. In *Roe v. Wade*, the Supreme Court defined viability as the point when the unborn is "potentially able to live outside the mother's womb, albeit with artificial aid."[1] The critical issue in when this point is reached is the development of the child's lungs.

But why make worthiness to live dependent upon the development of the child's lungs? Why not say he becomes human in the fourth week because that's when his heart beats? Or the sixth week because that's when he has brain waves? (Both are also arbitrary, yet both would eliminate all abortions currently performed.) Someone could argue that personhood begins when the unborn first sucks his thumb or responds to light and noise. Or why not say personhood begins when the child takes his first step or is potty trained?

There is only one objective point of origin for any human being—only one point at which there was not a human being a moment ago, and there is now. That point is conception.

6c. The point of viability constantly changes because it depends on technology, not the unborn herself. Eventually babies may be viable from the point of conception.

Like all points other than conception, viability is arbitrary, but it is even more arbitrary than most. The point at which heart and brain develop—though unscientific as measurements of personhood—at least remain fairly constant. Yet in the last three decades, viability has been reduced from thirty weeks to less than twenty weeks of development. A child has actually been born at nineteen weeks and survived.

Viability depends not only on the child but on the ability of our technology to save his life. What will happen when we are able to save lives at fifteen weeks or less? Will they suddenly become human and worthy to live? Can we honestly believe that children at twenty-one weeks were not human twenty years ago but are human now, simply because of improved technology? Or can we believe that the unborn at eighteen weeks, who is just barely nonviable, is not a human being, but ten years from now he will be because hospitals will have better equipment?

Does the baby's nature and worth also depend on which hospital—or country—he is in since some hospitals are equipped to save a nineteen-week developed child, and others could save a child no earlier than twenty-eight weeks? Technologies change, babies do not. Surely we cannot believe that the sophistication of life support systems determines the reality or worth of human life!

Dr. Landrum Shettles, a pioneer in fertility and sperm biology and contributor to fifty medical textbooks, made this assessment of the Supreme Court's arguments based on viability:

> An abortion law truly based on "viability" would require constant redefinition. What was not considered protectable human life last year might be this year. If we were to take the Court at its word, we would find ourselves with a law that makes last year's "abortions" this year's homicides in some cases. I have maintained human embryos in "laboratory wombs" for several days. . . . It appears inevitable that the day will come when the unborn will *always* be potentially viable outside the womb.[2]

"Test-tube" babies have already survived for days outside the womb before implantation. Shouldn't proponents of the viability theory then maintain that they were human from the point of conception since they were viable all along? As Dr. Shettles suggests, viability is ultimately an argument for the humanity of all preborn children since eventually science may find a way for an entire "pregnancy" to take place outside of a mother.

Despite all this, the Supreme Court cited viability as the point where the state has a compelling interest in the welfare of the unborn. (Ironically, the wording of the decision allowed abortion after viability anyway.) However, in the 1989 *Webster v. Reproductive Health Services* decision, the Supreme Court began to dismantle the illogical conclusions of *Roe v. Wade* when it said, "We do not see why the State's interest in protecting potential human life should come into existence only at the point of viability."

6d. In a broad sense, many born people are not viable because they are incapable of surviving without depending on others.

If viability is viewed in its broadest sense as the capacity to live without depending on other human beings, many people in our society are not viable. The premature baby still has to depend on someone for human care, even if it's a team of doctors and nurses who hover over him day and night.

What do the sick, the handicapped, Alzheimer's victims, infants, two-year-olds, many elderly, and the unborn all have in common? First, they are people. Second, they are not viable; they are dependent upon other people to live.

Many accident victims can't survive on their own without medical help. Is the person whose lungs are punctured now a nonperson? I am an insulin-dependent diabetic. I can't survive on my own. Without insulin I will die. Does that mean I'm not a person? The ability to survive without someone's help is a poor criterion by which to evaluate his humanity.

An infant won't survive two days without adult care. A two-year-old can't survive on his own either. Though these children can be very inconvenient and interfere with the desires and lifestyles of adults, most of us do not believe their parents have the right to kill them. I say "most of us" not facetiously but in the interests of accuracy. Psychiatrist and anthropologist Virginia Abernethy of Vanderbilt University's School of Medicine said in *Newsweek*: "I don't think abortion is ever wrong. As long as an individual is completely dependent upon the mother, it's not a person." The article goes on to explain:

In this view, which is shared by other pro-choice theorists, an individual becomes a person only when he or she becomes a responsible moral agent—around three or four, in Abernethy's judgment. Until then, she thinks, infants—like fetuses—are nonpersons; defective children, such as those with Down's syndrome, may never become persons.[3]

Those who doubt the logical and inevitable consequences of the pro-choice position should consider carefully these words. Even *Newsweek*, which has never been known as a mouthpiece for the prolife movement, cannot help but point out what a short jump there is from abortion to infanticide.

6e. Someone's helplessness or dependency should motivate us to protect her, not to destroy her.

The issue of viability is that if someone is dependent upon an adult to survive, somehow she does not deserve to live. Yet this is contrary to our sense of what is right:

> Normally when we see someone mistreated, our sense of outrage, our urge to protect, is inversely related to the person's ability to protect himself: The more *dependent* he or she is, the more protective we become. With "viability" as our guide, we act completely contrary to our normal sense of moral responsibility. Rather than appealing to our best instincts, "viability" brings out the very worst in us.[4]

Some years ago the attention of our entire nation was turned to Baby Jessica, the little girl trapped at the bottom of a deep well. The amount of human resources poured into saving her was vast, but no one doubted whether she was worth it. What touched our hearts more than anything was her helplessness and vulnerability.

When we are thinking accurately, we realize that a helpless person deserves help precisely because she is helpless. It is a sad commentary on society when a child's helplessness and dependence on another is used as an argument against her right to live.

7. "Obviously life begins at birth. That's why we celebrate birthdays, not conception days, and why we don't have funerals following miscarriages."

7a. Our recognition of birthdays is cultural, not scientific.

The Chinese calculate a person's age from the estimated time of his conception. Other societies celebrate birthdays because this is when the already living child enters our world. Now we can see, touch, and hold him. He has not come into being at this point, he has simply joined us on the outside. A birthday is not the beginning of a life, but the beginning of a face-to-face relationship.

7b. Some people *do* have funerals after a miscarriage.

A nonreligious couple came to me when their baby died before birth. The mother told me that she and her preborn daughter had become very close during her pregnancy. She said calmly, "No matter what anyone else says, I have lost a baby. We named her Mary Beth, and she will always be our daughter." There was no birth or death certificate, but this couple knew without a doubt their preborn child was a human being. They asked to have a funeral. It was unforgettable. There wasn't a dry eye anywhere—everyone knew a child had died.

7c. Funerals are an expression of our own subjective attachment to those who have died, not a measurement of their true worth.

Funerals are for the living, not the dead. The baby that dies in a miscarriage is a real baby, but we haven't gotten to know her yet. Therefore the sense of loss, though real, is often much less than if she had been born and we had bonded with her. The difference, however, is not in her, but in *us*. Whether born or preborn, the less we know a person, the less we grieve her death. That's why we would have been devastated if a close friend died today, but weren't devastated at the thousands of equally valuable people who did die today. Surely the fact that we do not grieve does not in any way lessen their personhood or worth.

7d. There is nothing about birth that makes a baby essentially different than he was before birth.

In October 1983 a physician was accused of murder because he killed a baby who survived his attempt to abort him. Envision this scenario as it actually happened. Before the attempted abortion, the baby was normal and healthy. Five minutes later, he had been disfigured, poisoned, and burned with salt, all of which was perfectly legal. But since this child had been moved a few feet from where he was before (inside his mother), he was now considered a person.

The same physician, who is now a director of Planned Parenthood Federation of America, had full legal right to poison and kill the child moments earlier, but was now considered a murderer. Why? Simply because he bungled his assigned task of killing inside the womb and finished the same job on the outside. Does anyone really believe that one of these attempted killings was right and the other was wrong?

I spent the night in a city where the news was dominated by the frightful story of a murdered infant estimated at three pounds. Only the top half of the child's body had been found. Doctors examining the baby said he could have been born prematurely or aborted, but it was impossible to tell. The reason this was so newsworthy is that if it could be determined the child had been born, it would have been a murder of the worst kind.

But children of this size are killed by abortion every day, and it is a ho-hum affair to the media. Those who oppose the abortions that kill these children are regarded as anti-choice and anti-rights. Yet anyone who would defend the bloody slaying of the child in the news—a child essentially no different than all aborted children of the same age—would be regarded as a monster. *What's the difference?*

If our concern is for the innocent child, why should anyone be relieved to find out that the child was aborted rather than murdered? The point is he was killed, and killed brutally! There would be no less pain, no less horror, and death would be no less real if this baby had been killed inside his mother by the doctor's knife or outside her by the knife of a psychopath.

There is simply no magic that somehow changes the nature and value of a child just because he has moved from inside his mother to outside.

8. "No one can really know that human life begins before birth."

8a. Children know that human life begins before birth.

I heard a radio news report of some children who found a dumpster full of aborted fetuses. But according to the report when they ran to their parents in shock and fear, they said they had found "dead babies." They stated the obvious. For one not to believe the obvious, one has to be taught not to believe it. These children were too young to know not to believe what they saw.

Feminist Jean Garton tells the moving story of her three-year-old, who wandered into her room late at night and inadvertently saw a photo of a ten-week abortion. His mother describes his reaction:

> His small voice was filled with great sadness as he asked, "Who broke the baby?"
>
> How could this small, innocent child see what so many adults cannot see? How could he know instinctively that this which many people carelessly dismiss as tissue or a blob was one in being with him, was like him? In the words of his question he gave humanity to what adults call "fetal matter"; in the tone of his question he mourned what we exalt as a sign of liberation and freedom. With a wisdom which often escapes the learned, he asked in the presence of the evidence before his eyes, "Who broke the baby?"[1]

8b. Pregnant women know that human life begins before birth.

When have you ever heard a pregnant woman say, "The blob of tissue kicked me" or, "That product of conception kicked me" or even, "My fetus kicked me"? It's always, "My *baby* kicked me." Many pregnant women have worn T-shirts with big arrows pointing to their unborn child. Always they say, "Baby." Have you ever seen one that says "Blob," "POC," or "Fetus"?

My wife and I were outside an abortion clinic one dark, overcast day. Three women in a row came out of the clinic wearing sunglasses. We could see that all three had been crying. My wife said, "You don't grieve like that when you've just had a lump of tissue removed. You grieve like that when you've lost your baby."

8c. Doctors know that human life begins before birth.

Talk to any good doctor and he will say that when he is treating a pregnant woman he has two patients, not just one. He shows great care and concern not only for the mother, but for the smaller less visible patient, checking his movement, his position, his heartbeat.

After a life-saving surgery on an unborn child, the surgeon stated that such surgeries "make it clear that the fetus is a patient."[2] Associated Press accompanied the story with a diagram from the *New England Journal of Medicine*, clearly showing the unborn to be a baby.

A remarkable 1991 cover story from *Discover* magazine was called "Surgery Before Birth." It describes surgery on an unborn child:

> A precise dose of anesthetic had put both the mother and the 24-week-old fetus safely and limply to sleep. And now, lifting the little arm gently to rotate the one-pound body into position, pediatric surgeon Michael Harrison poised his scalpel just under the rib cage. This astonishing intrusion on an unborn life took place on June 15, 1989; it was necessary because this tiny patient's diaphragm had failed to close as it should have.[3]

Note the reference to the unborn as "patient." If the unborn is not a person, who is the patient being operated on? If the surgery is unsuccessful and the unborn's heart stops beating, did the patient die? The patient is referred to as "an unborn life." His arm, rib cage, and diaphragm are referred to by name. An anesthetic was used to put him to sleep. Elsewhere in the article, the author refers to his gender, and occasionally comes right out and calls him a "baby." The article ends by saying, "While fetal therapists wrestle with protocols . . . their efforts to save tiny lives continue." Yet that same tiny life, not to be born for another four months, can be legally killed by abortion up to the moment of birth.

A prochoice editorial in *California Medicine* recognized that the position that human life does not begin at conception is politically and socially expedient for the prochoice movement, but that "everyone" knows it is simply untrue:

> Since the old ethic has not been fully displaced it has been necessary to separate the idea of abortion from the idea of killing, which continues to be socially abhorrent. The result has been a curious avoidance of the scientific fact, which everyone really knows, that human life begins at conception and is continuous whether intra- or extra-uterine until death.[4]

8d. Society knows that human life begins before birth.

Public service advertisements urge women not to smoke, drink alcohol, or take drugs while pregnant because they could harm their unborn babies. A front-page headline of the *Oregonian* read, "Judge sends mother to jail to protect unborn child."[5] The same has happened in Washington, D.C. Judges are taking radical steps to protect the lives of the unborn, even to the point of incarcerating women who take drugs or otherwise endanger their babies before birth. In Illinois a pregnant woman who takes an illegal drug can be prosecuted for "delivering a controlled substance to a minor." This is an explicit recognition that the unborn is a person with rights of her own.

But that same women who is prosecuted and jailed for endangering her child is perfectly free to abort her child. In America today, *it is illegal to harm your preborn child, but it is perfectly legal to kill him.*

If this sounds incredible, consider a pro-abortion *Newsweek* article that warns against do-it-yourself attempts at abortion. Caution should be used with taking drugs to induce abortion because of the danger of "depriving the fetus of oxygen and causing fetal brain damage instead of abortion." The writer states, "Sadly, many home remedies could damage a fetus instead of kill it."[6] A damaged unborn child is a tragedy; a dead unborn child is a remedy. Does *Newsweek* understand what it is saying?

Several states have laws requiring that aborted babies be disposed of in a "humane" fashion. One does not dispose of tonsils or gall stones in a humane fashion. Similarly, the state of Minnesota has a law that requires hospitals and abortion clinics to bury or cremate aborted babies. Who but human beings are required to be buried or cremated?

A prolife speaker was detained by police for carrying with him the preserved body of an aborted baby. He was told it was illegal to transport human remains across state lines without special permission. When he realized this meant the state would have to argue in court that the bodies of aborted babies are in fact human remains, he welcomed prosecution! The state dropped the charges. Though they knew these were human remains, how could a state that defends and funds abortions publicly admit—much less attempt to prove—that abortion kills human beings?

In 1988 a man stabbed a woman in the abdomen, thereby killing the "fetus" within her. Though the woman lived, the man was convicted of taking a human life, and his conviction was upheld in a higher court. Yet it was entirely legal for the woman to hire an abortionist to kill the same child. Why is an action that results in the death of the same preborn person considered murder on the one hand and a perfectly acceptable action on the other? This is society's schizophrenia about abortion—though it approves of it, there is an underlying knowledge that it kills children.

8e. The media know that human life begins before birth.

The evening news showed films of riots in another country. The reporter said that a number of innocent men and women had been shot down. Then with a look of horror he added, "Among those shot down was a pregnant woman."

Why was this any more tragic than shooting down the other women? Would anyone have reported, "They shot down a woman with a blob of tissue inside"? Of course not. The reason for the horror is because the bullet that killed the pregnant woman thereby killed a child. Ironically, the same newscaster is probably not at all horrified that over four thousand babies are deliberately cut to pieces in his country each day. Like 90 percent of his colleagues in the media, he was probably decidedly "prochoice."[7] Yet, his reaction to the killing betrayed a gut level realization that no amount of propaganda to the contrary could take from him—inside every pregnant woman is an innocent child.

A *Time* magazine article arguing against drug use and for better prenatal care says, "Courts will never be able to ensure real protection to an unborn child. That will have to come from mothers who take responsibility for the lives they carry within them."[8] If the subject were abortion rather than drug use, would mothers be exhorted to "take responsibility for the lives they carry within them"?

In October 1990 both Chrysler and Volvo ran ads in major newsmagazines promoting their new cars equipped with air bags. The fullpage Volvo ad showed a large ultrasound image of a preborn child, with the single message at the bottom: "Is Something Inside Telling You to Buy a Volvo?"[9] The Chrysler ad, two full pages, pictured a pregnant woman who had survived a serious automobile accident several months earlier. It said:

Susan Reed was on her way to work when a drunk driver crashed into Susan's 1990 Dodge Spirit. Both cars were totally destroyed. But Mrs. Reed was wearing her lap/shoulder belt, and the Dodge Spirit was equipped with a driver's air bag. It worked. It saved her life. And it saved another life. Her baby's.[10]

Above another picture of the mother, this time with her newborn in arms, the large caption reads, "One Chrysler Air Bag, Two Lives Saved."

If a prolife organization had run these ads, they would have been dismissed as propaganda. Yet nothing a prolife ad could have said would have expressed more precisely the central message of the prolife movement. The ads simply stated what every thinking person knows if he allows himself to realize it—*inside every pregnant woman is an innocent human being whose life is worthy of protection.*

8f. Prochoice advocates know that human life begins before birth.

A woman who was on television defending her abortions said, "I always carried my babies low." Despite her stated position, in the unguarded moment she showed her realization that her abortions had killed her babies.

A prochoice political candidate openly defended abortion. Yet in a television interview about his family he proudly said, "I'm a grandfather," even though his first grandchild was not due to be born for several months.

We visited a prochoice rally where one of the largest signs said, "My Body, My Baby, My Business." Think of what this message means. After birth the baby would still be hers. Would society then say it was her business what she did to him? If she has the right to kill her baby before birth, why not kill the same baby after birth? This demonstrator hadn't yet learned the cardinal rule of the prochoice movement: "Don't call them babies. Always pretend they aren't really children. Once you admit they are, your argument could be seen for what it is—an argument for baby-killing."

An editorial in the *New Republic* concedes the humanity of the unborn and admits that there is no essential difference between born and unborn. It then draws a conclusion refreshingly candid but chilling in its implications:

> There clearly is no logical or moral distinction between a fetus and a young baby; free availability of abortion cannot be reasonably distinguished from euthanasia. Nevertheless we are for it. It is too facile to say that human life always is sacred; obviously it is not.[11]

Psychologist and prochoice advocate Magda Denes wrote, "I do think abortion is murder—of a very special and necessary sort. And no physician ever involved with the procedure ever kids himself about that."[12]

For many people, prochoice thinking is not primarily the result of ignorance but of denial or ignorance-by-choice. What we all know to be true we refuse to admit or act upon as truth, because of the difficulty it may create for us. By heaping up argument upon argument—illogical and inconsistent though they be—we try to bury the truth so deep it will not resurface. And when it does, we quickly push it back down, hoping that our wishing it to go away will make it go away. But no matter how we ignore or deny it, the truth will still be the truth: Human life begins long before birth, and abortion kills children.

Rights and Fairness

PART TWO

ARGUMENTS CONCERNING
RIGHTS AND FAIRNESS

ARGUMENTS CONCERNING
RIGHTS AND FAIRNESS

---

9. "Even if the unborn are human beings, they have fewer rights than the woman. No one should be expected to donate her body as a life support system for someone else."

9a. Once we grant that the unborn are human beings, it should settle the question of their right to live.

One prochoice advocate, in the face of the overwhelming evidence, admitted to me that the unborn are human beings. He then added, "But that's irrelevant to the issue of a woman's right to have an abortion."

But how can one's humanity be irrelevant to the question of whether someone has the right to kill him? Wasn't the black person's humanity relevant to the issue of slavery, or the Jew's humanity relevant to the ethics of the holocaust? Not only is the unborn's humanity relevant, *it is the single most relevant issue in the whole abortion debate.*

In the *Roe v. Wade* decision, Justice Harry Blackmun stated, "We need not resolve the difficult question of when life begins." First, this question is not difficult at all, as the many scientists quoted under *Argument 1* attest. But second, no matter what answer we come to, isn't the question of whether living children are being killed by abortion *precisely* the question we must resolve?

Writing in the *New York Times*, Barbara Ehrenreich says, "A woman may think of her fetus as a person or as just cells depending on whether the pregnancy is wanted or not. This does not reflect moral confusion, but choice in action."[1]

In this Alice-in-Wonderland approach, one's choice is not made in light of scientific and moral realities. One's choice is itself the only important reality, overshadowing all matters of fact. But if society operated this way, every killing of a person would be justifiable. The real issue would not be the worth of the person killed, but the free choice of the one doing the killing. If a man doesn't want his wife, he can think of her as a nonperson. When he chooses to kill her this is not "moral confusion" but "choice in action."

Ms. Ehrenreich goes on to say, "Moreover, a woman may think of the fetus as a person and still find it necessary and morally responsible to have an abortion."[2] We must not miss the implications of this viewpoint. It says that one may acknowledge the personhood of a fellow human being, yet feel that for one's personal benefit it is legitimate—even "morally responsible"—to kill that other person. Though this is a logical conclusion of abortion-rights thinking, if carried out in our society it would mean the end of human rights and social justice.

9b. The right to live doesn't increase with age and size, otherwise toddlers and adolescents have less right to live than adults.

One author justifies some abortions based on his belief that "human worth and human rights grow with the physiological development."[3] If this is true, then human worth and rights continue to grow after birth, since we know physiological development continues after birth. Physical development continues year after year and takes on dramatic changes during adolescence. If human worth and rights grow with physiological development, then adults have a greater right to live than adolescents, who have a greater right to live than infants. It is morally preferable to kill an infant than a toddler, a toddler than a teenager, and a teenager than an adult.

In their argument for letting handicapped infants die, two scientists and ethicists say this:

> Pro-life groups are right about one thing: the location of the baby inside or outside the womb cannot make such a crucial difference. . . . The solution, however, is not to accept the pro-life view that the fetus is a human being with the same moral status as yours or mine. The solution is the very opposite: to abandon the idea that all human life is of equal worth.[4]

Can we accept a logic that ties human worth and rights to physiological development? Why are we so outraged when we read of child abductions and murders? Why do they seem even worse to us than when the same thing is done to an adult? Isn't it because children are small, vulnerable, and innocent? The idea of an older, stronger person using them, considering them expendable, is horrid and despicable. The right to live—the right not to be cut to pieces—is a basic right of every person. Surely it is no less a right for a child, whether born or unborn, than an adult.

The moral fabric of our society is woven around a premise stated in the Declaration of Independence: "We hold these truths to be self-evident that all men are created equal, that they are endowed by their Creator with certain unalienable rights, that among these are life, liberty and the pursuit of happiness." Our forefathers did not say, "After a certain level of physiological development human beings gradually become equal, but until they do it's OK to take from them life, liberty and the opportunity to pursue happiness." The concept that all are created equal stands in stark contrast to the notion that human rights evolve with age, size, or social status.

9c. The comparison between baby's rights and mother's rights is unequal. What is at stake in abortion is the mother's lifestyle, as opposed to the baby's life.

Of course a child does not have more rights than her mother. Any two people are equal, and any two people have equal rights. Hence, a mother has every bit as much right to live as any child. But in nearly all abortions, the woman's right to live is not an issue because her life is not in danger. (See Argument 29.)

The mother has not only the right to live, but also the right to the lifestyle of her choice—as long as that choice does not rob other people of even more fundamental rights, the most basic of which is the right to live. The right to a certain lifestyle is never absolute and unconditional. It is always governed by its effects on others.

Planned Parenthood states, "The desire to complete school or to continue working are common reasons women give for choosing to abort an unplanned pregnancy."[5] Completing school and working are desirable things in many cases, and pregnancy can make them difficult. But a woman normally can continue school and work during pregnancy. If she gives up a child for adoption she need not give up school or work. If she chooses to raise the child herself there are childcare options available if she must work outside the home. I am not suggesting this is ideal, nor do

I say it callously, as I have worked with single mothers and know their difficulties. I am simply pointing out that there are alternatives, any one of which is preferable to an innocent child's death. Regardless of the challenges, *one person's right to a preferred lifestyle is not greater than another person's right to a life.*

9d. It is reasonable for society to expect an adult to live temporarily with an inconvenience if the only alternative is killing a child.

Abortion-rights advocate Judith Jarvis Thomson invented an analogy that has been widely quoted in prochoice literature and debates. She compares pregnancy to a situation in which someone wakes up strapped to a famous but unconscious violinist. Imagine, Thomson says, that some group called the Society of Music Lovers has "kidnaped" you because you have a certain blood type. Now you are being forced to stay "plugged in" to the violinist's body for nine months until he is viable, or able to live on his own.

Thomson then asks, what if it was not just nine months but nine years or considerably longer? (Apparently this is a comparison to having to raise a child once he is born.) Thomson assumes that readers would find such a situation "outrageous," and would not consider it their obligation to be subjected to nine months—at least—of bondage and misery for the sake of the violinist, who is little more than a human parasite.[6]

This analogy is worth a closer examination, both because of its popularity and because it is typical of the way the abortion issue is framed by prochoice advocates. Here are six fallacies of this argument that cut to the heart of the abortion debate:

1. Over 99 percent of all pregnancies are the result of sexual relations in which both partners have willingly participated. One is rarely coerced into pregnancy. (See Argument 31, "What about a woman who is pregnant due to rape or incest?") Though prolifers may be in Thomson's mind, neither they nor anyone else is parallel to the Society of Music Lovers. No one is going around forcing people to get pregnant. The outrage the reader feels at the idea of being kidnaped and coerced is an effective emotional device, but it is a distortion of reality.

2. Pregnancy is a much different experience than the analogy depicts. Pregnancy is portrayed as a condition in which one is unable to leave the room, to socialize, to have a job, or even to get out of bed. Carrying a child is depicted as a horrid, degrading, and debilitating situation. Both medical science and the personal experience of millions of women argue against this bleak and twisted picture. Carrying a child is a natural condition in which there is some inconvenience. But few women are bedridden during their pregnancies. Most are socially active, capable of working, traveling, and exercising almost to the day the child is delivered.

3. Even when pregnancy is unwanted or difficult, it is a temporary condition. Since the great majority of abortions take place from seven weeks to six months of development, the actual difference between the woman who aborts her child and the woman who doesn't is not nine months but three to seven months. The analogy to nine years or even a lifetime of being chained to someone is obviously invalid since after birth a woman is free to give up her child to one of the hundreds of thousands of families waiting to adopt infants in this country. While pregnancy is a temporary condition, abortion produces a permanent condition—the death of a child.

4. In this scenario, mother and child are pitted against each other as enemies. The mother is at best merely a life support system, and at worst the victim of a crime. The child is a leech, a parasite unfairly taking advantage of the mother. Love, compassion, and care are nowhere present. The bonding between mother and child is totally ignored. The picture of a woman waking up in a bed, strapped to a strange unconscious man is bizarre and degrading to women whose pregnancy and motherhood are natural.

5. The child's presence during pregnancy is rarely more inconvenient than his presence after birth. The burden of a born child is usually greater on a woman than the burden of an unborn. Yet if a parent of a two-year-old decides he is tired of being a parent and no one has the right to expect him to be one any longer, society recognizes he nonetheless has certain responsibilities toward that child. He can surrender him for foster care or adoption, but he cannot abuse, neglect, or kill the child. If the solution to the stresses of pregnancy is killing the preborn child, is killing not also the solution to the stresses of parenting the preschooler?

6. Even when there is no felt obligation there is sometimes real obligation. If a woman is being raped or murdered, what do we think of those who make no effort to rescue the woman? Don't we recognize that there is moral responsibility toward saving a life, even if it involves an inconvenience or risk we did not ask for or want?

For the woman carrying a child, isn't it a significant consideration that her own mother made the same sacrifice for her? Can we forget that every one of us was once that "leech," that "parasite," that "violinist" dependent on our mothers in order to live? Aren't you glad your mother looked at pregnancy—and looked at you—differently than portrayed by this prochoice analogy?

10. "Every person has the right to choose. It would be unfair to restrict a woman's choice by prohibiting abortion."

10a. Any civilized society restricts the individual's freedom to choose whenever that choice would harm an innocent person.

When I present the prolife position on school campuses, I often begin by saying:

> I've been introduced as being prolife, but I want to make clear that I'm really prochoice. I believe that a person has the right to do whatever she wants with her own body. It's none of our business what choice she makes, and we have no right to impose our morals on others. Whether I like someone's choices or not is irrelevant. She should have the freedom to make her own choices.

I'm normally greeted by surprised looks and audible affirmation, including smiles, nods, and even applause. I have used the sacred buzzwords of the prochoice movement—rights, freedom, and choice. I have sounded tolerant, open-minded, and fair. Then I say this:

> Yes, I'm prochoice. That's why I believe every man has the right to rape a woman if that is his choice. After all, it's his body, and neither you nor I have the right to tell him what to do with it. He's free to choose, and it's none of our business what choice he makes. We have no right to impose our morals on him. Whether I like the choice or not, he should have the freedom to make his own choices.

After I let the shock settle in a bit, I explain that I am not really prochoice when it comes to rape. I ask them to point out the fallacy of the "it's his body and he can choose what he wants" argument. They realize that in emphasizing the man's right to choose I have completely ignored the rights of the innocent woman. My hope is that they also realize it is not always a virtue to be prochoice.

Laws against false advertising restrict a businessman's right to free speech. Laws against discrimination infringe on the freedom of choice of those who would treat minorities unfairly. When others' rights are at stake—and particularly when their very lives are at stake—any decent society must restrict the individual's freedom of choice. Is an innocent person being damaged by a woman's choice to have an abortion? If not, no problem. If so, it is a major problem that society cannot afford to ignore.

10b. "Freedom to choose" is too vague for meaningful discussion; we must always ask, "Freedom to choose *what?*"

It is absurd to defend a specific choice merely on the basis that it is a choice. Yet if you read the literature and listen to the talk shows, you know that this is constantly done by prochoice activists. "The right to choose" is a magic slogan that seems to make all choices equally legitimate.

All of us are in favor of free choice when it comes to where people live, what kind of car they drive, and a thousand matters of personal preference that harm no one else. We are also prochoice in matters of religion, politics, and lifestyle, even when people choose beliefs and behavior with which we don't agree. But most of us are decidedly not prochoice when it comes to murder, rape, kidnaping, armed robbery, and child abuse. When we oppose the "right to choose" rape or child abuse we aren't opposing a "right" we're opposing a "wrong." And we're not narrow minded and bigoted for doing so. We're just decent people concerned for the rights of the innocent. To be prochoice about someone's right to kill is to be anti-choice about someone else's right to live.

Whenever we hear the term *prochoice*, we must ask the all-important question, "What choice are we talking about?" Given the facts about abortion, the question really becomes, "Do you think people should have the right to choose to kill innocent children if that's what they want to do?"

10c. People who are prochoice about abortion are often not prochoice about other issues with less at stake.

After I spoke at a public high school on the prolife position, the prochoice instructor took me to the faculty lounge for lunch. He pointed to a table where four teachers were smoking and said, "Fortunately, this is the last week smoking will be allowed in here. We've finally gotten the district to make the teacher's lounge nonsmoking." Good naturedly I said, "I see you're not really prochoice." With a surprised look he explained, "But cigarette smoke hurts other people." I said, "So does abortion."

Many people who are prochoice about abortion support laws requiring people to wear seat belts. They are anti-choice about seat belts because seat belts save lives. When lives are at stake, "freedom to choose" can and is legitimately restricted by society.

10d. The one-time choice of abortion robs someone else of a lifetime of choices and prevents him from ever exercising his rights.

How to deal with a pregnancy is one among thousands of choices a woman will make in her lifetime. But if that choice is abortion, her child will never have the opportunity to make any choices of his own. A woman will have opportunity to exercise many legal rights. But if one of those is abortion, her child will never be able to exercise a single right.

10e. Everyone is prochoice when it comes to the choices prior to pregnancy and after birth.

Men and women are free to choose to abstain from sex or to use birth control or to do neither. But when a woman is pregnant, the choice she has made has produced a new human being. As one woman points out, "After a woman is pregnant, she cannot choose whether or not she wishes to become a mother. She already is, and since the child is already present in her womb, all that is left to her to decide is whether she will deliver her baby dead or alive."[1] Once the baby is born, the woman is again free to choose—she can keep the child or give him up for adoption. The choice prolifers oppose is the choice that takes an innocent life.

10f. Nearly all violations of human rights have been defended on the grounds of the right to choose.

The slaveowners in this country a century and a half ago were pro-choice. They said, "You don't have to own slaves if you don't want to, but don't tell us we can't choose to. It's our right." Those who wanted slaveholding to be illegal were accused of being anti-choice and anti-freedom, and of imposing their morality on others.

The civil rights movement, like the abolitionist movement one hundred years earlier, vehemently opposed the exercise of personal rights that much of society defended. It was solidly anti-choice when it came to racial discrimination. Whites historically had a free choice to own slaves, and later to have segregated lunch counters if they so chose. After all, America was a free country. But the civil rights movement fought to take away that free choice from them. Likewise, the women's movement fought to take away an employer's free choice to discriminate against women.

Nearly every movement of oppression and exploitation—from slavery, to prostitution, to pornography, to drug dealing, to abortion—has labeled itself prochoice. Likewise, opposing movements offering compassion and deliverance have been labeled anti-choice by the exploiters. At least with prostitution, pornography, and drugs, the victim usually has some choice. In the case of abortion, the victim has no choice. He is society's most glaring exception to all the high-sounding rhetoric about the right to choose and the right to live one's life without interference from others.

The prochoice position always overlooks the victim's right to choose. The women don't choose rape. The blacks didn't choose slavery. The Jews didn't choose the ovens. And the babies don't choose abortion.

11. "Every woman should have control over her own body. Reproductive freedom is a basic right."

11a. Abortion assures that 750,000 females each year do *not* have control over their bodies.

Since about half of aborted babies are females, approximately three-quarters of a million females per year have their lives taken by abortion in America. Nearly fifteen million females have died from abortion since it was legalized. A female who continues to be pregnant can still exercise basic control, though not absolute control, over her body and life. A female who is killed by abortion, however, no longer has a body or a life, and will never have the privilege of controlling one.

11b. Not all things done with a person's body are right, nor should they all be legally protected.

A man is not permitted to expose himself in public. Many places have laws against public urination. Prostitution is usually illegal. So is taking certain drugs. Most of us agree with these laws, yet they all restrict our freedom to do certain things with our bodies. My hand is part of my body, but I am not free to use it to strike you or steal from you or to hurt an innocent child. The key question is whether what is done with one person's body brings significant harm to others. Clearly, abortion does.

11c. Prolifers consistently affirm true reproductive rights.

Reproduction takes place at conception, not at birth. The only people I have heard argue against the right to reproduce are radical prochoice advocates who believe in sterilizing the mentally disabled and the poor with large families, who are often minorities. Prolifers do not oppose the right to reproduce. What they oppose is the right to kill a child after reproduction has taken place. "Abortion rights" are not reproductive rights, but child-killing rights.

11d. Even prochoicers must acknowledge that the "right to control one's body" argument has no validity if the unborn is a human being.

Prochoice philosopher Mary Anne Warren admits:

The fact that restricting access to abortion has tragic side effects does not, in itself, show that the restrictions are unjustified, since murder is wrong regardless of the consequences of prohibiting it; and the appeal to the right to control one's body, which is generally construed as a property right, is at best a rather feeble argument for the permissibility of abortion. Mere ownership does not give me the right to kill innocent people whom I find on my property, and indeed I am apt to be held responsible if such people injure themselves while on my property. It is equally unclear that I have any moral right to expel an innocent person from my property when I know that doing so will result in his death.[1]

11e. Too often "the right to control my life" becomes the right to hurt and oppress others for my own advantage.

Whenever one group of human beings affirms its rights in determining the fate of other human beings, this is the beginning of oppression. Whites used blacks to enhance their own quality of life, but did so at the expense of blacks. Men have often used women to live their lives as they wanted, but at the expense of the women.

Ironically, the same oppression women have sometimes endured from men is inflicted upon unborn children in abortion. Some men have used their greater size and strength to justify their mistreatment of women, as if one's size gives him the right to control another. Today some women use their greater size and strength to justify taking away the rights and lives of unborn children.

11f. Control over the body can be exercised to prevent pregnancy in the first place.

Except in the rare case of pregnancy by rape, a child-carrying woman has made choices of control over her body that have resulted in the pregnancy. She has chosen whether to have sex and whether to use birth control. She has the full right to make these choices, and I would not want to see those rights taken from her. But these control-choices she has already made have ushered in a whole new scenario in which not simply her personal preferences but also the life of another human being is now at stake.

The mother's first two matters of control—sex and birth control—were personal and private. The issue of abortion is not personal and private. It directly involves the life of another person, and therefore becomes the concern of a decent society. As society would protect the life of the mother if someone tried to kill her, so it must protect the life of the child if someone tries to kill him.

11g. It is demeaning to a woman's body and self-esteem to regard pregnancy as an unnatural, negative, and "out of control" condition.

One feminist group states:

When women feel that a pregnant body is a body out of control, deviant, diseased, they are internalizing attitudes of low self-esteem toward the female body. These attitudes contradict the rightful feminist affirmation of pregnancy as a natural bodily function which deserves societal respect and accommodation.[2]

12. "Abortion is a decision between a woman and her doctor. It's no one else's business. Everyone has a constitutional right to privacy."

12a. The Constitution does not contain a right to privacy.

There is nothing constitutional about the right to privacy, because that right is nowhere to be found in the United States Constitution. It was declared by the Supreme Court in 1973 as a right higher than an unborn child's right to live. Those who wrote the Constitution would be shocked to learn their document, which was dedicated to ensure justice and compassion for all people, would one day be claimed by some to guarantee a right to kill preborn children. Is privacy a right? Of course, but society recognizes that some rights are higher than others. Does one person's right to privacy outweigh another person's right to live? Of course not.

12b. Privacy is never an absolute right, but is always governed by other rights.

What would we think of a man who defended wife-beating on the grounds that "what I do in the privacy of my home is no one's business but mine." The question is, "Does abortion kill babies?" Killing done in private is no more acceptable nor less destructive than killing done in public.

An undated fund-raising letter from Planned Parenthood, signed by Faye Wattleton, attacks the prolife movement by saying, "We thought that what we did in our bedrooms was nobody else's business." Her primary argument for abortion is the right to privacy. The rest of the letter portrays prolifers as hateful, anti-sex, and a serious threat to society.

As I have written elsewhere, sex is a wonderful gift of God, a positive dimension of life that he intended a husband and wife to enjoy together.[1] Many prolifers believe that sex outside of marriage is destructive to individuals and society. Others do not share this belief, but still oppose the killing of children, since that is not the same issue. Though Wattleton's claim may generate both hostility and money, neither I nor the vast majority of prolifers I know have ever tried to monitor or regulate what goes on in other people's bedrooms. Those who oppose abortion are pro-choice about choices before a baby is conceived, and prolife about choices thereafter.

The truth is, abortion isn't done in the bedroom. And even if it was, child-killing in a bedroom would be no different than child-killing in the streets. The issue isn't sex. The issue is whether an innocent child deserves to live or die.

12c. The encouragement or assistance of a doctor does not change the nature, consequences, or morality of abortion.

A physician's advice is authoritative when it comes to tonsils, gall bladders, and cancers. These are questions of physiology and pathology, not morality. Doctors are trained in medicine and sometimes in surgery, but their moral opinions are not always as reliable as their physical diagnoses (which themselves are not always accurate either). Many doctors are conscientious people who place human welfare above expedience and money. Others, unfortunately, do not. Still others are sincere, but have embraced the prochoice party line without having thought the matter through scientifically, logically, or morally.

That physicians are capable of profoundly incompetent moral judgments was decisively demonstrated by many German doctors during World War II. Robert Jay Lifton, in his powerful book *The Nazi Doctors: Medical Killing and the Psychology of Genocide*, documents how normal and intelligent medical professionals endorsed and participated in cruel and deadly surgeries with shocking ease.[2] They were the best-trained medical personnel in Europe, but they were poor sources of moral guidance.

Doctors who actually perform abortions are surely the least objective people with whom to discuss abortion. Their personal and monetary interests in abortion disqualify them. One does not go to a tobacco company executive for guidance on whether to smoke cigarettes.

12d. The father of the child is also responsible for the child and should have a part in this decision.

On the one hand, a man is told he should take responsibility for an unwanted pregnancy and give the mother financial help and emotional support. He should take ownership of a situation he helped cause by regarding the baby not just as the woman's but as his own. On the other hand, the same man is told that abortion is none of his business, only the mother's and doctor's. Given this mixed message, how can we expect a man to act responsibly toward the mother and child?

Ironically, abortion allows and even encourages men to sexually exploit women without the fear of having to take responsibility for any children that are conceived. If the woman does get pregnant, the man can hand over three hundred dollars and buy a dead child. When the man is long gone, with no child to have to support, the woman is left with the burden of having killed her child. "Abortion rights" bring out not the best but the worst in men.

12e. The father will often face serious grief and guilt as a result of abortion. Since his life will be significantly affected, shouldn't he have something to say about it?

The implication of the "just between a mother and her doctor" argument is that no one else will have to deal with the consequences of the decision. On the contrary, abortion has powerful long-term effects on men. In an article in *Esquire* magazine, twelve men speak candidly on the price they have paid because of abortion.[3] Some agreed to the decision to abort, some didn't. Some pushed the decision to abort, but now desperately wish they hadn't:

> It's her body, but I had her brainwashed. I made all the decisions. Once it was over, we never talked about it again. We kept our mouths shut. She did have some real prophetic words, though. She said, "Wagner, you're going to regret this all your life." I told her, "No, no." But inside me something would spark and cling to that. She was right. I'll never forget it. I'll never forgive myself.

Reflecting on his experience, one man simply said, "An abortion is a terrible thing." Many of the men commented on the disastrous effects on their relationship with their wife or girlfriend. One says, "Everything just dissolved after she had the abortion." A married man reflects:

We tried to figure out why we weren't getting along so well. It occurred to one of us that it was a year since the abortion. That was the first time we realized that we felt we had killed something that we had made together and that it would have been alive and might have been our child. . . . We talked and shared how disturbed about it we both had been. . . . We hadn't known that we were angry and upset and hadn't been willing to face the facts.

One man reluctantly agreed to an abortion he did not feel good about. Years later he says:

I've got to think of the pain and the damage it did to her, because I know about the pain that it does to me, and it wasn't my decision. I was part of the cause and I certainly didn't resist in any way. I can't help but think, am I guilty of being an accomplice in the taking of a life, or at least in not bringing it to fruition? There's guilt, but more than anything, there's just sadness.

One last man demonstrates an understanding that not only women but many men come to years after an abortion. In light of such testimonies, surely we should consider not only the welfare of the children and mothers, but also of fathers.

I've had a hell of a time dealing with it, actually. To this day I still think about it. I'll go to bed and I'll think about it and say to myself, "Man, what a terrible thing to do. What a cop-out. You don't trade human life for material niceties." Which is what I was doing, because I was hoping for a better future, more goods I could buy.

I don't have a good rationalization for it either. I'm not one of those people who believe that it's only potential life. I've come to believe more and more that the baby in the womb is just that—a human life. I wish I didn't. I wish I could make myself believe differently, but I can't. It would make it easier to deal with mentally. When you have the opposite view and you go through with the abortion anyway, well, that's worse than anything.

So, you see, I'm kind of stuck. She did it for me. I feel like I murdered somebody. I wish I could do it over again, if I could just go back in time and relive those years. If she'd had the child, even if we'd got married and everything, it wouldn't have been that bad. I've seen other people do it. Reality's such a bitch sometimes, you know?

13. "It's unfair for an unmarried woman to have to face the embarrassment of pregnancy or the pain of giving up a child for adoption."

13a. Pregnancy is not a sin. Society should not condemn and pressure an unmarried mother into abortion, but should help and support her.

No matter what one's view of sex outside of marriage, clearly pregnancy per se is not wrong. It is not a moral but a biological reality. Society should not treat the mother as a "bad girl" or pressure her to "solve her problem" by aborting her child. Rather, it should love her and help her through the pregnancy and the post-birth options available to her.

Society should affirm a woman for not taking the "easy out" of abortion to preserve her image and avoid some inconvenience, but at the cost of someone's life. Whenever I see an unmarried woman carrying a child, my first response is one of respect. I know she could have taken the "quick fix" without anyone knowing, but she chose instead to let an innocent child live.

13b. The poor choice of premarital sex is never compensated for by the far worse choice of killing an innocent human being.

Abortion may cover up a problem, but it never solves it. The poor choice of premarital sex can be learned from, reconsidered, and not repeated. The poor choice of killing an innocent human being by abortion is more serious, more permanent, and more unfair. It causes one person to pay for another's mistake. Furthermore, it forces the young woman to live with the guilt of her decision, and gives her an even worse mistake to cover up. Not only the young woman, but all society suffers from the attitudes fostered by the abortion alternative. We send the message to her and to everyone, "The individual's comfort and happiness comes first—even if you have to disregard the rights of an innocent person to get it." This attitude emerges in a thousand arenas, big and small, which cumulatively tear apart the moral fabric of society.

13c. One person's unfair or embarrassing circumstances do not justify violating the rights of another person.

It is unfortunate to lose one's job, and it may also be unfair and embarrassing. But this difficult situation does not justify armed robbery in order to pay one's bills. We must commit ourselves to finding workable solutions that treat a pregnant, unmarried woman with dignity and do not require others to suffer or die.

13d. Adoption is a fine alternative that avoids the burden of child raising, while saving a life and making a family happy.

I am amazed at the negative light in which adoption is often portrayed in prochoice literature. Prochoice advocates Carole Anderson and Lee Campbell say of adoption, "The unnecessary separation of mothers and children is a cruel, but regrettably usual, punishment that can last a lifetime."[1] It is not adoption that is cruel; what is cruel is an innocent child's death, and a woman's lifelong guilt when she realizes she has killed her child. Adoption is hardly a "punishment" to a woman carrying a child. It is a heaven-sent alternative to raising a child she is unprepared to raise, or to killing that same child.

According to the National Committee for Adoption, there are 1.5 million American couples wanting to adopt children.[2] With proper education and a positive portrayal of adoption, even this number could be increased. Yet each year, while 1.6 million children are being killed by abortion, only 50,000 new children are made available for adoption. This means that for every new adoptable child, thirty others are killed. For every couple that adopts, another forty wait in line.[3] Tragically, most women with unwanted pregnancies are not given accurate information about the adoption alternative:

> A 1984 study by Edmund Mech showed that nearly 40 percent of pregnancy counselors did not include adoption as an option in their counseling. Another 40 percent were uncertain or provided inaccurate information on adoption. Conversely, 68 percent could provide accurate information on abortion clinic locations.[4]

The adoption option is much more healthy for everyone involved, not only for the child but for the adoptive parents, society, and the pregnant woman herself. By carrying a child to term, a young woman accepts responsibility for her choices and grows and matures. She can then look back with pride and satisfaction that she did the right thing by allowing her child both life and a good family. (Of course, adoption is only one alternative—the young woman may choose to keep the baby and raise him herself. Either alternative is viable. The one that isn't is the one that kills a baby.)

13e. The reason that adoption may be painful is the same reason that abortion is wrong—a human life is involved.

I have talked with several women considering abortions who had identical reactions to the suggestion of adoption: "What kind of mother would I be to give up a child for adoption?" The irony is that a mother who would not give away her child because he is too precious will instead kill that same child. The question she should ask herself is not, "How could I give up my baby for adoption?" but, "How could I kill my baby by abortion?" Even if she cannot care for her child herself, she will want to allow him to live so that another mother can love and raise him.

Because she has not yet bonded with the child the abortion may seem like an easy solution, while parting with her child after birth may be emotionally difficult. But the child's life is just as real before bonding as after. The woman has three choices—have her child and raise him, have her child and allow another family to raise him, or kill her child. Two of these options are reasonable. One is not.

We took a pregnant teenage girl into our home. Though she had two abortions, this time she chose to have her baby and give him up for adoption. It was not easy, but this wonderful woman recently (ten years, a husband, and three more children later) told me: "I look back at the three babies I no longer have, but with very different feelings. The two I aborted fill me with grief and regret. But when I think of the one I gave up for adoption, I'm filled with joy, because I know he's being raised by a wonderful family that wanted him."

14. "Abortion-rights are fundamental for the advancement of women. They are essential to having equal rights with men."

14a. Early feminists were prolife, not prochoice.

Susan B. Anthony was a radical feminist, standing for women at a time when they were not even allowed to vote. She referred to abortion as "child murder" and viewed it as a means of exploiting both women and children:

> I deplore the horrible crime of child murder. . . . No matter what the motive, love of ease, or a desire to save from suffering the unborn innocent, the woman is awfully guilty who commits the deed . . . but oh! thrice guilty is he who drove her to the desperation which impelled her to the crime.[1]

Anthony's newspaper, *The Revolution*, made this claim: "When a woman destroys the life of her unborn child, it is a sign that, by education or circumstances, she has been greatly wronged."[2]

Another leading feminist, Elizabeth Cady Stanton, said this about abortion: "When we consider that women are treated as property, it is degrading to women that we should treat our children as property to be disposed of as we wish."[3]

These women were later followed by a new breed of feminists. Most prominent of these was Margaret Sanger, founder of Planned Parenthood, who advocated abortion as a means of sexual freedom, birth control, and eugenics. (See Answer 19d.)

Sanger and others who followed her tried to tie the abortion agenda to the legitimate issues of women's rights. The same thing happened in the sixties. Dr. Bernard Nathanson says he and his fellow abortion-rights strategists deliberately linked the abortion issue to the women's issue so it could be furthered not on its own merits but on the merits of women's rights.[4] Because of the legitimate concerns for women's rights, the abortion issue was pulled along on its coat-tails.

Early feminists such as Susan Anthony would have been appalled and angered to think that abortion—which they deplored as the killing of innocent children—would one day be linked in people's minds with the cause of women's rights!

14b. Some active feminists still vigorously oppose abortion.

Alice Paul drafted the original version of the Equal Rights Amendment. She also referred to abortion as "the ultimate exploitation of women."[5]

Feminists for Life of America (FFL) was started in the early 1970s. FFL supported the Equal Rights Amendment and has labored for other feminist goals, but is adamantly prolife.[6] One FFL member, Mary Ann

Schaefer, has labeled the attempt to marry feminism to abortion as "terrorist feminism." In her words, it forces the feminist to be "willing to kill for the cause you believe in."[7]

Both men and women should be free to affirm certain platforms of the feminist movement without affirming others. One may support some or most feminist ideals, while wholeheartedly opposing abortion because it kills children.

14c. Women's rights are not inherently linked to the right to abortion.

Kate Michelman, president of the National Abortion Rights Action League (NARAL), says: "We have to remind people that abortion is the guarantor of a woman's . . . right to participate fully in the social and political life of society."[8] But a pregnant woman *can* fully participate in society. And if she can't, the solution is changing society, not killing babies. (Notice that abortion is called "*the* guarantor" of women's rights. Are there no women's rights unless there is license to kill unborn children?)

"How can women achieve equality without control of their reproductive lives?" Feminists for Life responds:

> How can women ever lose second-class status as long as they are seen as requiring surgery in order to avoid it? The premise of the question is the premise of male domination throughout the millennia—that it was nature which made men superior and women inferior. Medical technology is offered as a solution to achieve equality; but the premise is wrong. . . . It's an insult to women to say women must change their biology in order to fit into society.[9]

14d. The basic premises of the abortion-rights movement are demeaning to women.

Rosemary Bottcher, an analytical chemist and environmentalist, wrote an essay titled, "Feminism: Bewitched by Abortion."[10] Bottcher thinks women are much different than the way the feminist movement portrays them. If women can't handle the stress and pressures of pregnancy, Bottcher wonders how they could ever handle the stress and pressures of the presidency. Here is the crux of her argument, as summarized by D. James Kennedy:

A man is expected to be mature when he fathers a child; he is expected to endure inconvenience and hardship, if necessary, to provide the means to bring a child up and go through college, even if this requires taking an extra job or working late at night. He is expected to do this because he is supposedly mature.

But the woman, according to feminists, is so selfish, immature, irrational and hysterical that she cannot stand the fact of nine months of inconvenience in order to bring life to another person or to bring happiness, perhaps, to some other family who might adopt that child.[11]

14e. Some of the abortion-rights strategies assume female incompetence and subject women to ignorance and exploitation.

Across the country prochoice groups are opposing efforts to require by law that abortion be treated like every other surgery when it comes to informing the patient of its nature and risks. They do not seem to believe that women are capable of making intelligent choices after being presented with the facts.

The Supreme Court ruled against the legality of states requiring information to be given to a woman considering an abortion because, the Court argued, such information "may serve only to confuse her and heighten her anxiety."[12] The message is, "Don't tell women the whole truth—they can't handle it." Instead, abortion clinics are free to tell women whatever they want in order to sell abortions. As Feminists for Life points out, "This attitude is patronizing to women's decision-making abilities, and essentially establishes for women a constitutional 'right' to ignorance."[13]

It is also amazing that prochoice advocates oppose having even the most common-sense health and disclosure regulations at abortion clinics. For whom are they concerned? Abortions or women? Again, Feminists for Life comments,

Those seriously concerned about women's rights should at the very least support consumer protection regulations. Abortion is the most remarkably unregulated medical procedure in the country. Why are abortionists given such free reign in a procedure which, after all, involves only women? Women are deserving of better protection.[14]

14f. Abortion has become the most effective means of sexism ever devised, ridding the world of multitudes of unwanted females.

One of the great ironies of the women's movement is that by its advocacy of abortion it has endorsed the single greatest tool to rob women of their most basic right—the right to live. Abortion has become the primary means of eliminating unwanted females across the globe. A survey of a dozen villages in India uncovered a frightening statistic—out of a total population of ten thousand, only fifty were girls.[15] The other girls, thousands of them, had been killed by abortion when prenatal tests revealed they were females, who are considered an economic liability. *Newsweek* reported that in six clinics in Bombay, of eight thousand amniocentesis tests indicating the babies were female, all but one were killed by abortion.[16] *Time* gives this alarming report:

> In South Korea, where fetal testing to determine sex is common, male births exceed female births by 14%, in contrast to a worldwide average of 5%. In Guangdong province, the China news agency Xinhua reported, 500,000 bachelors are approaching middle age without hopes of marrying, because they outnumber women ages 30 to 45 by more than 10 to 1.[17]

The same thing is now happening in America. Amniocentesis is being used to detect the gender of a baby. If you want a boy, you don't have to go through months of inconvenience till you can get a reliable ultrasound. You can tell within a month or two, then kill your little girl by abortion and start over again. *Medical World News* reported a study in which ninety-nine mothers were informed of the sex of their children. Fifty-three of these preborns were boys and forty-six were girls. Of this number, only one mother elected to kill her boy, while *twenty-nine* elected to kill their girls.[18]

As the husband of a wonderful woman and the father of two precious girls, I cannot understand why anyone would not want to have a daughter! But for reasons that reflect some irrational bias against women, females are being targeted for extinction. And the tool for this destruction of women is staunchly defended by those who call themselves "pro-woman."

Since many more girls than boys are being killed by the amniocentesis-abortion connection, some outraged feminists have labeled the practice "femicide."[19] Ironically, the term betrays what those who use it deny: The unborn are people, and to kill an unborn female is to kill a young woman. There can be no equal rights for all women until there are equal rights for unborn women.

15. "The circumstances of many women leave them no choice but to have an abortion."

15a. Saying they have no choice is not being prochoice, but pro-abortion.

One of the great ironies of the prochoice movement is that it has left many women feeling they have no choice but abortion. This is because abortion is constantly portrayed as the preferred choice. Having been taught that abortion is the easiest way out of a difficulty, fathers, mothers, boyfriends, husbands, teachers, school counselors, doctors, nurses, media, and peers often pressure the pregnant woman into making a choice that is more theirs than hers. One young woman reflects back on her own pregnancy:

> There were plans racing through my mind of where we would live, what we'd name it, what it would look like. . . . But, on his father's advice of "it'll ruin your life," [my boyfriend] opted for an abortion. I was in shock, so I went along with him when he said that there was no way I could have it alone and that I'd be kicked out of the family.

> Reality set in, and the choice was not mine. That's the heartache—the choice was not *mine*—it was his, my family's, society's. It was his choice because he would have been the only financial support. It was my family's because of the rejection of me and the unborn. And it was society's because of the poverty cycle I would enter as a teenage mother.[1]

Studies confirm that many women feel pressured into abortions:

> Altogether, fully 64 percent of the aborted women surveyed described themselves as "forced into abortion because of their particular circumstances at that time." . . . Abortion was simply the most obvious and fastest way to escape from their dilemmas. Over 84 percent state that they would have kept their babies "under better circumstances."[2]

15b. Those who are truly prochoice must present a woman with a number of possible choices, rather than just selling the choice of abortion.

If we are prochoice, why are doctors, schools, family planning clinics, and abortion clinics not required to present women with facts about available choices, including adoption? A friend of mine who was formerly an abortion clinic counselor says:

> I was totally uninformed of available alternatives to abortion. I never recommended adoption or keeping the child. Furthermore, I was completely unaware of the medical facts, including the development of the fetus. I received no training in factual matters—my job was just to keep women happy and make sure they went through with an abortion.

With this kind of "counseling," how many women will choose anything other than abortion? Former owners and employees of abortion clinics have stated it was their job to "sell abortions" to pregnant women. Some clinics even hire professional marketing experts to train their staff in abortion sales.[3] (See Answer 28c.)

Feminists for Life maintains, "If we could limit abortion to only those women who truly decided to have one, with adequate information without unfair and unjust pressures, we could cut the abortion rate dramatically."[4]

15c. "Abortion or misery" is a false portrayal of the options; it keeps women from pursuing—and society from providing—positive alternatives.

It is a terrible thing to present pregnant women with inadequate choices, leaving them in an apparent no-win situation.

> This is not a choice between vanilla and chocolate. This is a choice like "Do you want me to break your arm, or your leg?" This is a choice that says, "Do you want to see your life derailed, see your dreams turn to ashes—or do you want to undergo a humiliating, invasive operation and have your own child die?" "Do you want to sacrifice your life plans, or would you rather sacrifice your offspring?" It's a lousy choice. Women should not be forced into making such a choice. We should be able to keep both mother and child's lives and bodies intact.[5]

We must reject this trap of presenting the choice between abortion and misery, as if there were no misery in abortion, and as if there were no alternatives. Why does Planned Parenthood, with all its hundreds of millions of dollars from tax revenues and foundations, not devote itself to a third alternative, such as adoption? Instead of helping with adoptions, why is Planned Parenthood the largest abortion provider in the country?[6] And because it makes millions of dollars from abortions every year, giving it huge vested interests in abortion, how can Planned Parenthood be expected to offer real and objective choices to pregnant women in need?

We cannot improve the abortion alternative—it will always result in the death of an innocent child. But we can surely work to promote adoption and to free adoption agencies from the red tape that sometimes clogs the process. We can work to improve the quality of children's services and aid to unmarried mothers. We can open our homes to women in crisis pregnancies. To not do so is to leave women with the tragic perception that abortion is their only choice.

16. "I'm personally against abortion, but I'm still prochoice. It's a legal alternative and we don't have the right to keep it from anyone."

16a. To be prochoice about abortion is to be proabortion.

Suppose drug-dealing were legalized, as some have advocated. Then suppose you heard someone argue this way for selling cocaine:

> I'm personally not in favor of drug-dealing, but this is a matter for a drug-dealer to decide between himself and his attorney. Lots of religious people are against drug-dealing, but they have no right to force the anti-cocaine morality on others. We don't want to go back to the days when drug-dealing was done in back alleys and people died from poorly mixed cocaine, and when only rich people could get drugs and poor people couldn't. It's better now that qualified drug dealers can safely give cocaine to our children. I personally wouldn't buy drugs, so I'm not pro-drugs, you understand, I'm just prochoice about drug-dealing.

There is no significant difference between people who are in favor of drug-dealing and people who don't like it personally but believe it should be an option. Someone who is prochoice about rape might argue that this is not the same as being pro-rape. But what is the difference, since being prochoice about rape allows and effectively promotes the legitimacy of rape?

Those who were prochoice about slavery fancied that their moral position was sound since they personally didn't own slaves. Yet it was not just the pro-slavery position, but the prochoice about slavery position, that resulted in the exploitation, beatings, and deaths of innocent people in this country. Similarly, most people in Germany did not favor the killing of Jews, but they did nothing to stop that killing.

In ancient Rome it was legal for fathers to kill their newborn children by setting them out to die of exposure or to be eaten by wild beasts. While many people would not do this to their own children, they recognized the rights of others to do so. The early Christians saw this "right" as a wrong, and when they found such children, they took them into their homes to care for them.

Some people have the illusion that being personally opposed to abortion while believing others should be free to choose it is some kind of compromise between the proabortion and prolife positions. It isn't. Prochoice people vote the same as proabortion people. Both oppose legal protection for the innocent unborn. Both are willing for children to die by abortion and must take responsibility for the killing of those babies even if they do not participate directly. To the baby who dies it makes no difference whether those who refused to protect her were pro-abortion or merely prochoice.

16b. The only good reason for being personally against abortion is a reason that demands we be against other people choosing to have abortions.

If abortion doesn't kill children, why would someone be opposed to it? If it does kill children, why would someone defend another's right to do it? Being personally against abortion but favoring another's right to abortion is self-contradictory and morally baffling. It's exactly like saying, "We're personally against child abuse, but we defend our neighbor's right to abuse his child if that is his choice."

16c. What is legal is not always right.

One of the weakest arguments for the legitimacy of abortion is that it is legal. Civil law does not determine morality. Rather, the law should reflect a morality that exists independently of the law. Can anyone seriously believe that abortion was immoral on January 21, 1973, and moral on January 23, 1973? If abortion killed children before the law changed, it continues to kill children after the law changed. Law or no law, either abortion has always been right and always will be, or it has always been wrong and always will be.

In the last century, slaveowners argued that the slaves were theirs and they had the right to do with them as they wished. They claimed that their personal rights and freedom of choice were at stake. They said slaves were not fully persons. They said they would experience economic hardship if they were not allowed to have slaves, and they developed slogans to gain sympathy for their cause. They maintained that others could choose not to have slaves, but had no right to impose their anti-slavery morality on them. Above all, they argued, slavery was perfectly legal, so no one had the right to oppose it.

This point of view was given further legal support in the Dred Scott decision of 1857. The Supreme Court determined in a 7-2 decision that slaves were not legal persons and were therefore not protected under the Constitution. In 1973, the Supreme Court, by another 7-2 decision, would determine that unborn children also were not legal persons and therefore not protected under the Constitution. In 1857 the chief justice of the Supreme Court said, "A black man has no right which the white man is bound to respect."[1] Despite slavery's legality, however, Abraham Lincoln challenged its morality. "If slavery is not wrong," he said, "then nothing is wrong."[2]

In the 1940s a German doctor could kill Jews legally, while in America he would have been prosecuted for murder. In the 1970s an American doctor could kill unborn babies legally, while in Germany he would have been prosecuted for murder. Laws change. Truth and justice don't.

PART THREE

ARGUMENTS CONCERNING SOCIAL ISSUES

Arguments Concerning Social Issues

17a. Every child is wanted by someone—there is no such thing as an unwanted child.

One and a half million American families want to adopt, some so badly that the scarcity of adoptable babies is a source of major depression. There is such a demand for babies that a black market has developed where babies have been sold for as much as $35,000.[1] Not just "normal" babies are wanted—many people request babies with Down's syndrome, and there have been lists of over a hundred couples waiting to adopt babies with spina bifida.[2]

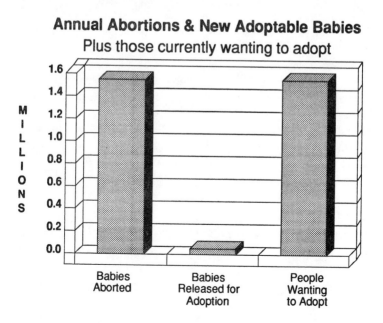

Annual Abortions & New Adoptable Babies
Plus those currently wanting to adopt

Would the demand for babies keep up with the supply if abortion were made illegal? The National Committee for Adoption (NCA) maintains most women would choose to keep their babies, but 11 percent of the children that would have been aborted would be given up for adoption. The NCA's president says, "If abortion were totally outlawed, we would guess the numbers to be 68,400 more white infants and 3,960 non-white infants needing adoptive homes."[3] Those waiting to adopt would still have to wait in line, but the wait would be shorter and less agonizing.

17b. There is a difference between an unwanted pregnancy and an unwanted child.

Many children who are at first unwanted by their mothers are very much wanted later in the pregnancy, and even more so at birth. Unfortunately, many women who would have bonded with and wanted the child by their six month of pregnancy get an abortion in their third month.

Furthermore, many children wanted at birth are *not* wanted when they are crying at 2:00 A.M. six weeks later. Shall whether or not the parents want the baby still determine whether she deserves to live? If that is a legitimate standard before birth, why not after?

17c. "Unwanted" describes not an actual condition of the child, but an attitude of adults.

The problem is not unwanted children but unwanting adults. "Wanting" is simply one person's subjective and changeable feeling toward another. The "unwanted" child is a real person regardless of anyone else's feelings toward her. For years women were degraded when their value was judged by whether or not they were wanted by men. Just as a woman's value is real whether or not a man recognizes it, so a baby's value is real whether or not his mother or father recognizes it. "Every woman or child a wanted woman or child" is a good goal, but if a woman or child is not wanted it does not justify killing her.

17d. The problem of unwantedness is a good argument for wanting children, but a poor argument for aborting them.

Planned Parenthood argues that unwanted children "get lower

grades, particularly in language skills." It says unwanted adolescents "perform increasingly poorly in school" and are "less likely to excel under increased school pressure." And, "they are less than half as likely as wanted children to pursue higher education."[4]

I do not question the accuracy of these findings. They tell us what we should already know—the importance of wanting our children. Instead, prochoice advocates use such research to justify aborting the "unwanted." They say the solution to having unwanted children who don't perform well in school is eliminating them. But isn't this a backwards approach? Aren't there better ways to cure the disease than killing the patient?

In another Planned Parenthood publication, abortion is defended on the basis that "children need love and families who want and will care for them."[5] This is a fine argument for providing prenatal care for women in need. But according to its own 1990 annual report, Planned Parenthood performed 122,191 abortions while managing, out of its $300 million annual budget, to provide prenatal care for only 4,732 women.[6] Even without counting the innumerable abortions referred to other abortion clinics, this is thirty abortions for every one woman helped to have or care for a child. Saying children need love and families is also a great argument for adoption. But Planned Parenthood and other prochoice groups don't promote adoption. They promote abortion.

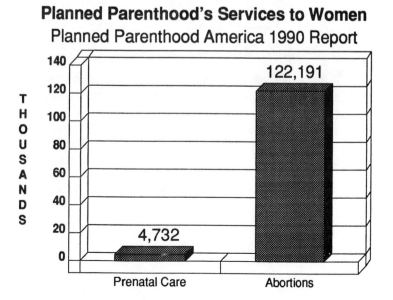

Planned Parenthood's Services to Women
Planned Parenthood America 1990 Report

Planned Parenthood's slogan, "Every child a wanted child," is something we can all agree with. Where we disagree is in the proper way to finish the sentence. Check the box that indicates how you think the sentence should be finished:

☐ Every child a wanted child, so let's place children for adoption in homes where they are wanted, and let's learn to want children more. (Eliminate the "unwanted" in "unwanted children.")

☐ Every child a wanted child, so let's identify unwanted children before they're born and kill them by abortion. (Eliminate the "children" in "unwanted children.")

Everyone agrees that children should be wanted. The question is whether we should eliminate the "unwanted" or the children. When it comes to the unborn, the prochoice position is captured in a different slogan: "Every unwanted child a dead child."

17e. What is most unfair to "unwanted" children is to kill them.

One day my wife was calmly sharing with a prochoice woman why she is prolife. The woman looked at Nanci and said, "Haven't you seen the homeless kids on the streets of our city? It's *cruel* for them to have to live in a world like this!" My wife said, "Okay, why don't you and I get some guns and go kill those children right now. Let's put them out of their misery." The woman was shocked, but Nanci made her point. It isn't an act of love and fairness to kill people just because they're unwanted.

One of the most misleading aspects of prochoice argumentation is making it appear that abortion is in the best interests of the baby. This is so absurd as to be laughable were it not so tragic. A little person is torn limb from limb, never to see the light of day, for her benefit? Slave owners argued that slavery was in the best interest of the blacks, since they couldn't make it on their own. Today people say, "I can't have this child because I can't give it a good life." And what is the solution to not being able to give him a good life? To take from him the only life he has. Exploiting people and stripping them of their rights is always easier when we tell ourselves we're doing it for *their* good rather than our own.

18. "Having more unwanted children results in more child abuse."

18a. Most abused children were wanted by their parents.

A landmark study of 674 abused children was conducted by University of Southern California professor Edward Lenoski. He discovered that 91 percent were from planned pregnancies; they were definitely wanted by their parents. What is startling is that, in society in general, 63 percent of pregnancies are planned. Hence, *among abused children, a significantly higher percentage were wanted children compared to the percentage of wanted children in society at large.*[1]

Dr. Lenoski also discovered, again to his surprise, that the mothers of abused children had begun wearing maternity clothes at 114 days, compared to 171 days in the control group. This showed they looked forward to having the child more than most women. Furthermore, fathers named later-to-be-abused boys after themselves 24 percent of the time, compared to only 4 percent in the control group. However we explain these findings, the best study done to date indicates that many more "wanted" children are abused than are "unwanted" children! The prochoice argument that more unwanted children are destined for abuse may sound logical, but solid research demonstrates it is not true.

18b. Child abuse has not decreased since abortion was legalized, but has dramatically increased.

Statistics reveal a sharp rise in child abuse in countries that legalize abortion. In 1973, when abortion was legalized, child abuse cases in the United States were estimated at 167,000.[2] By 1982 the number had risen to 929,000.[3] *In the first ten years after the legalization of abortion in America, child abuse increased over 500 percent.*[4] By 1991 there were 2.5 million reported child abuse cases, fifteen times more than in 1973. While the increased attention on child abuse in the mideighties no doubt accounted for the reporting of abuse that was already happening, the rise was extraordinary prior to this point. The experts agree that child abuse—not just the reporting of it—has dramatically increased since the early seventies.

111

Rise in Child Abuse Since Legal Abortion
Annual cases (not including abortions)

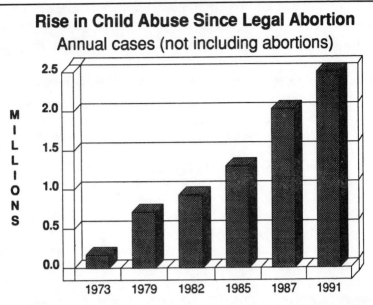

Natl. Cent. of Child Abuse & Neglect; U.S. Dept. Health; Child. Def. Fund

The actual increase in child abuse is even more dramatic than it appears, however, since abortion has left us over twenty-eight million fewer children in America to abuse. Furthermore, these children were abused to death by abortion, so they also should be counted as victims of child abuse.

18c. If children are viewed as expendable before birth, they will be viewed as expendable after birth.

"Studies indicate that child abuse is more frequent among mothers who have previously had an abortion."[5] Dr. Philip G. Ney's studies indicate that this is partially due to the guilt and depression caused by abortion and its hindering of the mother's ability to bond with future children.[6] Writing in a psychiatric journal, Dr. Ney documents that having an abortion may decrease a parent's natural restraint against feelings of rage felt toward small children.[7]

A parent overcomes her natural impulse to care for a child's helplessness when she chooses abortion. Having suppressed the preserving instinct once

112

before, that instinct may become less effective in holding back rage against the helplessness of a newborn or the crying of a toddler or the defiance of a preschooler.[8]

The attitude that results in abortion is exactly the same attitude that results in child abuse. The pressure to abort is a pressure to reject the child. Even if she doesn't abort, the mother can look at her baby and think, "I could have aborted you," or even, "I *should* have aborted you." The child owes her everything; she owes the child nothing. This can cause resentment for any demands or needs of the child that require parental sacrifice. The logic, whether conscious or unconscious, is inescapable—if it was all right to kill the same baby before birth, is it really so bad to slap him around once in a while now?

Of the five thousand "born children" in this country murdered every year, 95 percent are killed by one or both of their parents.[9] Once the child-abuse mentality grips a society, it does not restrict itself to abusing only one group of children. If preborn children aren't safe, neither are born children.

18d. It is illogical to argue that a child is protected from abuse through abortion since abortion *is* child abuse.

The solution to battered children outside the womb is not butchered children inside the womb. More babies already dead means fewer babies to abuse now, but this is hardly cause for encouragement. The solution to child abuse is not doing the abusing earlier, but not abusing at all. Abortion is the earliest form of child abuse, and there is none more deadly.

19. "Restricting abortion would be unfair to the poor and minorities, who need it most."

19a. It is not unfair for some people to have less opportunity than others to kill the innocent.

Planned Parenthood claims "laws restricting abortion discriminate against low-income women and minority women."[1] Because rich white people can afford something and others can't makes it neither right nor advantageous. Rich people have greater access to cocaine and can more easily commit any crime. Is the solution to subsidize a harmful activity so all can have equal opportunity to do it? Shall we make burglary legal so it would be a more viable alternative for the poor and minorities?

The question is whether or not abortion kills children. Neither economics nor race have anything to do with it. If the rich kill their children it does not make child-killing a virtue that should be available to all. Equal rights does not mean equal opportunity to destroy the innocent.

19b. The rich and white, not the poor and minorities, are most committed to unrestricted abortion.

The abortion rate among white women is 22.5 per 1000. The abortion rate among blacks and other minorities is 53.7 per 1000.[2]

Hispanic women are 60 percent more likely than non-Hispanic women to have abortions.[3] This leads many to conclude that minorities are generally pro-abortion. The truth is, however, that many of the same poor and minority women getting abortions do not consider abortion a decent alternative. They feel trapped into abortion because it is the only alternative they know. One feminist compares the choice of abortion to a trapped animal's choice to gnaw off its own leg.[4]

Studies show that "abortion finds its heaviest support not among lower or lower-middle class women, but among white upper-middle class women for whom child-bearing may conflict with career goals."[5] Appealing to the "poor and minority" issue diverts attention from the actual reasons most prochoice advocates favor convenience abortions.

It is the poor and minorities—not the rich and white—who foot the physical and psychological bill for their abortions. The facts suggest that what is behind prochoice arguments is not concern *for* the poor and minorities but concern *about* them. What better way to control the numbers of blacks, Hispanics, and other minorities than by providing the means for them to eliminate their preborn children? The poor and minorities do not want abortion for themselves nearly as much as the rich and white want abortions for them.

19c. Prochoice advocates want the poor and minorities to have abortions, but oppose requirements that abortion risks and alternatives be explained to them.

Regulations requiring the giving of complete and accurate information to women getting abortions are consistently opposed by prochoice groups. Since minorities have many more abortions, they suffer most from misinformation. Prochoice groups do not favor the poor and minorities making informed choices; they favor the poor and minorities having abortions.

19d. Planned Parenthood's abortion advocacy was rooted in the eugenics movement and its bias against the mentally and physically handicapped and minorities.

Margaret Sanger was the direction-setter and first president of Planned Parenthood, the world's largest abortion promoter and provider. Although in her earlier writings she condemned abortion, ultimately her organization ended up viewing abortion as just one more means of controlling the birthrate of those considered inferior. I have in front of me a stack of Sanger's original writings, as well as copies of her magazine, *Birth Control Review*. I encourage readers to review these writings and decide for themselves the beliefs and attitudes that gave birth to Planned Parenthood and the American abortion movement.[6]

Margaret Sanger spoke of the poor and handicapped as the "sinister forces of the hordes of irresponsibility and imbecility," claiming their existence constituted an "attack upon the stocks of intelligence and racial health."[7] She warned of "indiscriminate breeding" among the less fit that would bring into the world future voters "who may destroy our liberties, and who may thus be the most far-reaching peril to the future of civilization."[8] She called the less priviledged members of society "a dead weight of human waste."[9]

In a chapter called the "Cruelty of Charity" Sanger argued that groups dedicated to helping pregnant women decide to give birth to their children were "positively injurious to the community and the future of the race."[10] She claimed, "the effect of maternity endowments and maternity centers supported by private philanthropy would have, perhaps already have had, exactly the most dysgenic tendency."[11] Her use of the technical term *dysgenic* clearly indicates her belief that these woman-helping efforts violated Darwin's doctrine of the survival of the fittest, by which the weaker were naturally eliminated by virtue of their inferiority.

This same spirit permeates Sanger's magazine, *Birth Control*

Review. It is full of articles with titles such as "The World's Racial Problem," "Toward Race Betterment," and "Eugenic Sterilization: An Urgent Need."[12] The latter article was written in 1933 by Dr. Ernst Rudin, a leader in the German eugenics movement that was at the time busily laying the foundation for the Nazi's acts of "racial improvement" and "ethnic cleansing." Elsewhere in that issue an article titled "Defective Families" calls the "American Gypsies" a "family of degenerates" started by a man and "a half-breed woman," and warns "their germ plasm has been traced throughout seven middle-western states."[13] Also in the same issue, in his article "Birth Control and Sterilization," Sanger's companion and lover Dr. Havelock Ellis stated, "sterilization would be...helpful, although it could not be possible in this way to eliminate the mentally unfit element in the population. It would only be a beginning."[14] Students of history know where that "beginning" ended only a decade later, under the leaderhsip of a eugenic devotee name Adolf Hitler. (Though Sanger did not write these specific articles herself, as founder and director she was responsible for the content and ideas promoted by the magazine.)

In fact, the international eugenics movement, of which Margaret Sanger was inarguably a part, was openly praising Nazi racial policies at least as late as 1938.[15] Sanger gave the welcoming address to a 1925 international eugenics conference.[16] According to researcher Marvin Olasky, Margaret Sanger's "Negro Project" of the 1930s was "hailed for its work in spreading contraception among those whom eugenicists most deeply feared."[17] When it became evident that contraceptives were not sufficiently curtailing the black population and other target groups, the eugenicists turned to abortion as a solution to the spread of unwanted races and families.[18]

In Margaret Sanger's own words, to help the weaker and less priviledged survive and to allow them to reproduce was to take a step backward in human evolution—"Instead of decreasing and aiming to eliminate the stocks that are most detrimental to the future of the race and the world, it tends to render them to a menacing degree dominant."[19] These "stocks" were the poor and uneducated, a large portion of whom were ethnic minorities. Sanger was more interested in "aiming to eliminate" these "stocks" (read *people*) than in helping them.

This history helps to explain why to this day Planned Parenthood does virtually nothing to promote adoption or help poor and minority women who choose to give their children life rather than abort them. Planned Parenthood has even brought legal action to shut down alternative pregnancy centers which give women other choices besides abortion. Though I have read many Planned Parenthood materials, I have never seen any that renounce or apologize for Sanger's blatant eugenicism, her bias against the poor and the mentally and physically handicapped, and her implicit racism, all of which characterized Planned Parenthood's social philosophy from its inception. The fact that there are some highly visible blacks and other minority leaders in Planned Parenthood does not change its heritage or philosophy. It simply makes it easier to carry out its policies among target groups.

I do not believe Margaret Sanger was insincere or incorrect in everything she said and did. Nor do I believe most people who support abortion rights are racists, any more than I believe there are no racists among prolifers. I do believe that regardless of motives, a closer look at both the history and present strategies of the prochoice movement suggests that "abortion for the minorities" may not serve the cause of racial equality nearly as much as the cause of upperclass white supremacy.

20. "Abortion helps solve the problem of overpopulation and raises the quality of life."

20a. The current birth rate in America is less than what is needed to maintain our population level.

In 1957 the average American woman in her reproductive years bore 3.7 children. Taking into account all causes of death and the increases in average life span, zero population growth requires that the average woman bears 2.1 children. Since 1972 the average in America has been 1.8 children.[1] For two decades we have been below zero population growth. Every day more people die in America than are born. Any increases in population since 1972 have been due to immigration. The sociological perils we face are not those of population explosion, but population reduction.

Prochoice advocates warn the American people that the prolife movement is trying to outlaw contraceptives. This is untrue. Some confusion may stem from the opposition to some forms of contraception, specifically the intrauterine device (IUD),[2] Norplant, and certain low-dose oral contraceptives, which often do not prevent conception but prevent implantation of an already fertilized ovum.[3] The result is an early abortion, the killing of an already conceived individual. Tragically, many women are not told this by their physicians, and therefore do not make an informed choice about which contraceptive to use.

Opposition to specific abortion-causing agents is not the same as opposition to true contraceptives, which do not cause abortions. It is true that among prolifers there is honest debate about contraceptive use and the degree to which people should strive to control the size of their families. But on the matter of controlling family size by killing a family member, we all ought to agree. Solutions based on killing people are not viable.

20b. The dramatic decline in our birth rate will have a disturbing economic effect on America.

A reducing population is a serious threat to social and economic prosperity. Most western European countries are now experiencing economic problems that their governments attribute to population reduction. France offers child-bearing incentives that include monthly financial payments to families with more than a certain number of children. Why would a government pay its people to have children? Because it recognizes any society needs a continuous influx of the young in order to remain healthy.

The problem of a shrinking population propagates itself. Because today's women have fewer children, there will be fewer parents tomorrow, resulting in still fewer children. Fewer and fewer people having fewer and fewer children adds up to a dying society.

The legalization of abortion resulted in a drastic reduction of the number of children in this country. By 1980 there were 6.5 million fewer school-age children in America than just a decade earlier. This required the closing of nine thousand elementary schools.[4]

Legalized abortion has resulted in over twenty million fewer tax payers in America to support the elderly. "Population loss from abortion on demand is already responsible for past and future economic, employment and tax revenue losses and is eroding the solvency of Social Security."[5] The imbalance of older and younger is shaping into a chronological civil war. By 2025 there will be twice as many grandparents as young children.[6] Some experts predict Social Security taxes will rise from 25 to 40 percent of total income.[7] In 1980 there were over four people of wage-earning age for each retired person, while in 2020 there will be only two. By 2040 there will be one and a half.[8]

Having endorsed abortion as a means of decreasing the young, will society be compelled toward euthanasia as a means of reducing the old? If back in the 1980s the governor of Colorado could tell old people they have a duty to "step aside" (die), what will happen in the 2010s? If the elderly don't step aside, will society begin setting them aside?

Former Surgeon General C. Everett Koop stated publicly his fears about mandatory euthanasia eventually resulting from the unwillingness of the younger generation to support the elderly. He said, "My fear is that one day for every Baby Doe in America, there will be ten thousand Grandma Does."

20c. Overpopulation is frequently blamed for problems with other causes.

In the sixties there was a widespread fear that the world was swarming with people and we were quickly running out of space. Yet the truth is that in 1992 Marilyn vos Savant calculated that the entire world population of 5.4 billion people, standing several feet apart, would cover an area of less then eight hundred square miles—the size of Jacksonville, Florida.[9] Every single global inhabitant could be placed in one gigantic city within the borders of the state of Texas, with a population density less than many cities around the world.[10] The rest of the globe would be completely empty of people.

Does this mean that there is no overcrowding and that our resources are infinite? Of course not. The world is full of problems, including poverty and starvation. But studies consistently show that plenty of food is presently produced to feed every person on the planet. The problem of starvation is a combination of many factors, including natural disasters, wars, lack of technology, misuse of resources, waste, greed, government inefficiency, and failure to distribute food properly. None of these has a direct cause and effect link to overpopulation. It is simplistic and inaccurate to attribute most of our global problems to overpopulation. Having fewer people alive to experience social problems is not a solution to those problems.

20d. If there is a population problem that threatens our standard of living, the solution is not to kill off part of the population.

Suppose there *is* a severe overpopulation problem. Suppose it could be demonstrated that the standard of living is higher in America because 1.5 million children are killed each year. The philosophy of a Hitler can increase the standard of living—for those, that is, who are allowed to live. We must ask ourselves whether we want to live in a society where the standard of living was bought with the blood of the innocent.

20e. Sterilization and abortion as cures to overpopulation could eventually lead to mandatory sterilization and abortion.

China's one-child policy places extreme pressure on women pregnant with a second child to get abortions. Not only are they punished economically, but in some cases they are physically forced to get abortions. In 1981 abortion "posses" rounded up expectant mothers and took them to abortion clinics. In a single town, nineteen thousand abortions were performed in fifty days, all in the name of population control.[11]

If anyone imagines this could not happen in America, a closer look at the direction of the prochoice movement should cause us to think again. The president of a scientific affiliation looks forward to the day when the government will require "that no parents will in the future have a right to burden society with a malformed or mentally incompetent child."[12] Molly Yard, past president of the National Organization for Women (NOW), has said, "We are going to have to face, as China has faced, the policy of controlling the size of families."[13] As George Grant points out, Planned Parenthood has been supportive of China's abortion policy:

> The truth is that from its very inception, Planned Parenthood has sought mandatory population control measures—measures carefully designed to *deny* the freedom to choose. Over the years it has proposed that our government implement such things as "compulsory abortion for out-of-wedlock pregnancies," federal entitlement "payments to encourage abortion," "compulsory sterilization for those who have already had two children," and "tax penalties" for existing large families.[14]

20f. The "quality of life" concept is breeding a sense of human expendability that has far-reaching social implications.

"Quality of life" is a euphemism when applied to those not allowed to live. There is no quality of life for those whose lives are taken. For those allowed to live, life can only become more precarious. Variables such as age, health, or handicap may take one out of the position of privilege, making him a potential victim of others' quality of life. As Mother Teresa has said, "If a mother can take her child in the womb, what is to stop me from taking you and you from taking me?"

The slippery slope starts with the concept that some lives have more quality than others. Historically, this has always slid society into further human exploitation. Dr. Leo Alexander was a consultant to the secretary of war at the Nuremberg Trials. Writing in the *New England Journal of Medicine*, he points out that the holocaust began with a subtle shift in medical ethics:

> Whatever proportions these crimes finally assumed, it became evident to all who investigated them that they had started from small beginnings. The beginnings at first were merely a subtle shift in emphasis in the basic attitude of the physicians. It started with the acceptance of the attitude . . . that there is such a thing as life not worthy to be lived. This attitude in its early stages concerned itself merely with the severely and chronically sick. Gradually the sphere of those to be included in this category was enlarged to encompass the socially unproductive, the ideologically unwanted, the racially unwanted and finally all non-Germans.[15]

21. "Even if abortion were made illegal, there would still be many abortions."

21a. That harmful acts against the innocent will take place regardless of the law is a poor argument for having no law.

There are laws against burglary, rape, and armed robbery, yet every one of these crimes continues to happen in our society. That these things still happen should not convince us to make them legal. Laws should exist to discourage bad things from happening, not conform to them simply because they happen.

21b. The law can guide and educate people to choose better alternatives.

It is true that hearts and minds—not just laws—need to change in relation to abortion. Yet, we often underestimate the power of law to mold thought as well as action. When slavery was abolished people gradually began to think differently. The civil rights movement brought about further changes in law, and further changes in people's thinking. The law is a moral guide, a tutor that helps shape the conscience of society.

Even when law doesn't change attitudes right away, it does affect the actions of many. Martin Luther King, Jr., said, "Morality cannot be legislated but behavior can be regulated. Judicial decrees may not change the heart, but they can restrain the heartless."[1]

21c. History shows that laws concerning abortion have significantly influenced whether women choose to have abortions.

There were abortions in this country before abortion was legal, but the number skyrocketed once it was legalized. There are now fifteen times more abortions annually in this country than there were the year prior to *Roe v. Wade*.[2] The laws that once restrained abortion now encourage it.

A change in abortion laws, from restrictive to permissive, appears—from *all data* and in *every country*—to bring forward a whole class of women who would otherwise not have wanted an abortion or felt the need for one.... Women can be conditioned (and are in many places) to want and feel the need for abortions. Evidence from those countries where abortion-on-request has been long available (Russia, Japan, Hungary, for instance) shows that the subjectively felt stress that leads women to seek an abortion is socially influenced.[3]

In one survey of women who had abortions, 72 percent said they would definitely not have sought an abortion if doing so were illegal.[4] Though making abortion illegal again would not stop all abortions, it would encourage the larger number of women to pursue available alternatives.

22. "The anti-abortion beliefs of the minority shouldn't be imposed on the majority."

22a. Major polls clearly indicate it is a majority, not a minority, who believe there should be greater restrictions on abortion.

In 1989 the *Boston Globe*, a pro-abortion newspaper, reported the results of its own survey: "Most Americans would ban the vast majority of abortions performed in this country."[1] The *Globe* found that "while 78 percent of the nation would keep abortion legal in limited circumstances, those circumstances account for only a tiny percentage of the reasons cited by women having abortions."[2] The "limited circumstances" were rape, incest, danger to the mother's life, and deformity of the child. But in cases where pregnancy poses financial or emotional strain, or when the woman is alone or a teenager—in other words, in 97 percent of actual situations—an overwhelming majority of Americans believe abortion should be illegal.

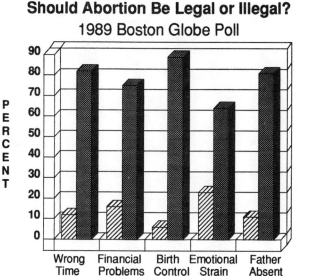

Should Abortion Be Legal or Illegal?
1989 Boston Globe Poll

A *Los Angeles Times* poll indicated that 61 percent believe abortion is immoral, and 57 percent believe it is murder.[3] A 1989 *New York Times* poll indicated 79 percent of the population opposes the current policy of unrestricted abortion.[4] A 1990 *USA Today* poll showed that 63 percent believe laws should be changed to allow greater restrictions on abortion.[5]

A 1989 *Newsweek* poll indicated strong support for legislation restricting abortion.[6] The question was asked, "Would you support or oppose the following restrictions that may come before state legislatures?" Nearly two out of three supported the restriction, "No public funds for abortion, except to save a woman's life." Three out of four supported the restriction, "Teenagers must have parent's permission to get an abortion." And an overwhelming nine out of ten affirmed support for a law saying, "Women seeking abortions must be counseled on the dangers and on alternatives to abortion." Significantly, most of these restrictions are not in place in most states, even though the overwhelming majority of Americans support them.

Support for Abortion Restrictions
1989 Newsweek Poll

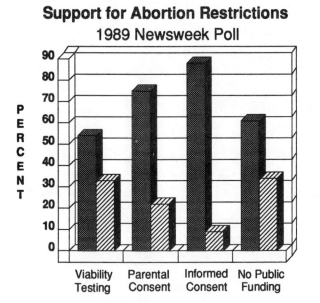

The most comprehensive abortion survey ever taken was a Gallup Poll released in 1991. It showed that 77 percent of Americans believe abortion takes a human life.[7] Only 17 percent of the country is "strongly prochoice," while 26 percent is "strongly prolife."[8] Only one out of four Americans "seldom disapprove of abortion," another one out of four "consistently disapprove of abortion," and the remaining half "often disapprove of abortion."[9]

U.S. Disapproval of Abortion
1991 Gallup Poll

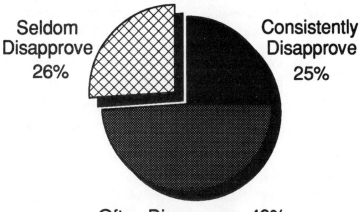

Seldom Disapprove 26%

Consistently Disapprove 25%

Often Disapprove 49%

When asked when the child's right to life outweighs the woman's right to choose, a full 50 percent said "conception." Only 7 percent said "birth," the position that most closely corresponds to current law.[10] A clear majority of Americans approves of almost every kind of legislative proposal restricting abortions.[11] For instance, 73 percent support the banning of all abortions in the second and third trimester; 69 percent support parental consent laws; an overwhelming 84 percent believe health and safety standards should be imposed on abortion clinics; and 86 percent believe the law should require that a woman receive information regarding fetal development and alternatives to abortion before she may obtain one.[12]

In summary, "The Survey data yield the unmistakable conclusion: Americans generally disapprove of abortion in most circumstances under which it is currently performed."[13]

22b. Many people's apparent agreement with abortion law stems from their ignorance of what the law really is.

In reference to the 1991 Gallup poll, the *Washington Times* asked and answered a critical question: "So why has there been no tidal wave of opposition to the legal status quo of abortion-on-demand? Simply this: Americans don't know what the abortion laws say."[14]

The most startling discovery of the Gallup poll was that *only 11 percent of Americans have an accurate understanding that abortion is available throughout all nine months of pregnancy.*[15] Interestingly, the one in four who "seldom disapprove" of abortion were the most likely to say they were "very familiar" with *Roe v. Wade* and abortion law.[16] But of those who considered themselves "very familiar" with the law, only 24 percent accurately understood what the law is![17]

What Americans Think about Abortion
When it's legal and when it isn't (under Roe v. Wade)

Percent believing abortion is legal for:

- Never Legal
- 1st Trimester, Mother's Health
- 1st Trimester, Any Reason
- Any Time or Reason (Correct)
- Uncertain
- Total incorrect
- Total correct

1991 Gallup Poll

In the words of Victor Rosenblum, past president of the Association of American Law Schools, the poll revealed that "an overwhelming majority of Americans simply do not understand what is allowed under current law. In many cases, it appears that people who consider themselves 'prochoice' simply don't know what they're supporting."[18] The poll shows that if they did know, many would not support it.

Of the six major polls I have cited, none was conducted by an organization with a prolife slant, and only one was even commissioned by such a group. Five of the six were conducted by publishers with a clear prochoice slant. *Yet all six polls demonstrate that if Americans had their way, abortion would be severely restricted in this country.* These restrictions would not impose a minority morality on the nation. On the contrary, they would reflect what a majority of Americans already believe.

22c. Beliefs that abortion should be restricted are embraced by a majority in each major political party.

The 1991 Gallup poll also categorized abortion beliefs according to political party. The differences were much less significant than most people would anticipate. For instance, 55 percent of Republicans believed that the unborn's right to be born outweighed the mother's right to choose at the point of conception. Among Democrats, 51 percent said the same, as did 43 percent of Independents and 57 percent of "other parties."[19] Only 17 percent of Republicans believe abortion is acceptable when pregnancy would interrupt a professional career, and only 20 percent of Democrats believe the same. Only 26 percent of Republicans believe abortion is acceptable because of low income and financial burden, and only 31 percent of Democrats believe the same. Only 26 percent of Republicans, 28 percent of Democrats, and 29 percent of Independents believe abortion is acceptable when a woman is abandoned by her partner.[20]

Among voters who identified themselves as either "strongly prolife" or "strongly prochoice" (those who would "withhold their vote from a political candidate with whom they largely agree, but with whom they disagree on abortion"), the "strongly prolife" outnumber the "strongly prochoice" among Democrats, Republicans, and Independents.[21]

22d. In 1973 the Supreme Court imposed a minority morality on the nation, ignoring the votes of citizens and the decisions of state legislatures.

Abortion was illegal in every state in America until 1967, when some abortions became legal in Colorado. Fourteen other states followed, permitting abortion under very restrictive conditions. In 1970 New York became the first state to have abortion-on-demand, though even that was limited to twenty-four weeks. In the following two years, *thirty-three states debated the issue in their legislatures and all thirty-three voted against legal abortion.* Even New York repealed its own abortion law, but because of a veto by Governor Nelson Rockefeller, the law remained in force.[22]

After being stopped in legislatures and in state courts, proabortion advocates proposed ballot measures in Michigan and North Dakota in the November 1972 election. Michigan had been claimed to be 60 percent proabortion, yet 63 percent voted against legalizing abortion. Prochoice leaders claimed the Catholic church was behind anti-abortion sentiments, so North Dakota, with only 12 percent Catholics, seemed an ideal place to pass a referendum legalizing abortion. But an overwhelming 78 percent of the state's citizens voted against the measure.[23]

Only two months later, the Supreme Court imposed abortion-on-demand upon every state, making it illegal for states to restrict abortion in any meaningful way. The opinions of seven men imposed a radical new morality on the entire nation.

Bob Woodward and Scott Armstrong's *The Brethren* is a well-researched and compelling account of the inner workings of the Supreme Court from 1969 to 1975. It discusses the subjective and arbitrary rulings of the court, most notably *Roe v. Wade.* Judge Harry Blackmun, the author of *Roe,* was heavily influenced by his wife, who actually told her husband's proabortion clerk that while he was lobbying Blackmun in the office, she was working on the judge at home.[24] Such influence helps explain the fact that the decision had no basis in law but merely reflected personal preference in a changing moral climate. Speaking of *Roe,* Woodward and Armstrong say, "As a constitutional matter, it was absurd."[25] Even with its prochoice bias, *Newsweek* summarizes *Roe* this way: "With a wave of the judicial wand, abortion had become a constitutional right, without an accounting of why."[26]

The Supreme Court determined in *Roe v. Wade* that no state could put any legal restrictions on abortion in the first three months of pregnancy. It said abortion was allowed until birth provided only that one physician considered it necessary for the mother's "health." In an adjoining case, *Doe v. Bolton, health* was defined so as to embrace almost any consideration. Abortions were legal "in the light of all factors—physical, emotional, psychological, familial and the woman's age—relevant to the well being of the patient. All these factors may relate to health."[27]

Hence, *what was imposed on America was not only legalized abortion, but the most liberalized abortion policy conceivable.* The first major step in correcting this policy was the 1989 *Webster* decision, which gave back to the states some of the power abruptly taken from them sixteen years earlier.[28]

Ronald Reagan summarized the issue this way: "Our nation-wide policy of abortion-on-demand through all nine months of pregnancy was neither voted for by our people nor enacted by our legislators—not a single state had such unrestricted abortion before the Supreme Court decreed it to be national policy in 1973."[29] According to dissenting Justice White, the *Roe v. Wade* decision was nothing but "an act of raw judicial power."[30]

Not only the Constitution, but also the beliefs of the majority of citizens, and the laws and votes of the states and their legislatures, have never been more blatantly disregarded. *The prochoice position was forcibly imposed upon the largely unwilling citizens of America.* Any change in that law is not the imposition of a new minority morality, but the restoration of an old majority morality.

23. "The anti-abortion position is a religious belief that threatens the vital separation of church and state."

23a. Many nonreligious people believe that abortion kills children and that it is wrong.

The polls cited under the previous argument show that an anti-abortion position, at least to a certain extent, is held by a majority of citizens. Many of these citizens are not religious, and those that are belong to a wide variety of religious groups that transcend political parties. As the

Washington Times states, "Women and men and people of varying religious faiths and races tend to support the right to life in equal measure."[1]

A study of thirty women who considered their abortions highly stressful yielded this revealing insight: "Though 72% of the subjects reported no identifiable religious beliefs at the time of the abortion, 96% regarded abortion as the taking of a life or as murder subsequent to their abortion."[2] One does not have to subscribe to a particular religion to have a conscience, or an innate sense that killing the innocent is wrong.

Nat Hentoff is a creator and editor of New York's ultra-liberal *Village Voice*. He is a self-described "atheist, a lifelong leftist, and a card-carrying member of the ACLU."[3] He detests most of the policies of conservative administrations. He is also an outspoken prolife advocate, who takes constant heat for publicly calling abortion the killing of children.[4]

In the most widely listened to radio talk show in history, host Rush Limbaugh regularly argues against abortion. He appeals not to religious beliefs but to scientific, historical, and common sense realities. And to many listeners—nonreligious and religious—he makes a lot of sense.

Dr. Bernard Nathanson was an atheist when his first-hand involvement in abortion made him realize it was the killing of the innocent. He argued that abortion falls far short of the most profound tenet of human morality, spoken by Jesus Christ: "Do unto others as you would have them do unto you."[5] Responding to the charge that this was some sectarian religious tenet, Nathanson said:

> On the contrary, it is simply a statement of innate human wisdom. Unless this principle is cherished by a society and widely honored by its individual members, the end result is anarchy and the violent dissolution of the society. This is why life is always an overriding value in the great ethical systems of world history. If we do not protect innocent, nonaggressive elements in the human community, the alternative is too horrible to contemplate. Looked at this way, the "sanctity of life" is not a theological but a secular concept, which should be perfectly acceptable to my fellow atheists.[6]

Writing in another context, Nathanson stated:

> I think that abortion policy ought not be beholden to a sectarian creed, but that obviously the law can and does encompass moral convictions shared by a variety of religious interests. In the case of abortion, however, we can and must decide on the biological evidence and on fundamental humanitarian

grounds without resorting to scriptures, revelations, creeds, hierarchical decrees, or belief in God. Even if God does not exist, the fetus does.[7]

The abortion issue is really a human life issue, a civil rights issue. It is not simply a religious issue, any more than the rights of Jews and blacks is simply a religious issue. Though most governments are secular, there is hardly a nation in the world where abortion was legal prior to World War II. You do not need to be a Christian, nor to subscribe to any religion, to believe that the unborn are children and that it should not be legal to kill them.

23b. Morality must not be rejected just because it is supported by religion.

William Carey, known as the "father of Christian missions," faced the terrible practice of widow burning in India. He labored long and hard to make this killing illegal, and finally succeeded. While trying to be sensitive to the Indian culture, Carey didn't think it inappropriate to bring to bear his Christian morality when the lives of innocent people were at stake.

Every law establishes a certain moral position as a social norm. Every society can and must implement legislation that defines what is right and wrong, and what citizens should and should not do. Whether it is from the Bible or elsewhere, all law must come from somewhere. Most of our laws are rooted in the Judeo-Christian religion.

The Bible says, "You shall not steal." Should we get rid of our laws against stealing because they impose a Judeo-Christian morality? Shall we invalidate all moral standards that are founded on religious principles? If we did, what moral standards would be left?

23c. America was founded on a moral base dependent upon principles of the Bible and the Christian religion.

If our goal is to keep religion from dictating the moral principles and laws of our country, we are hundreds of years too late. Virtually every significant document that defines the values of the United States of America—including the Declaration of Independence, the Constitution, and the Bill of Rights—leans heavily on a belief in God and the moral authority of the Bible.[8]

George Washington said, "It is impossible to rightly govern the world without God and the Bible."[9] In his farewell address, Washington reminded the country that religion and morality are inseparable: "Let us with caution indulge the supposition that morality can be maintained without religion. . . . Reason and experience both forbid us to expect that national morality can prevail in exclusion of religious principles."

Noah Webster warned, "The moral principles and precepts contained in the Scriptures form the basis of all our civil constitution and laws. All the miseries and evils which other nations suffer from vice, crime, ambition, injustice, oppression, slavery, and war, proceed from their despising or neglecting the precepts contained in the Bible."[10]

It is impossible to reject the moral framework of the Scriptures, including the sanctity of human life, and to simultaneously affirm the values of freedom and human rights that distinguish the United States of America.

23d. Laws related to church and state were intended to assure freedom *for* religion, not freedom *from* religion.

Neither the words "separation of church and state" nor the concept as we now know it are found in the Constitution. The First Amendment's establishment of religion clause was devised to protect religious liberty, not to banish religion's influence on society. But even if we adopt the later terminology of a separate church and state, the "church" that was to be separate from the state was a single denomination or sectarian group, not religion in general. The founders of our country did not want one church or denomination to control the state. They definitely *did* want religion, specifically the Christian religion, to influence the moral principles and laws of the state.[11] America's colonists came here to have freedom *of* religion, not freedom *from* religion. Their intention was that the moral principles founded in religious beliefs should permeate the social order.

23e. Religion's waning influence on our society directly accounts for the moral deterioration threatening our future.

In their book, *The Day America Told the Truth*, James Patterson and Peter Kim put their fingers on the moral pulse of the nation. By their own testimony, many of the results were alarming.[12]

Three out of four Americans say, "I will steal from those who won't really miss it." Two-thirds say, "I will lie when it suits me, so long as it doesn't cause any real damage." Over half say, "I will cheat on my spouse—after all, given the chance, he or she will do the same." One-third acknowledged, "I will put my lover at risk of disease. I sleep around a bit, but who doesn't?"

Only one-third of Americans agree with the statement "Honesty is the best policy." When asked what they would do for ten million dollars, 25 percent said they would abandon their entire family, 23 percent said they would become prostitutes for a week or more, and 7 percent—one out of fourteen—said they would murder a stranger. "Americans believe that our country has become a colder, greedier, meaner, more selfish and less caring place."

To what can we attribute this startling unraveling of the moral fiber of our nation? Patterson and Kim say, "In the 1950s 75% of Americans believed that religion was very important. Today the figure is 54%." They say Americans now live in a moral vacuum:

> Americans of the 1990s stand alone in a way unknown to any previous generation. When we want to answer a question of right and wrong, we ask ourselves. . . . The overwhelming majority of people (93%) said that they—and nobody else—determine what is and what isn't moral in their lives. They base their decisions on their own experience, even on their daily whims. . . .
>
> We are a law unto ourselves. . . . What's right? What's wrong? When you are making up your own rules, your own moral codes, it can make the world a confusing place. Most Americans are very confused about their personal morals right now.[13]

Patterson and Kim say this about the relationship between religion and morality in this country:

> People describing themselves as "very religious" (14 percent) definitely make better citizens. . . . Religion appears to play a strong role in building moral character. We found that people who defined themselves as religious showed a much stronger commitment to moral values and social institutions than did nonreligious people.[14]

Based on their interviews Patterson and Kim maintain, "A let down in moral values is now considered the number one problem facing our country. Eighty percent of us believe that morals and ethics should be taught in our schools again." But no suggestion is made as to what these morals and ethics could be based upon if not what they always were in our past—the Judeo-Christian morality rooted in the Scriptures.

When traveling in the Soviet Union in 1991, I had the opportunity to talk with two public school principals. Both were Communists who had followed the strict practice of keeping religion out of the classrooms. They now realized there was a moral crisis in the Soviet Union. One of them said, "Our children have nothing to believe in, no morality, no reason to be honest, good citizens. We want to bring the Christian religion back to our young people, back to our classrooms, so we can have a moral society again." Though these men had no strong religious faith, they recognized what we in America have forgotten—the essential connection between a society's morality and its religious beliefs.

PART FOUR

_____

ARGUMENTS CONCERNING HEALTH AND SAFETY

ARGUMENTS CONCERNING HEALTH AND SAFETY

24. "If abortion is made illegal, tens of thousands of women will again die from back-alley and clothes-hanger abortions."

24a. For decades prior to its legalization, 90 percent of abortions were done by physicians in their offices, not in back alleys.

Fifteen years before abortion was legal in America, around 85 percent of illegal abortions were done by "reputable physicians in good standing in their local medical associations."[1] In 1960, Planned Parenthood stated that "90% of all illegal abortions are presently done by physicians."[2] The vast majority of abortions were not done in back alleys but in the back offices of licensed physicians.

Were these doctors "butchers," as prochoice advocates claim? The majority of physicians performing abortions *after* legalization were the same ones doing it *before* legalization. Neither their training nor their equipment improved when abortion was decriminalized. Either they were not butchers before legalization, or they continued to be butchers after legalization. It cannot be argued both ways.

24b. It is not true that tens of thousands of women were dying from illegal abortions before abortion was legalized.

Former abortion-rights activist Bernard Nathanson admits that he and his cofounders of NARAL fabricated the figure that a million women were getting illegal abortions in America each year. The average, he says, was actually ninety-eight thousand per year. Nonetheless, the abortion advocates fed their concocted figures to the media, who eagerly disseminated the false information. Nathanson says he and his associates also invented the "nice, round shocking figure" for the number of deaths from illegal abortions:

It was always "5,000 to 10,000 deaths a year." I confess that I knew the figures were totally false, and I suppose the others did too if they stopped to think of it. But in the "morality" of our revolution, it was a useful figure, widely accepted, so why go out of our way to correct it with honest statistics? The overriding concern was to get the laws [against abortion] eliminated, and anything within reason that had to be done was permissible.[3]

Research confirms that the actual number of abortion deaths in the twenty-five years prior to 1973 averaged 250 a year, with a high of 388 in 1948.[4] In 1966, before the first state legalized abortion, 120 mothers died from abortion.[5] By 1972 abortion was still illegal in 80 percent of the country, but the use of antibiotics had greatly reduced the risk. Hence, the number dropped to 39 maternal deaths from abortion that year.[6] Dr. Christopher Tietze, a prominent statistician associated with Planned Parenthood, maintained that these are accurate figures, with a margin of error no greater than 10 percent.[7]

However, suppose that only one out of ten deaths from illegal abortion was properly identified. This would mean that the number of women dying the year before abortion was legalized would be less than four hundred, still only a fraction of the five to ten thousand claimed by prochoice advocates.

24c. Women still die from *legal* abortions in America.

Abortion is normally not life-threatening to the mother. However, the fatality rate is much higher than many prochoice advocates admit. For instance, a widely disseminated prochoice video produced in the late 1980s states, "By 1979 the Federal Government could not identify a single woman anywhere in this country who died of abortion."[8]

This is an amazing statement, since many sources document a number of deaths from legal abortion. According to the *American Journal of Obstetrics & Gynecology*, "the New York City Department of Health reported seven legal abortion-related deaths that occurred between 1980 and 1985. The cause of death in all cases was attributed directly to general anesthesia."[9] (These were seven deaths in a single city.) There were four abortion-caused deaths in a single Florida clinic between 1979 and 1983.[10] In 1986, four doctors and researchers presented a study of no less than 193 deaths by legal abortion between 1972 and 1985.[11] One researcher has uncovered the tragic cases of some 300 women who have died as a result of legal abortion.[12]

Since public health officials stopped looking for abortion-caused deaths after abortion was legal, the opportunity to overlook or cover up abortion-caused deaths is now much greater. A former abortion clinic owner says, "A woman died because of an abortion at our clinic, but the public never heard about it, and it wasn't reported to the authorities as abortion related."[13] When the *Chicago Sun-Times* investigated Chicago-area abortion clinics in 1978 it uncovered the cases of twelve women who died of legal abortion but whose deaths had not been reported as abortion-related. Twelve unreported deaths from abortion in one small part of the country is a revealing number when the official statistics indicated twenty-one deaths from abortion *in the entire country* the previous year![14]

Statistics on death by abortion are dependent on the voluntary reporting of abortion clinics, who have much to lose and nothing to gain by doing so.[15] What makes abortion-related deaths hard to trace is that the majority of the deaths do not occur during the surgery but afterward. Hence, any number of secondary reasons are routinely identified as the cause of death:

> Consider the mother who hemorrhaged, was transfused, got hepatitis, and died months later. Official cause of death? Hepatitis. Actual cause? Abortion. A perforated uterus leads to pelvic abscess, sepsis (blood poisoning), and death. The official report of the cause of death may list pelvic abscess and septicemia. Abortion will not be listed. Abortion causes tubal pathology. She has an ectopic pregnancy years later and dies. The cause listed will be ectopic pregnancy. The actual cause? Abortion.[16]

In his novel *Prophet*, Frank Peretti masterfully portrays the web of deception and complicity surrounding legal abortion and its dangers.[17] Family members, doctors, the media, and political figures all have vested interests in this cover-up. Six weeks ago I attended the funeral of a woman who died from "treatment" at a Portland abortion clinic. There has been no media coverage.

Legalized abortion has resulted in fifteen times more women having abortions. This means that if it is fifteen times safer than illegal abortion, the number of women dying remains the same. Writing in the *American Journal of Obstetrics and Gynecology*, Dr. Dennis Cavanaugh stated that since abortion has been legalized, "there has been no major impact on the number of women dying from abortion in the U.S. . . . After all, it really makes no difference whether a woman dies from legal or illegal abortion,

139

she is dead nonetheless. I find no comfort in the fact that legal abortion is now the leading cause of abortion-related maternal deaths in the U.S."[18]

24d. If abortion became illegal, abortions would be done with medical equipment, not clothes hangers.

One woman told me, "People must think women are stupid. If abortion were illegal and I wanted one, I sure wouldn't use a clothes hanger." Since 90 percent of pre-1973 illegal abortions were done by doctors, it's safe to assume many physicians would continue to give abortions. "Self-help" abortion kits are being widely promoted and distributed by pro-abortion groups, who have vowed they will step up their efforts if abortion is made illegal again.[19] Sadly, many women would continue to have abortions. But the "many" might be a quarter of a million rather than one and a half million. The result would be over a million mothers and babies annually saved from abortion.

Clothes hangers make effective propaganda pieces at prochoice rallies, but they do not accurately reflect what would happen if abortion were made illegal again. Clothes hangers would be used for baby clothes, not abortions.

24e. We must not legalize procedures that kill the innocent just to make the killing process less hazardous.

From the child's point of view there is no such thing as a safe, legal abortion. It is always deadly. For every two people who enter an abortion clinic, only one comes out alive.

Rape is a horrible attack on an innocent human being, so we do not attempt to make rape safe and legal. If abortion kills children, our goal should not be to make it as safe and easy as possible, but to provide alternatives and legal restrictions that help avoid it in the first place.

24f. The central horror of illegal abortion remains the central horror of legal abortion.

Unfortunately, every horror that was true of illegal abortion is also true about legalized abortion. Many veterans of illegal abortion, however, do not realize this. Instead, they cling to the belief that all the pain and problems they suffered could have been avoided if only abortion had been legal. They imagine that if their abortions had been legal, their lives would somehow be better today. Instead of recognizing that it is the very nature of abortion itself which caused their problems, they blame their suffering on the illegality of abortion at that time.[20]

Abortion is horrible primarily because it is a process in which instruments of death invade a woman's body and kill her innocent child. Neither laws nor slogans nor attractive waiting rooms nor advanced medical equipment can change the nature of abortion. What it is it will always be—the killing of children.

25. "Abortion is a safe medical procedure, safer than full-term pregnancy and childbirth."

25a. Abortion is not safer than full-term pregnancy and childbirth.

Less than one in ten thousand pregnancies results in the mother's death.[1] Government statistics indicate the chances of death by abortion are even less. But while deaths from childbirth are accurately reported, many deaths by legal abortion are not. This completely skews the statistics. Furthermore, "abortion actually increases the chance of maternal death in later pregnancies."[2] This means some maternal deaths in full-term pregnancies are actually caused by earlier abortions, creating a double inaccuracy.

But even if abortion did result in fewer maternal deaths, that wouldn't make it safer. The nonfatal but significant complications of abortion are much more frequent and serious than those of full-term pregnancy. One researcher states, "The evidence overwhelmingly proves that the morbidity and mortality rates of legal abortion are several times higher than that for carrying a pregnancy to term."[3]

25b. Though the chances of a woman's safe abortion are now greater, the number of suffering women is also greater because of the huge increase in abortions.

No one doubts that legal abortion is marginally safer than illegal abortion, but neither is there any doubt that decriminalization has encouraged more women to undergo abortions than ever before. Risk goes down, but numbers go up. . . . This combination means that though the odds of any particular

141

woman suffering ill effects from an abortion have dropped, the total number of women who suffer . . . from abortion is far greater than ever before.[4]

25c. Even if abortion were safer for the mother than childbirth, it would still remain fatal for the innocent child.

Having a baby is a low-risk undertaking, but suppose the risk were much higher. When an innocent life is at stake, isn't there a moral obligation to take risk? Childbirth is much safer than trying to rescue a drowning child in the ocean, or trying to rescue a woman who is being beaten or raped. An adult swimming to shore from a capsized boat has a much greater chance of survival if he doesn't try to save a child. But does that mean he shouldn't?

25d. Abortion can produce many serious medical problems.

Ectopic pregnancies occur when gestation takes place outside the uterus, commonly in a fallopian tube. Though usually not fatal, such pregnancies are nonetheless responsible for 12 percent of all pregnancy-related maternal deaths.[5] Studies show that the risk of an ectopic pregnancy is twice as high for women who have had one abortion, and up to four times as high for women with two or more previous abortions.[6] There has been a 300 percent increase of ectopic pregnancies since abortion was legalized. In 1970 the incidence was 4.8 per 1,000 births; by 1980 it had risen to 14.5 per 1,000 births.[7]

Pelvic Inflammatory Disease is an infection that leads to fever and infertility. Researchers state, "Pelvic infection is a common and serious complication of induced abortion and has been reported in up to 30% of all cases."[8] A study of women having first-trimester abortions demonstrated that "women with postabortal pelvic inflammatory disease had significantly higher rates of . . . spontaneous abortion, secondary infertility, dyspareunia, and chronic pelvic pain."[9] Other infectious complications, as well as endometriosis, follow approximately 5 percent of abortion procedures.[10]

Because of the rapid growth of breast tissue in early pregnancy, a premature cessation of pregnancy (such as that caused by abortion) creates an unnatural condition. Consequently, women who have first-trimester abortions face twice the risk of contracting breast cancer as those who complete their pregnancies and give birth.[11]

Internal bleeding is normal following abortions, but in some cases it is severe due to a perforated uterus. This can cause sterility and other serious and permanent problems. A perforated uterus was the cause of at least twenty-four deaths among U.S. women having abortions between 1972 and 1979.[12] Numerous scientific studies demonstrate that the chance of miscarriages significantly increases with abortion, as much as ten-fold.[13] Tragically, some women are unable to conceive after having abortions. Tubal infertility has been found to be up to 30 percent more common among women who have had abortions.[14] Having taken the life of a child they did not want, they will never be able to carry a child they do want.

The health of future children is also at risk, as both premature births and low birth weights are more common among women who have had abortions.[15] Malformations, both major and minor, of later children are increased by abortion.[16] For various reasons, the frequency of early death for infants born after their mothers have had abortions is between two and four times the normal rate.[17]

Placenta previa is a condition occurring when the placenta covers the cervix, preventing the baby from passing through the birth canal. It usually requires a Caesarean section and can threaten the life of both mother and child. Placenta previa is seven to fifteen times more common among women who have had abortions than among those who have not.[18]

Calculations of abortion complication rates vary considerably, but even the lower estimates are significant: "The reported immediate complication rate, alone, of abortion is no less than 10 percent. In addition, studies of long-range complications show rates no less than 17 percent and frequently report complication rates in the range of 25 to 40 percent."[19] After carefully studying the vast body of the world's medical literature on the subject, Dr. Thomas W. Hilgers concluded, "The medical hazards of legally induced abortion are very significant and should be conscientiously weighed."[20]

25e. The statistics on abortion complications and risks are often understated due to the inadequate means of gathering data.

It is not only abortion deaths that go unreported. Researchers warn that studies are likely to underestimate the risks and complications of abortion, because of the reluctance of women to report prior abortions and the difficulty of following up women who may have been injured through abortions.[21] A former director of several abortion clinics told me, "Most abortion complications are never made known to the public, because abortion has a built-in cover up. Women want to deny it and forget it, not talk about it."[22]

Furthermore, the accuracy of reported complications is largely dependent upon the willingness of abortion clinics to give out this information.[23] An abortion clinic director told me of a young woman at her clinic whose uterus was perforated during her abortion. The abortionist proceeded to accidentally pull out her bowel with the abortion instrument. No ambulance was called, because the clinic didn't want the bad publicity. The girl was driven to the hospital in a clinic worker's car. The damage was permanent, and she had to have a colostomy. Yet this was not reported as an abortion-related incident.[24]

25f. The true risks of abortion are rarely explained to women by those who perform abortions.

It is common to talk to women physically or psychologically damaged by abortions, who say, "I had no idea this could happen; no one told me about the risks." Many people do not realize the privileged status of abortion clinics:

> Abortion is the only surgery for which the surgeon is not obligated to inform the patient of the possible risks of the procedure, or even the exact nature of the procedure. Indeed, abortion providers are the only medical personnel who have a "constitutional right" to withhold information, even when directly questioned by the patient.[25]

The large body of evidence indicating significant abortion risks has been suppressed and ignored. This suppression is made possible by pro-choice advocates who zealously oppose any information-giving requirements for abortion clinics. This "immunity to stating the facts" enjoyed by abortion clinics increases their profits, but only at the expense of women who are not allowed to make an informed choice.

> The Court guarantees "freedom of choice" but denies the right to "informed choice." Abortionists can legally withhold information, or even avoid their clients' direct questions, in order to ensure that the patient will agree to an abortion which will be, they assume, "in her best interests."

> Why is there such widespread silence about the dangers of legal abortion?

Wasn't abortion legalized in order to *improve* health care for women rather than to encourage them to take unnecessary risks?[26]

Some abortion clinics may object that they voluntarily offer consent forms which patients must sign. Yet many patients testify that they did not read these forms, that the forms did not give specific information, or that they did not understand what they signed. The few who do ask questions are assured by clinic workers that any references to possible complications are just a formality, and there is nothing to worry about. Because of the nervous anxiety associated with an abortion, and the desire to get it over with, signing such a form is no different than not signing a form at all—except that it absolves the clinic of legal responsibility for the health problems the woman may suffer later.

The evidence indicates that the only way to avoid the risks of abortion is not to have one.

26. "Abortion is an easy and painless procedure."

26a. The various abortion procedures are often both difficult and painful for women.

There are several different kinds of abortion procedures, each creating its own kind of pain and difficulty. In a D & C, a tiny hoe-like instrument is inserted into the womb. The abortionist then scrapes the wall of the uterus, cutting the baby's body to pieces, which are pulled out piece by piece through the cervix. The scraping of the uterus typically involves some bleeding and other possible side effects that some women find quite painful.

In a suction abortion, a powerful suction tube is inserted through the cervix into the womb. The baby and the placenta are torn to pieces and sucked out into a jar. Sometimes this method follows a D & C. Infections, damage, and pain in the cervix and uterus can result.

In a saline abortion, a long needle is inserted through the mother's abdomen and a strong salt solution is injected directly into the amniotic fluid which surrounds the child. The salt is swallowed and absorbed into the baby, burning his skin and resulting in his death some hours later. The baby's death causes the mother to go into labor and expel a shriveled and visibly burnt baby.[1] (See photograph #5 at the center of this book.) The baby's thrashing, caused by his trauma, can be physically painful to his mother, and is often psychologically devastating. Sometimes the baby is born alive, writhing in pain because of severe burns. In such cases, the emotional consequences to the mother are considerable.

In a prostaglandin or chemical abortion, hormone-like compounds are injected or applied to the muscle of the uterus, causing it to contract and force the baby out. "This injection results in a very painful abortion for the mother."[2] In D & E, dilatation and evacuation, a forceps is used to crush the head of the unborn, and to pull out body parts from the uterus. This places a stress on the woman's body that can create various complications.[3]

A hysterotomy or C-section abortion is used in the last trimester. The womb is entered by surgery through the wall of the abdomen. It is the same as a live delivery except the baby is killed in the uterus, or is allowed to die from neglect if he is not yet dead upon removal. This is a major surgery with inherent difficulties, possible complications, and a potentially painful recovery.

A biologist states, "Unnatural abortions are violent and abusive to the human body."[4] Each of the abortion methods is unnatural and invasive; any of them can cause acute anxiety. One clinic manager told me she has seen a distraught woman getting an abortion who had to be held to the table by six people.[5] While this is not the norm, it demonstrates the extent of abortion's potential difficulty.

26b. Abortion is often difficult and painful for fathers, grandparents, and siblings of the aborted child.

One man who decided to abort his child has this to say:

Abortion is presented to you as something that is easy to do. It doesn't take very long. It doesn't cost very much money nowadays, for a middle-class person. You say, "Well, it's okay." But it wasn't okay. It left a scar, and that scar had to be treated tenderly and worked on in order for us to get on with our lives. I don't think abortion is easy for anybody. The people who say it's easy either don't want to face the pain of it or haven't been through it, because it's really a tough experience.[6]

A school teacher in her forties says, "Advising my daughter to have an abortion led me into a long, suicidal siege. I'm not over it yet. I can picture a baby who never even existed."[7] (Or does the guilt stem from the knowledge that a baby *did* exist, but was killed by the abortion?)

Imagine this conversation between a six-year-old girl and her mother who aborted one of the child's siblings, or who the child knows to be prochoice:

Daughter: Mom? Why didn't you abort me?

Mother: Darling, how can you say such a thing? I wanted you! You're my little girl!

Daughter: But what if you hadn't wanted me?

Mother: But I did!

Daughter: But what if you stopped wanting me?

Mother: But I won't!

Daughter: But how can you be sure? What if you *do* stop wanting me?[8]

Whether on the conscious or subconscious level, these questions have to be asked by any child aware of his mother's choice to abort a sibling or of his parents' support of abortion. This cuts to the core of the child's own sense of security in his parents' love. Such questions cannot be painless or inconsequential to the child.

26c. Abortion is often difficult and painful for clinic workers.

A veteran abortionist and his nurse assistant presented to the Association of Planned Parenthood Physicians a troubling report on reactions to the dilation and evacuation abortion procedure. They stated that the dismemberment of the fetus is "more traumatic for the operator and assistants than for the patient."[9] (Unlike the staff, the patient is not allowed to see the baby's body parts.) They followed a questionnaire with in-depth interviews of twenty-three present and former staff members of their abortion clinic:

Many subjects reported serious emotional reactions which produced physiological symptoms, sleep disturbances, effects on personal relationships, and moral anguish. . . . Reactions to viewing the fetus ranged from "I haven't looked" to shock, dismay, amazement, disgust, fear and sadness. . . . Two felt that it must eventually damage [the doctor] psychologically. . . .

147

Two respondents described dreams which they had had related to the procedure. Both described dreams of vomiting fetuses along with a sense of horror. Other dreams revolved around a need to protect others from viewing fetal parts, dreaming that she herself was pregnant and needed an abortion or was having a baby. . . . The more direct the physical and visual involvement (i.e. nurses, doctors), the more stress experienced.[10]

Because of their lack of understanding of what abortion really is, it is hard for many people to understand such reactions. This firsthand description of an abortion facility's "saline unit," written by a prochoice advocate, should shed some light:

I am drawn to the unit, irresistibly, by my reactions of disbelief, sorrow, horror, compassion, guilt. The place depresses me, yet I hang around after working hours. When I leave, I behave outside with the expansiveness of one who has just escaped a disaster. I have bad dreams. My sense of complicity in something nameless grows and festers. I consider giving up the research. . . .

I remove with one hand the lid of a bucket. . . . I look inside the bucket in front of me. There is a small naked person there floating in a bloody liquid—plainly the tragic victim of a drowning accident. But then perhaps this was no accident, because the body is purple with bruises and the face has the agonized tautness of one forced to die too soon. Death overtakes me in a rush of madness.[11]

When the same woman watched an abortion for the first time from the surgeon's end of the table her shock went even deeper:

[The doctor] pulls out something, which he slaps on the instrument table. "There," he says. "A leg.". . . I turn to Mr. Smith. "What did he say?" "He pulled a leg off," Mr. Smith says. "Right here." He points to the instrument table, where there is a perfectly formed, slightly bent leg, about three inches long. It consists of a ripped thigh, a knee, a lower leg, a foot, and five toes. I start to shake very badly, but otherwise, I feel nothing. Total shock is passionless. . . .

"There, I've got the head out now.". . . There lies a head. It is the smallest human head I have ever seen, but it is unmistakably part of a person. My vision and my hearing though disengaged, continue, I note, to function with exceptional clarity. The rest of me is mercifully gone.[12]

Abortion clinic workers may cover twinges of conscience with flippancy, apparent indifference, or morbid joking about their profession.

Beneath this veneer, however, they often suffer guilt, which manifests itself in destructive behavior. Bernard Nathanson says doctors in his own clinic suffered from nightmares, alcoholism, drug abuse, and family problems leading to divorce.[13] Carol Everett says the same was true in her clinics.[14]

Dr. George Flesh confessed, "Extracting a fetus, piece by piece, was bad for my sleep. . . . I stared at the sad face in the mirror and wondered how all those awards and diplomas had produced an angel of death."[15] Dr. David Brewer states, "My heart got callous against the fact that I was a murderer, but that baby lying in a cold bowl educated me to what abortion really was."[16] Dr. McArthur Hill confesses, "I am a murderer. I have taken the lives of innocent babies and I have ripped them from their mothers' wombs with a powerful vacuum machine."[17]

26d. Abortion is difficult and painful for the unborn child.

Surgeon Robert P. N. Shearin states:

As early as eight to ten weeks after conception, and definitely by thirteen-and-a-half weeks, the unborn experiences organic pain. . . . First, the unborn child's mouth, at eight weeks, then her hands at ten weeks, then her face, arms, and legs at eleven weeks become sensitive to touch. By thirteen-and-a-half weeks, she responds to pain at all levels of her nervous system in an integrated response which cannot be termed a mere reflex. She can now experience pain.[18]

When President Ronald Reagan stated in 1984 that during an abortion "the fetus feels pain which is long and agonizing," it set off a furious reaction by prochoice advocates. They did not want to believe this, nor did they want the public to believe it. But twenty-six medical authorities, including two past presidents of the American College of Obstetricians and Gynecologists, stepped forward with a letter documenting that *the unborn does in fact feel pain during an abortion.* Their letter says in part:

Mr. President, in drawing attention to the capability of the human fetus to feel pain, you stand on firmly established ground. . . . That the unborn, the prematurely born, and the new-born of the human species is a highly complex, sentient, functioning, individual organism is established scientific fact. . . . Over the last eighteen years, real time ultrasonography, fetoscopy, study of the fetal EKG (electrocardiogram) and the fetal EEG (electroencephalogram) have demonstrated the remarkable responsiveness of the human fetus to pain, touch, and sound.[19]

Pioneer fetologist Albert Liley, of the University of Auckland, says that by the fifty-sixth day after conception, the baby's spinal reflexes are sufficiently developed to feel pain. He adds, "When doctors first began invading the sanctuary of the womb, they did not know that the unborn baby would react to pain in the same fashion as a child would. But they soon learned he did."[20]

Dr. Liley's observation is graphically demonstrated in Dr. Bernard Nathanson's film, "The Silent Scream."[21] The film is an ultrasound of an actual abortion. It shows a child serenely resting in her mother's womb. Suddenly the child is alarmed because of the intruding abortion device. She moves as far away as she can, trying desperately to save her life. Just before her body is torn to pieces and sucked out through the vacuum tube, her tiny mouth opens in an unheard scream of terror. After the abortion the doctor who performed it was invited to view the ultrasound. He was so upset with what he saw that he left the room. Though he had performed over ten thousand abortions, he never performed another one.[22]

The fact that anesthesia is routinely used on preborn children during fetal surgery is an obvious commentary on the unborn's capacity to feel pain. Despite the prochoice rhetoric, it is clear that for one person, at least, no abortion is ever easy or painless.

26e. Even if abortion were made easy or painless for everyone, it wouldn't change the bottom-line problem that abortion kills children.

If in the future "improved" procedures make abortion painless—or at least less painful—for both mother and child, this will do nothing to change the moral issue. While it is more horrible for a man to torture his wife before killing her, no jury would feel good about his decision to kill her painlessly while she slept. Improving the ease and efficiency of killing does nothing to lessen the reality and the tragedy of the lost life.

27. "Abortion relieves women of stress and responsibility, and thereby enhances their psychological well-being."

We've never talked about it since. Never. It was only mentioned once. Just before our first child was born, out of the blue she said, "If I hadn't had the abortion, that child would be five years old now." We both let it drop. . . . For all I know there is a lot of psychological damage hidden behind the silence.[1]

These words speak for many women and married couples. The shadow of abortion hangs over them the rest of their lives.

27a. The many post-abortion therapy and support groups testify to the reality of abortion's potentially harmful psychological effects.

Women Exploited by Abortion (WEBA) has over thirty thousand members in more than two hundred chapters across the United States, with chapters in Canada, Germany, Ireland, Japan, Australia, New Zealand, and Africa.[2] Other post-abortion support and recovery groups include Victims of Choice, Post Abortion Counseling and Education (PACE), Healing Visions Network, Counseling for Abortion Related Experiences (CARE), Women of Ramah, Project Rachel, Open Arms, Abortion Trauma Services, and American Victims of Abortion. (For further information on these and other groups, see Appendix D, "Prolife Resources.") The existence of such groups testifies to the mental and emotional needs of women who have had abortions.

I recently read an editorial comparing abortion to a root canal or to having one's tonsils or appendix removed. But why are there no ongoing support groups for those who have had tonsillectomies, appendectomies, and root canals? Because abortion takes a toll on women that normal surgeries do not. And no wonder—normal surgeries do not take a life.

27b. The suicide rate is significantly higher among women who have had abortions than among those who haven't.

Feelings of rejection, low self-esteem, guilt and depression are all ingredients for suicide, and the rate of suicide attempts among aborted women is phenomenally high. According to one study, women who have had abortions are nine times more likely to attempt suicide than women in the general population.[3]

Women's World reports a study of aborted women in which 45 percent said they had thoughts of suicide following their abortions.[4] The article quotes women who describe the aftermath of abortion as "devastating," "insidious," "misery," and "prolonged anguish." One woman says, "I was completely overwhelmed with grief." Another says, "I was so depressed, nothing mattered," and "I wished I were dead."

27c. Postabortion syndrome is a diagnosable psychological affliction.

In 1981 Nancy Jo Mann came to terms with her abortion of seven years earlier, then went public and established Women Exploited by Abortion. After hearing the stories of thousands of women, she was the first to identify consistent psychological consequences of abortion. Terry Selby runs a residential treatment program for those suffering from Postabortion syndrome (PAS). Dr. Vincent Rue and Dr. Susan Stanford-Rue head the nonprofit Institute for Abortion Recovery and Research, which was founded to provide accurate information on the psychological effects of abortion.[5]

Though the American Psychiatric Association (APA) has not taken a position on PAS (doing so would be highly unpopular in a field dominated by prochoice thinking), it nevertheless lists abortion as a stressor event that can trigger post-traumatic stress disorder (PTSD).[6] Hence, in an indirect way, it recognizes the reality of PAS.

> The woman who suffers heavily from PAS becomes severely depressed and loses pleasure in almost everything in life. She is likely to experience poor appetite, sleep disturbance, agitation of behavior, loss of pleasure in usual activities, such as her sexual relationship(s), loss of energy, inappropriate guilt, a diminished ability to concentrate, and recurrent thoughts of suicide ("I just want to sleep" or "I wish to join my baby").[7]

Keeping in mind that some women experience fewer of these than others, Dr. Vincent Rue offers this list of identified consequences of induced abortion:

> Guilt, depression, grief, anxiety, sadness, shame, helplessness and hopelessness,

lowered self-esteem, distrust, hostility toward self and others, regret, sleep disorders, recurring dreams, nightmares, anniversary reactions, psychophysiological symptoms, suicidal ideation and behavior, alcohol and/or chemical dependencies, sexual dysfunction, insecurity, numbness, painful reexperiencing of the abortion, relationship disruption, communication impairment and/or restriction, isolation, fetal fantasies, self-condemnation, flashbacks, uncontrollable weeping, eating disorders, preoccupation, confused and/or distorted thinking, bitterness, and a sense of loss and emptiness.[8]

27d. Many professional studies document the reality of abortion's adverse psychological consequences on a large number of women.

Prochoice advocates often claim that former Surgeon General C. Everett Koop issued a report that there were no adverse psychological effects of abortion on women. This is not true. Dr. Koop stated after the report that as a physician he *knows* abortions are dangerous to a woman's mental health—he said, "There is no doubt about it."[9]

What Dr. Koop actually said, in a three-page letter to the president, was that the available studies were flawed because they did not examine the problem of psychological consequences over a sufficiently long period. Based on his own experience and knowledge he says, "Any long term studies will add more credibility to those people who say there are serious detrimental health effects of abortion."[10]

Because abortion has been legal for only twenty years, it is difficult to prove its long-term effects. But many studies and expert observations indicate serious short- and mid-term effects on some women. Furthermore, other significant studies have been done since Dr. Koop's letter to the president. A study by clinical psychologist Catherine Barnard, released in 1991, indicated 18.8 percent of post-aborted women interviewed showed diagnosable post-traumatic stress disorder. Another 39 to 45 percent had sleep disorders, hyper-vigilance, flashbacks, and other high stress reactions. Dr. Barnard concluded that nearly half of women who have had an abortion may be suffering some type of emotional trauma as a result.[11]

Prochoice advocates often cite a 1977 study by Brewer that concluded childbirth creates more psychiatric problems than abortion, but this study was seriously flawed. Dr. James L. Rogers says, "Brewer's study is riddled with severe methodological pitfalls."[12] He compares a 1981 study done by David, Rasmussen, and Holst, which is based on much sounder research, including the careful use and comparison of a control group. Rogers concludes, "The best study to date indicates that women who undergo abortion are at greater psychiatric risk than women who deliver at term."[13]

From a survey of psychiatric and psychological studies, the Royal College of Obstetricians and Gynecologists concluded, "The incidence of serious, permanent psychiatric aftermath [of abortion] is variously reported as between 9 and 59%."[14] Even taking a low figure, if one out of ten women getting abortions faced such "serious" and "permanent" psychiatric effects, this would be 160,000 women *per year*.

Columnist John Leo cites a researcher who says that "only" 1 percent of women who abort are "so severely scarred by post-abortion trauma that they become unable to function normally." Leo notes that this 1 percent is sixteen thousand "severely scarred" women per year,[15] and over a quarter of a million women "severely scarred and unable to function normally" since abortion was legalized. The percentage may be low, but the total numbers are staggering.

27e. Abortion can produce both short and longer term psychological damage, especially a sense of personal guilt.

The *British Medical Journal*, after reviewing psychological research on abortion, concluded that "almost all those terminated feel guilt and depression" for at least a brief period.[16] Research has indicated that "about half of all abortion patients" experience psychological disturbances lasting at least eight weeks, including guilt feelings, nervous symptoms, sleeplessness, and feelings of regret.[17]

Longer-term studies have found that 10 to 30 percent of abortion patients experience serious ongoing psychiatric problems.[18] In one five-year study, 25 percent of women who had undergone abortion surgery sought out psychiatric care, versus 3 percent of women with no prior abortions.[19] Another study found that psychiatric disorders were 40 percent more common among women who had abortions than among those who hadn't.[20] This is not definitive proof that abortion is a direct cause of such problems, but its relationship to some cases of psychological disorders is evident.

Interviews with women within a year of their abortions may indicate they are still glad they had an abortion, because of the relief it gave to their life situation. Often it is much later that reality sinks in and identifiable depression emerges:

> A woman that a six-month post-abortion survey declares "well-adjusted" may experience severe trauma on the anniversary of the abortion date, or even many years later. This fact is attested to in psychiatric textbooks which affirm that . . . "the psychiatrist frequently hears expressions of remorse and guilt concerning abortions that occurred twenty or more years earlier." In one study, the number of women who expressed "serious self-reproach" increased fivefold over the period of time covered by the study.[21]

Dr. C. Everett Koop tells this story of later emerging consequences of abortion:

> A woman had a pregnancy at about 38 or 39. Her kids were teenagers. And without letting either her family or her husband know, she had an abortion. At the moment, she said, "[The abortion was] the best thing that ever happened to me—clean slate, no one knows. I am all fine." Ten years later, she had a psychiatric break when one of those teenage daughters who had grown up, got married, gotten pregnant, delivered a baby, and presented it to her grandmother. . . . Unless you studied that one for ten years, you would say, "Perfectly fine result of an abortion."[22]

A 1989 *Los Angeles Times* poll found that 56 percent of aborted women had "a sense of guilt about having an abortion." The same poll found that almost two-thirds of men whose children are killed by abortion felt guilt.[23] Guilt and grief over abortion are sometimes more severe on the anniversary of the due date or the date of the abortion.[24] One study demonstrates that teenagers who have had an abortion sometimes attempt to kill themselves on the day corresponding to the birth date if the baby had been allowed to live.[25] (Appendix A, "Finding Forgiveness After an Abortion," is written for women who have had abortions, and shares the good news of how they can experience real and lasting forgiveness.)

27f. Most women have not been warned about and are completely unprepared for the psychological consequences of abortion.

A woman getting an abortion at three months relays her conversation with an abortion clinic counselor:

> "Are there psychological problems?" I continued.

"Hardly ever. Don't worry," I was told.

"What does a three-month-old fetus look like?"

"Just a clump of cells," she answered matter-of-factly."[26]

Later this same woman, now sterile as a result of her abortion, saw some pictures of fetal development. She said, "When I saw that a three-month-old 'clump of cells' had fingers and toes and was a tiny perfectly formed baby, I became really hysterical. I'd been lied to and misled, and I'm sure thousands of other women are being just as poorly informed and badly served."[27]

Psychologist Vincent Rue confirms that this kind of misinformation is common:

> I have seen hundreds of patients in my office who have had abortions who were just lied to by the abortion counselor. Namely: "This is less painful than having a tooth removed. It is not a baby." Afterwards the woman sees *Life* magazine and she breaks down and goes into a major depression.[28]

At age thirteen Kathy Walker, now president of Women Exploited by Abortion, had an abortion that was supposed to solve her problems. But Planned Parenthood misled her, and she paid a terrible psychological price that would haunt her for years:

> As soon as the needle went through my abdomen, I hated myself. I wanted to scream out, "Please don't do this to me!" I wanted to run as far away as I possibly could. . . . I felt my baby thrash around violently while he was being choked, poisoned, burned, and suffocated to death. I wasn't told any of that was going to happen.
>
> I remember talking to my baby and telling him I didn't want to do this, and that I wished he could live and that his mommy loved him and that I was so sorry. I prayed that he understood and that someday, if he could, he would learn to forgive me. He was dying, and there was nothing I could do to save him. I remember his very last kick. He had no strength left to fight.[29]

Karen Sullivan Ables also says she wasn't told the truth of what her abortion might do to her:

> I could feel the baby being torn from my insides. It was really painful. . . . Three quarters of the way through the operation I sat up. . . . In the cylinder I saw the bits and pieces of my little child floating in a pool of blood. I screamed and jumped up off the table. They took me into another room and I started vomiting. . . . I just couldn't stop throwing up. . . .
>
> I had nightmares and recurring dreams about my baby. I couldn't work my

job. I just laid in my bed and cried. Once, I wept so hard I sprained my ribs. Another time while crying, I was unable to breathe and I passed out. I was unable to walk on the beach because the playing children would make me cry. Even Pampers commercials would set me into fits of uncontrollable crying.[30]

An in-depth study of thirty women experiencing turmoil over abortion revealed this:

Eighty-five percent of the subjects were surprised at the intensity of their emotional reaction. In other words, these women were not anticipating or expecting significant personal response to their abortion. . . . Eighty-one percent of the subjects reported feeling victimized by the abortion process. Feelings of victimization were generally associated with either feeling coerced into the abortion or a belief that significant information regarding the pregnancy resolution and abortion procedure had been withheld.[31]

One researcher concludes, "For most women, abortion is not just an assault on their womb; it is an assault on their psyche."[32] It is a tragedy that the mental health of women is considered expendable by the pro-choice movement, which opposes laws requiring that women considering abortions be given accurate information on the risks of abortion.

Abortion may relieve a woman of some immediate stress and responsibility, but it often creates much more than it relieves. Ironically, those women who do not experience psychological consequences as a result of their abortion can maintain their mental health only through denial. They escape the emotional trauma that invariably comes with realizing you've killed a baby by simply choosing not to realize it. This is a tenuous situation, requiring a lifetime of running from reality. And reality has a way of pursuing and catching us.

Many women will testify that it is much easier to scrape a baby from a mother's uterus than to scrape him from her mind.

28. "Abortion providers are respected medical professionals working in the woman's best interests."

28a. Abortion clinics do not have to maintain the high standards of health, safety, and professionalism required of hospitals.

According to Planned Parenthood, "Most abortions are performed in specialized clinics, and only 10 percent are performed in hospitals . . . 4 percent in physicians' offices."[1] To understand the abortion business in America we must understand what goes on inside abortion clinics.

The Miami Herald found abominable conditions in abortion clinics, including mold growing on a suction machine.[2] Florida's Department of Health secretary examined four abortion clinics, finding no restrooms or hot water at one of the clinics, stirrups covered with blood, an oxygen mask with smeared lipstick from a previous patient, and disposable tubes used with bodily fluid, being reused on patient after patient. There wasn't any soap in one abortion clinic, so inspectors had to go to a building next door to wash their hands. One official stated, "It is hard to believe that places like this can exist in this age of modern medicine."[3]

The *Chicago Sun-Times* exposé of Illinois abortion clinics described an abortionist dashing from one woman to the next, "without washing his hands or donning sterile gloves."[4] *Sun-Times* reporters also discovered dirty and rusty instruments, instruments encrusted with "dried matter," and recovery room beds made with dirty linens. Surgical equipment, including the suction machine, were being cleaned with nothing more than plain water.[5] Abortionists were described as "cold," "mechanical," and even "sadistic" in their behavior.[6]

These are not stories of back-alley abortions, but of legal clinics doing legal abortions since 1973. Neither were they located in "sleazy" areas—the *Sun-Times* investigation centered on abortion clinics in Chicago's high rent district, where one third of all Illinois abortions are done. Abortion clinics can get away with such substandard conditions because they are not carefully regulated or monitored like hospitals.

Many people assumed that the *Sun-Times* exposé would "clean up" the abortion industry in that state. However, six years later a spokesperson for the Illinois Department of Public Health was unable to identify any lasting reform in abortion clinics.[7]

I have spoken with a number of former abortion clinic employees. This is a partial list of abuses they have described: falsified records, unreported injuries, unsanitary conditions, invalid licenses, no lab work, inadequate supervision of patients in recovery, illegal disposal of fetal remains and biohazardous wastes (e.g. body parts, needles, and bloody material in trash cans), unprofessional behavior of doctors toward patients, insurance fraud, medical advice and drugs dispensed by untrained and unlicensed employees, and use of illegal drugs and alcohol by clinic staff while on duty.

The contrast between abortion clinics and hospitals doing legitimate surgeries is conspicuous.[8] Abortions seldom include pathologic exams, while normal surgeries do. Abortion clinics aggressively advertise their "services," while real hospitals seldom do. The patient's informed consent is always required at hospitals, while abortion clinics almost never explain to women the full risks of abortion or the physiological development of the unborn. The consent of the parents of a minor is always required for an ethical surgery, but not for abortion (except in states with parental consent laws). Abortion clinics sometimes give kickbacks to family planning clinics that send them business, something ethical hospitals would not do.[9] Hospitals require detailed record keeping, abortion clinics records are often sketchy. The great majority of ethical surgeries are for true medical reasons, whereas 99 percent of abortions are for nonmedical reasons.[10]

28b. Many clinics are in the abortion industry because of the vast amounts of money involved.

Abortion is a five hundred million dollar a year industry in America alone.[11] Worldwide it is a ten billion dollar industry.[12] While the average annual income for a physician in the Portland, Oregon, area is just under $100,000, a local abortionist testified in court that in the previous year his income was $345,000. One physician says, "An abortionist, working only 20 or 30 hours a week, with no overhead, can earn from 3 to 10 times as much as an ethical surgeon."[13] Doctors who do abortions not only make more money, but they are not on call and usually don't have to worry much about malpractice lawsuits. Most women don't want others to know they've had an abortion and won't come forward no matter how badly they've been hurt. Performing abortions is a doctor's dream job—unless it bothers him to kill babies.

In its "Abortion Profiteers" investigative series, *Chicago Sun-Times* reporters spoke of "counselors who are paid not to counsel but to sell abortion with sophisticated pitches and deceptive practices." One clinic owner admitted, "No matter how you put it, we're in the business of selling abortions. Use a positive approach. It's not, 'Do you want a termination, but *when*?' "[14]

Dr. Beverly McMillan, who described herself as "a radical feminist," opened the first abortion clinic in Mississippi. She states that not only is there a lot of money in doing abortions, but many clinics don't report a significant amount of incoming funds to the government. Dr. McMillan says, "Why the IRS doesn't go after those guys, I don't know."[15]

Abortion clinic worker Nita Whitten says, "Every single transaction that we did was cash money. We wouldn't take a check, or even a credit card. If you didn't have the money, *forget it*. It wasn't unusual at all for me to take $10,000 to $15,000 a day to the bank—in cash." Whitten adds, "It's a lie when they tell you they're doing it to help women because they're not. They're doing it for the money."[16]

A personal and powerful behind-the-scenes look at the abortion industry is found in Carol Everett's autobiography, *Blood Money: Getting Rich Off a Woman's Right to Choose.*[17] Everett testifies that the motive of financial profit pervades the business of abortion, belying the noble-sounding rhetoric of "helping women in need."

28c. Clinic workers commonly prey on fear, pain, and confusion to manipulate women into getting abortions.

Nita Whitten says:

I was trained by a professional marketing director in how to sell abortions over the telephone. He took every one of our receptionists, nurses, and anyone else who would deal with people over the phone, through an extensive training period. The object was, when the girl called, to hook the sale so she wouldn't get an abortion somewhere else, or adopt out her baby, or change her mind.[18]

Abortion clinic staffer Debra Henry confesses, "We were told to find the woman's weakness and work on it. The women were never given any alternatives. They were told how much trouble it was to have a baby."[19]

From her inside experience in several abortion clinics, Carol Everett says:

Those kids, when they find out that they are pregnant, may not want an abortion; they may want information, but when they call that number, which is paid for by abortion money, what kind of information do you think they're going to get? Remember, they sell abortions—they don't sell keeping the baby, or giving the baby up for adoption, or delivering that baby. They only sell abortions.[20]

Sometimes clinics sell abortions to women who aren't even pregnant. The caption in one of the *Sun-Times* articles said, "Some are pregnant, some are not. Most will be sold abortions." Everett says that her clinics too gave false pregnancy test results, told women they were pregnant, then did fake abortions just for the money.[21]

28d. Clinic workers regularly mislead or deceive women about the nature and development of their babies.

Former clinic workers have told me they deliberately used euphemisms to suggest the unborn was not a baby. Among these were "cluster of cells," "product of conception," "blood clot," and "piece of tissue." Dr. Anthony Levatino, who performed abortions for years, claims that doctors doing abortions are less than forthright: "I want the general public to know that the doctors know that this is a person; this is a baby. That this is not some kind of blob of tissue. . . ."[22]

Dr. Joseph Randall says, "The picture of the baby on the ultrasound bothered me more than anything else. The staff couldn't take it. Women who were having abortions were never allowed to see the ultrasound."[23]

A Colorado abortionist stated,"We have reached a point in this particular technology where there is no possibility of denial of an act of destruction by the operator. It is before one's eyes. The sensations of dismemberment flow through the forceps like an electric current."[24]

My wife often does "sidewalk counseling" outside abortion clinics. She offers accurate medical information and also financial and practical support for women who feel they have no choice but abortion. Routinely clinic workers take this information away from women, or tell them, "It's a bunch of lies." Nanci has watched as workers tear the literature to pieces so the patient cannot read it later. (So much for "choice.") Obviously, it is the clinic employees—not prolife volunteers—who have vested financial interests in persuading the woman to make one particular choice and no other.

28e. Abortion clinics often exploit the feminist connection, making it appear their motive is to stand up for women.

Despite the huge amounts of money they make, abortion clinics actually receive volunteer help from feminist organizations because they are regarded as heroically pro-woman. Yet the attitude of the abortionists

—the vast majority of whom are men—toward the women coming for abortions tells a different story. A friend who formerly worked as an abortion clinic counselor shared one example of this. "One day the doctor was in a hurry to go play golf. This poor woman was crying because he was rushing the procedure to dilate her cervix. She was in a lot of pain and really afraid. He got angry and told her, 'Spread your legs! You've obviously spread them for someone else, now spread them for me.'"

Wichita abortionist George Tiller proudly advertises that he will do late-term abortions. To kill babies sixteen to twenty-two weeks he charges $750, for twenty-two to twenty-six weeks, $1800, and for beyond twenty-six weeks, $2200. Dr. Tiller says he averages two thousand abortions a year.[25] Estimating his average charge per abortion and multiplying by two thousand gives an idea of his annual income. Dr. Tiller's clinic brochure says this (the emphasis is his):

> Our purpose at Women's Health Care Services is to guide and support women through an experience which will allow them the opportunity to change the rest of their lives. We are here to help our patients make their DREAMS COME TRUE by maximizing their assets and minimizing their shortcomings. We are dedicated to providing the chance for women to live joyous, productive and free lives.

The brochure offers package deals that include a night in a nice Wichita hotel, with language that suggests an unforgettable get-away vacation rather than a traumatic life-taking procedure that will haunt women the rest of their lives. Tiller sells late-term abortion as something beautiful. Surely it should be offensive to true feminists that a man could grow rich by killing visibly human children, and crassly manipulating and exploiting women. But he does—and prochoice "feminists" hail him as a hero.

28f. Doctors doing abortions violate the fundamental creeds of the medical profession.

The fifth-century B.C. Hippocratic oath was a resolution intended to forever separate killing and healing in the medical profession. Previously killing and healing had been incongruously wedded together in the practices of pagan "doctors," who were more like witch doctors. In the Hippocratic oath, which was taken routinely by doctors for centuries, physicians swore they would never participate in inducing an abortion.

The Nazi doctors, with their program of euthanasia and cruel experiments on "undesirable" people, cast a dark shadow over the medical profession. Dr. Josef Mengele, the notorious "butcher of Auschwitz," epitomized the Nazi ideal of fastidious devotion to research and medicine, killing innocent people in the name of bettering humanity.[26] Recently opened Argentine files reveal that Dr. Mengele spent his postwar years performing abortions.[27]

In 1948, the Holocaust still fresh in its memory, the World Medical Association adopted the Declaration of Geneva that said, "I will maintain the utmost respect for human life, from the time of conception; even under threat, I will not use my medical knowledge contrary to the laws of humanity."[28] In 1949 the World Medical Association also adopted the International Code of Medical Ethics which said, "A doctor must always bear in mind the importance of preserving human life from the time of conception until death."[29]

The strongest statements of condemnation for doctors who perform abortions were made not by a religious group or a prolife organization, but by the American Medical Association. In the last century the AMA publicly called abortionists "monsters" and men of "corrupt souls," a "blight" on society and a "shame" to the medical profession.

What follows is a portion of the AMA's official position on abortionists, issued in 1871. Keep in mind that though abortion has been made legal, the nature of abortion—which the medical community found so repugnant—has not changed in any way:

> There we shall discover an enemy in the camp; there we shall witness as hideous a view of moral deformity as the evil spirit could present. . . . Men who seek not to save, but to destroy; men known not only to the profession, but to the public, as abortionists. . . .
>
> "Thou shalt not kill." This commandment is given to all, and applies to all without exception. . . . Notwithstanding all this, we see in our midst a class of men, regardless of all principle, regardless of all honor, who daily destroy that fair fabric of God's creation; who daily pull down what he has built up; who act in antagonism to that profession of which they claim to be members. . . .
>
> It matters not at what state of development his victim may have arrived—it matters not how small or how apparently insignificant it may be—it is a murder, a foul, unprovoked murder; and its blood, like the blood of Abel, will cry from earth to Heaven for vengeance. . . .

163

Every practicing physician in the land (as well as every good man) has a certain amount of interest at stake in this matter. . . . The members of the profession should form themselves into a special police to watch, and to detect, and bring to justice these characters. They should shrink with horror from all intercourse with them, professionally or otherwise. These men should be marked as Cain was marked; they should be made the outcasts of society.[30]

PART FIVE

_____

ARGUMENTS CONCERNING THE HARD CASES

ARGUMENTS CONCERNING
THE HARD CASES

---

29. "What about a woman whose life is threatened by pregnancy or childbirth?"

29a. It is an extremely rare case when abortion is required to save the mother's life.

While he was United States Surgeon General, Dr. C. Everett Koop stated publicly that in his thirty-eight years as a pediatric surgeon, *he was never aware of a single situation in which a preborn child's life had to be taken in order to the save the life of the mother.* He said the use of this argument to justify abortion in general was a "smoke screen."

Due to significant medical advances, the danger of pregnancy to the mother has declined considerably since 1967. Yet even at that time Dr. Alan Guttmacher of Planned Parenthood acknowledged, "Today it is possible for almost any patient to be brought through pregnancy alive, unless she suffers from a fatal illness such as cancer or leukemia, and, if so, abortion would be unlikely to prolong, much less save, life."[1] Dr. Landrum Shettles says that less than 1 percent of all abortions are performed to save the mother's life.[2]

29b. When two lives are threatened and only one can be saved, doctors must always save that life.

If the mother has a fast-spreading uterine cancer, the surgery to remove the cancer may result in the loss of the child's life. In an ectopic pregnancy the child is developing outside the uterus. He has no hope of survival, and may have to be removed to save his mother's life. These are tragic situations, but even if one life must be lost, the life that can be saved should be. More often than not that life is the mother's, not the child's. There are rare cases in later stages of pregnancy when the mother can't be saved but the baby can. Again, one life saved is better than two lives lost.

Friends of ours were faced with a situation where removing the mother's life-threatening and rapidly spreading cancer would result in the unborn child's death. It was heartbreaking, but they and we were confident the decision to save the mother's life was right. The pregnancy was still so early that there wasn't time for the child to become viable before both mother and child would die from the cancer. But it is critical to understand this was in no sense an abortion. The purpose of the surgery was not to kill the child but to save the life of the mother. The death of the child was a tragic and unintended secondary effect of lifesaving efforts. This was a consistently prolife act, since to be prolife does not mean being prolife just about babies. It also means being prolife about women, who are just as valuable as babies.

29c. Abortion for the mother's life and abortion for the mother's health are usually not the same issue.

The mother's *life* and the mother's *health* are usually two distinct considerations. A woman with toxemia will have adverse health reactions and considerable inconvenience, including probably needing to lie down for much of her pregnancy. This is a difficulty, but not normally a threat to her life. Hence, an abortion for the sake of "health" would not be life-saving but life-taking, since her life is not in jeopardy in the first place.

There are other situations where an expectant mother has a serious or even terminal medical condition. Her pregnancy may cause complications, but will not cause her death. If she is receiving radiation therapy, she may be told that the child could have handicaps as a result. It may be possible to postpone or reduce such treatment, but if it is essential to continue the treatment to save the mother's life, this is preferable to allowing her death or killing the child. Efforts can and should be made that value the lives of both mother and child.

29d. Abortion to save the mother's life was legal before convenience abortion was legalized, and would continue to be if abortion were made illegal again.

Even under restrictive abortion laws, the mother's right to life is never disregarded. Contrary to what some prochoice advocates have said, there is no danger whatsoever that women whose lives are in jeopardy will be unable to get treatment, even if such treatment tragically results in the death of an unborn child. Even prochoice *USA Today* acknowledges, "The National Right to Life Committee consistently has maintained that while abortion should be banned, there should be exceptions if an abortion is needed to save a woman's life."[3]

30. "What about a woman whose unborn baby is diagnosed as deformed or handicapped?"

30a. The doctor's diagnosis is sometimes wrong.

Many parents have aborted their babies because doctors told them their children would be severely handicapped. Others I have met were told the same thing, but chose to let their babies live. These parents were then amazed to give birth to normal children.

Just today I saw on the television news a woman who was diagnosed as having a growing tumor. The "tumor" turned out to be a child. The woman, who truly had cancer, had been under extensive chemotherapy for two years. Had her doctors known she was pregnant she almost certainly would have been advised to get an abortion on the assumption the child would be deformed. Yet the child was perfectly normal.

Some doctors suggest "terminating the pregnancy" if a couple's genetic history suggests a probable or even possible risk of abnormality. Ironically, "Of all eugenic abortions prescribed on the basis of genetic history, one-half to three-quarters of the unborn children destroyed are not affected by the disease. More normal children are killed than 'handicapped' children."[1]

30b. The child's deformity is often minor.

Planned Parenthood's Guttmacher Institute says 1 percent of women who have abortions have been advised by their doctors that the unborn has a defect.[2] But what are called deformities are sometimes easily correctable conditions, such as cleft lips and cleft palates. After reading in London's *Sunday Times* about these common cosmetic abortions, a mother of a five-year-old girl with a cleft lip and palate wrote to the editor:

> I was horrified to read that many couples now opt for abortion rather than risk having a baby with such a minor physical imperfection. My daughter is not some subnormal freak . . . she can, and does, lead a happy, fulfilled

life. . . . What sort of society do we live in when a minor facial deformity, correctable by surgery, is viewed as so abnormal as to merit abortion?[3]

30c. Medical tests for deformity may cause as many problems as they detect.

The standard test for possible deformities is done by amniocentesis. One study found a 1.5 percent rate of spontaneous miscarriage after amniocentesis.[4] This means that "a forty-year-old woman undergoing amniocentesis faces a greater risk of miscarrying a healthy child because of the procedure than she faces for having a Down's syndrome baby in the first place."[5]

Dr. Hymie Gordon, chairman of the Department of Medical Genetics at Minnesota's Mayo Clinic, says that in amniocentesis "a conservative estimate is that there is a 2 percent risk of either damaging the baby, tearing the uterus, introducing infection, or precipitating a miscarriage."[6] Furthermore, Dr. Gordon states the procedure is not always effective even when it is safe. In his extensive experience most women are not told of the risks and limitations of amniocentesis, and when they are the great majority of them elect not to have the procedure done.[7]

30d. Handicapped children are often happy, always precious, and usually delighted to be alive.

Often medical tests or doctors' predictions are accurate and the child *is* born with a serious deformity. To be sure, it will be hard to raise a handicapped child. He will require extra attention and effort. What makes this a "hard case," however, is not whether the child deserves to live or die. What is hard is the difficult responsibilities letting him live will require of his parents.

The film, *The Elephant Man*, depicts the true story of John Merick. He was a terribly deformed young man, rejected and ridiculed, until someone took time to know him and discover a wonderful human being. Merick said, "My life is full because I know that I am loved."

A young man born without a left leg and without arms below the elbows says, "When I was born, the first thing my dad said to my mom was that 'this one needs our love more.' "[8] Not only were these parents just what their son needed, he was just what they needed. Many families have drawn together and found joy and strength in having a child with mental or physical handicaps. It is significant that "there has not been a single organization of parents of mentally retarded children that has ever endorsed abortion."[9]

Some argue that it's unfair to bring a handicapped child into the world, because he will be unhappy. Yet studies show that suicide rates are no higher for the handicapped. Experience confirms that many people with severe handicaps are happy and well-adjusted, often more so than "normal" people. Dr. C. Everett Koop dealt with innumerable "deformed children" in his role as a pediatric surgeon. He says:

> I am frequently told by people who have never had the experience of working with children who are being rehabilitated into our society after the correction of a congenital defect that infants with such defects should be allowed to die, or even "encouraged" to die, because their lives could obviously be nothing but unhappy and miserable. Yet it has been my constant experience that disability and unhappiness do not necessarily go together. Some of the most unhappy children whom I have known have all of the physical and mental faculties and on the other hand some of the happiest youngsters have borne burdens which I myself would find very difficult to bear.[10]

The television series "Life Goes On" portrayed a teenager named Corky who has Down's syndrome. The starring role was played by a young man with Down's syndrome, and many people were touched by his winsome performance. Critics raved. But many of the same critics favor the killing of Down's syndrome children, just like "Corky," before they are born!

In 1982 "Infant Doe" was born in Bloomington, Indiana. A routine operation could have corrected the birth defect that would not allow food to pass into his stomach. But his parents and their doctors decided to let him starve to death because he had Down's syndrome. When word got out that the baby was dying, a dozen families came forward and said they would gladly adopt him. His parents said no. Some in the media labeled them "courageous." Though it would cost them no money, time, or effort to allow someone else to raise their child, the parents, their doctors, and the Supreme Court of Indiana said they had the right to allow the child to starve to death. Seven agonizing days after birth, he died.

A survey of pediatricians and pediatric surgeons revealed that more than two out of three would go along with parents' wishes to deny life-saving surgery to a child with Down's syndrome. Nearly three out of four said that if they had a Down's syndrome child they would choose to let him starve to death.[11] This is not only horrible, but baffling, for many Down's children are the happiest you will ever meet. We have good friends who have adopted three Down's children. Each is delightful. One of them sang "Jesus Loves Me" in church one morning and the applause was thunderous. These children require special care, of course, but surely they deserve to be born and to live as much as any of us.

Some argue, "It is cruel to let a handicapped child be born to a miserable and meaningless life." We may define a meaningful life one way, but we should ask ourselves what is meaningful to the handicapped themselves. A number of spina bifida patients were asked whether their handicaps made life meaningless and if they should have been allowed to die after birth. "Their unanimous response was forceful. Of course they wanted to live! In fact, they thought the question was ridiculous."[12]

Let's not kid ourselves. When adults kill a handicapped child, pre-born or born, we aren't doing it for his good, but for what we think is our own. We aren't preventing cruelty to the child—we're committing cruelty to the child in order to prevent difficulty for ourselves.

30e. Handicapped children are not social liabilities, and bright and "normal" people are not always social assets.

The Bible is one of the oldest sources of moral guidance in the world. It asks and answers these questions about the handicapped: "Who gave man his mouth? Who makes him deaf or mute? Who gives him sight or makes him blind? Is it not I, the LORD?" (Exodus 4:11). Jesus Christ said that a certain man was born blind "so that the work of God might be displayed in his life" (John 9:3). He also said, "when you give a banquet, invite the poor, the crippled, the lame, the blind, and you will be blessed. Although they cannot repay you, you will be repaid at the resurrection of the righteous" (Luke 14:13-14). The message to individuals and society is this: When it comes to the handicapped, ignore the bottom-line cost; take care of them, and God will take care of you.

A geneticist tells this thought-provoking story that challenges society's assumptions on the relative worth of the handicapped as opposed to "normal" people:

Many years ago, my father was a Jewish physician in Braunau, Austria. On one particular day, two babies had been delivered by one of his colleagues. One was a fine, healthy boy with a strong cry. His parents were extremely proud and happy. The other was a little girl, but her parents were extremely sad, for she was a [Down's syndrome] baby. I followed them both for almost fifty years. The girl grew up, living at home, and was finally destined to be the one who nursed her mother through a very long and lingering illness after a stroke. I do not remember her name. I do, however, remember the boy's name. He died in a bunker in Berlin. His name was Adolf Hitler.[13]

30f. Using dehumanizing language may change our thinking, but not the child's nature or value.

I heard a prochoice advocate say with disgust, "Should a woman be forced to bring a *monster* into the world?" Only by using such words long enough can we deceive ourselves into believing them. The term *vegetable* is another popular word for disadvantaged humans. This kind of terminology dehumanizes people in our eyes but does not change their true nature.

A bruised apple is still an apple. A blind dog is still a dog. A senile woman is still a woman. A handicapped child is still a child. A person's nature and worth are not changed by a handicap. Hitler called the Jews "useless eaters." This made it easier to kill them, but no less terrible.

30g. Our society is hypocritical in its attitude toward handicapped children.

On the one hand, we provide special parking and elevators for the handicapped. We talk tenderly about those poster children with MS, spina bifida, and leukemia. We are touched when we see the telethons, the March of Dimes, the United Way ads. We sponsor the Special Olympics and cheer on the Down's syndrome competitors, speaking of the joy and inspiration they bring us. We look with admiration at a television series that stars a Down's syndrome young man. But when we hear a woman is carrying one of these very children, we say, "Kill it before it is born."

30h. The adverse psychological effects of abortion are significantly more traumatic for those who abort because of deformity.

One study showed that of forty-eight women who terminated their pregnancies for genetic reasons, 77 percent demonstrated acute grief reactions and 45 percent continued in this grief six months after the abortion.[14] Another study showed a higher rate of depression for genetic abortion than for other kinds, and demonstrated post-abortion family disharmony and flashbacks.[15]

Still another study analyzed the reactions of children in families where the mother aborted after fetal abnormalities were detected. Even very young children—and children sheltered from knowledge of the event—showed negative reactions.[16] This may relate also to the finding that children who have siblings killed by abortion have psychological conflicts similar to those of children who survive disasters or have siblings who die of accidents or illness.[17]

30i. The arguments for killing a handicapped unborn child are valid only if they also apply to killing born people who are handicapped.

If we would abort children on the basis of their handicaps, this jeopardizes the rights of born people who are handicapped.

> People with disabilities have rightly been working hard to achieve recognition for their needs. To justify abortion on the grounds that the baby is or might be disabled is to express a bigotry against people with disabilities which should not be countenanced in an egalitarian, democratic society.[18]

Suppose your six-year-old becomes blind or paraplegic. He is now a burden to his parents and society. Raising him is expensive, inconvenient, and hard on your psychological health. Some would say he does not have a significant "quality of life." Should you put him to death? What if a law was passed that made it legal to put him to death? Would you do it then? If not, why not?

You would not kill your handicapped child because you know him. But killing an unborn child just because you have not held him in your arms and can't hear his cry does not change his value or reduce his loss when killed.

What about the anencephalic child who doesn't have a fully developed brain? Since he will die anyway, his parents often decide to have an abortion or allow his life to be taken in order to harvest his organs. It is one thing to know a child will probably die and another to choose to take his life. Many families have had precious and enriching experiences naming and bonding with an anencephalic baby. Then they experience healthy grief at the natural death of this family member. This is in stark contrast to the unhealthy grief and guilt that comes from denying a baby's place in the family, and actually taking his life.

The quality of a society is largely defined by how it treats its weakest and most vulnerable members. Killing the innocent is never justified because it relieves others of a burden. It is not a solution to inflict suffering on one person in order to avoid it in another. What defined Nazi Germany as an evil society was its wanton disregard for human life. That disregard surfaced in Hitler's killing of 275,000 handicapped people before he began killing the Jews. If abortion is wrong because it is killing a child, then whether or not the child is normal has no bearing on the matter—unless, of course, it is wrong to kill "normal" people but right to kill handicapped people.

30j. Abortions due to probable handicaps rob the world of unique human beings who would significantly contribute to society.

A medical school professor gave his students a case study in whether or not to advise an abortion. He laid out the facts like this: "The father had syphilis and the mother had tuberculosis. Of four previous children, the first was blind, the second died, the third was both deaf and dumb, and the fourth had tuberculosis. What would you advise the woman to do when she finds she is pregnant again?"

One student gave what seemed the obvious answer: "I would advise an abortion." The professor responded, "Congratulations . . . you have just killed Beethoven."

31. "What about a woman who is pregnant due to rape or incest?"

31a. Pregnancy due to rape is extremely rare, and with proper treatment can be prevented.

Studies conducted by Planned Parenthood's Guttmacher Institute indicate that two consenting and fertile adults have only a 3 percent chance of pregnancy from an act of intercourse. They also indicate that there are factors involved in a rape which further reduce these chances for rape victims.[1] The Guttmacher Institute says sixteen thousand abortions per year are due to rape or incest, which amounts to 1 percent of all abortions.[2] Other studies show that pregnancies due to rape are much rarer than is generally thought, perhaps as few as one in a thousand cases.[3] Furthermore, since conception doesn't occur immediately after intercourse, pregnancy can be prevented in nearly all rape cases by medical treatment that removes the semen before an ovum can be fertilized.[4]

So where does the misconception come from that many pregnancies are due to rape? Fearful young women will sometimes attribute their pregnancies to rape, since doing so gains sympathy and avoids condemnation. The young woman called "Roe" in the famous *Roe* v. *Wade* case—who elicited sympathy in the court and media because she claimed to be a rape victim—years later admitted she had lied and had not been raped at all.[5]

Prochoice advocates often divert attention from the vast majority of abortions by focusing on rape because of its inherent (and well-deserved) sympathy factor. Their frequent references to rape during discussions of the abortion issue leaves the false impression that pregnancy due to rape is common.

31b. Rape is never the fault of the child; the guilty party, not an innocent party, should be punished.

In those rare cases when a pregnancy is the result of rape, we must be careful who gets the blame. What is "hard" about this hard case is not whether an innocent child deserves to die for what his father did. What is hard is that an innocent woman has to take on childbearing and possibly mothering—if she decides to keep the child rather than choose adoption—for which she was not willing or ready. This is a very hard situation, calling for family, friends, and church to do all they can to support her. But the fact remains that none of this is the fault of the child.

Why should Person A be killed because Person B raped Person A's mother? If your father committed a crime, should you go to jail for it? If you found out today that your biological father had raped your mother, would you feel you no longer had a right to live?

Biblical law put it this way: "The soul who sins is the one who will die. The son will not share the guilt of the father" (Ezekiel 18:20). And, "Fathers shall not be put to death for their children, nor children put to death for their fathers; each is to die for his own sin" (Deuteronomy 24:16). Civilized people do not put children to death for what their fathers have done. Yet aborting a child conceived by rape is doing that exact thing. He is as innocent of the crime as his mother. Neither she nor he deserves to die.

Rape is so horrible that we easily transfer our horror to the wrong object. We must not impose the ugliness of rape or incest upon either the innocent woman or the innocent child. The woman is not "spoiled goods"—she is not "goods" at all but a precious human being with value and dignity that not even the vilest act can take from her. Likewise, the child is not a cancer to be removed but a living human being. By all means, let's punish the rapist. (I favor stricter punishment of the rapist than do the prochoice advocates I know.) But let's not punish the wrong person by inflicting upon the innocent child our rage against the rapist.

31c. The violence of abortion parallels the violence of rape.

One woman says, "When a woman exercises her right to control her own body in total disregard of the body of another human being, it is called abortion. When a man acts out the same philosophy, it is called rape."[6]

There is a close parallel between the violent attack on an innocent woman that happens in a rape, and the violent attack on a innocent child that happens in an abortion. Both are done in response to a subjective and misguided sense of need, and both are done at the expense of an innocent person. The woman may not hate her child the way the rapist may hate his victim, but this is no consolation to the child. Regardless of the motives or disposition of his mother, he is just as brutally killed.

The violence of abortion is no solution to the violence of rape. The killing of the innocent by abortion is no solution to the hurting of the innocent by rape.

31d. Abortion does not bring healing to a rape victim.

Imposing capital punishment on the innocent child of a sex offender does nothing bad to the rapist and nothing good for the woman. Creating

177

a second victim doesn't undue the damage to the first.

One feminist group says, "Some women have reported suffering from the trauma of abortion long after the rape trauma has faded."[7] It is hard to imagine a worse therapy for a woman who has been raped than to add the guilt and turmoil of having her child killed. Even if we convince ourselves and her that it isn't a real child or even *her* child, some day she will realize it was. Those who advised abortion will not be there then to help carry her pain and guilt.

31e. A child is a child regardless of the circumstances of his conception.

On a television program about abortion, I heard a man argue, "Anything of this nature has no rights because it's the product of rape." But how is the nature of this preborn child different from that of any other preborn child? Are some children more worthy of living because their fathers were better people? And why is it that prochoice advocates are always saying the unborn child is really the mother's, not the father's, until she is raped—then suddenly the child is viewed as the father's, not the mother's.

A child conceived by rape is as precious as a child conceived by love, because a child is a child. The point is not *how* he was conceived but *that* he was conceived. He is not a despicable "product of rape" but a unique and wonderful creation of God.

Women often think that a child conceived by such a vile act will be a constant reminder of their pain. On the contrary, the innocence of the child often has a healing effect. But in any case, the woman is free to give up the child for adoption, which may be the best alternative. Aborting the child is an attempt to deny what happened, and denial is never good therapy.

One woman told me, "A baby is the only beautiful thing that can come out of a rape." Having and holding an innocent child can do much more good for a victimized woman than the knowledge that an innocent child died in an attempt to deny or reduce her trauma.

31f. What about already-born people who are "products of rape"?

What if you found that your spouse or adopted child was fathered by a rapist? Would it change your view of their worth? Would you love them any less? If not, why should we view the innocent unborn child any differently?

After I shared similar thoughts in a lecture, a dear woman in her midtwenties came up to me in tears. I'll never forget what she said:

> Thank you. I've never heard anyone say that a child conceived by rape deserved to live. My mother was raped when she was twelve years old. She gave birth to me and gave me up for adoption to a wonderful family. I'll probably never meet her, but every day I thank God for her and her parents. If they hadn't let me live, I wouldn't be here to have my own husband and children, and my own life. I'm just so thankful to be alive.

Singer Ethel Waters was conceived after her twelve-year-old mother was raped. Waters touched millions through her life and music. Many other people, perhaps some of our dearest friends whose stories we'll never know, are what some disdainfully call "the product of rape."

31g. All that is true of children conceived in rape is true of those conceived in incest.

Incest is a horrible crime. Offenders should be punished, and young girls should be carefully protected from further abuse. Decisive personal and legal intervention should be taken to remove a girl from the presence of a relative who has sexually abused her. The abuser—not the girl or her child—is the problem. Intervention, protection, and ongoing personal help for the girl—not the death of an innocent child—is the solution. Despite popular beliefs, fetal deformity is rare in such cases. Even if the child has handicaps, however, he still deserves to live.

FINAL THOUGHTS ON THE HARD CASES

1. No adverse circumstance for one human being changes the nature and worth of another human being.

The hard cases are also sometimes called the exceptional cases. But the fundamental question remains, "Is there any exception to the fact that a preborn child is a human being?" As we demonstrated in the responses to Arguments 1 through 8, the scientific facts and common sense evidence conclusively demonstrate that the answer to this question is *no*. What is exceptional is the difficult situation of the mother, not the nature of the child.

Compassion for the mother is extremely important, but is never served through destroying the innocent. One person must not be killed under the guise of compassion for another. An alternative must be sought that is compassionate to both mother and child. Furthermore, true compassion to the mother considers her psychological well-being, which is not served by abortion. Instead of encouraging her to kill her child, we should do something that requires much more compassion and sacrifice. We should offer tangible support and sacrificial help.

Giving up the child for adoption to eagerly waiting families is often the answer in cases where the mother is too young and immature. The same is true if the baby's handicap is so great that it takes a special person to raise him. (But willing parents often find they become just such special people.)

In cases of rape and incest, family and friends need to offer compassionate support and help find counseling that can assist in personal healing. Society needs to protect the innocent by stiffer sentences and enforced restraining orders for sex offenders. Exposing the woman to further abuse is unjustifiable. So is making an unborn child the scapegoat for a crime he or she didn't commit.

2. Laws must not be built on exceptional cases.

Research shows that only 1 to 3 percent of abortions are performed for the reasons of rape, incest, deformity, or threat to the life of the mother.[1] If a building is burning, it is permissible for someone to break in to save lives or property. However, recognizing the legitimacy of this exception does not mean that we shouldn't have laws against the usual cases of forcible entry and trespassing. That an exception may exist does not invalidate the normal standard of behavior.

Suppose you disagree with my firm conviction that a handicapped child or a child conceived by rape or incest deserves to live and should be protected by law just like every other child. Nevertheless, surely you must recognize that even if there *were* legitimate grounds for abortion in the exceptional cases, it would in no way justify legal abortion for the vast majority of cases, which are matters of personal and economic convenience. These cases account for over 97 percent of abortions, while the "hard cases" account for less than 3 percent. (Of course, the deaths of those 3 percent are equally tragic.)

Some believe laws restricting convenience abortions could go a long way in protecting the lives of 1.5 million innocent children each year in America alone. Others believe that legislation allowing exceptions for rape and deformity are an unjustifiable compromise and would be badly abused, encouraging false claims to cover convenience abortions. In any case we must seek to find ways—personal, educational, and political—to save as many innocent lives as possible.

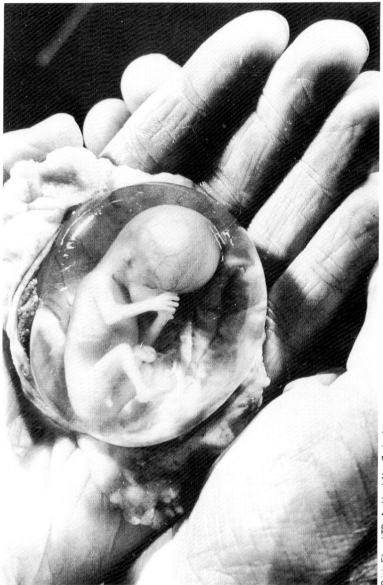

Photograph 1: Unborn child at ten weeks after conception. This miscarried baby, still in its amniotic sac, is held in a doctor's hand. The heart was beating since three weeks, brain waves measurable since six weeks.

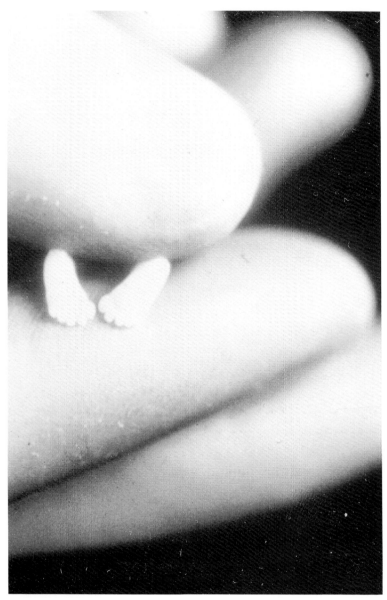

Photograph 2: Feet of miscarried child at ten weeks after conception. Note the perfectly formed toes, weeks before the end of the first trimester of pregnancy.

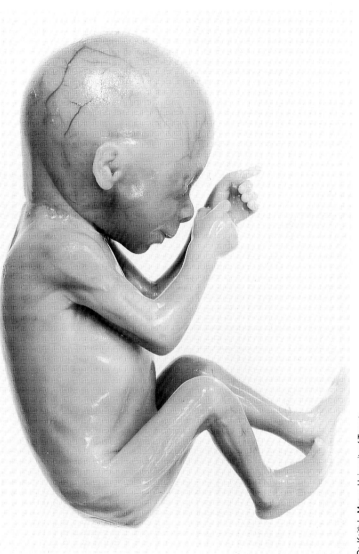

Photograph 3: Unborn child at seventeen weeks after conception. This is early in the second trimester.

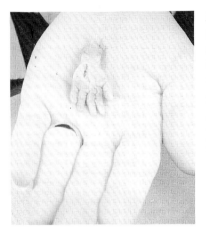

Photograph 4 (left): A hand taken from the discarded remains of an abortion, held in the hand of an adult. Decide for yourself if this was a potential or actual human life.

Photograph 5 (below): A preborn baby killed by saline abortion. A poisonous salt solution is injected into the amniotic sac, killing the child over a process of several hours, then bringing on the mother's labor and delivery of the dead baby.

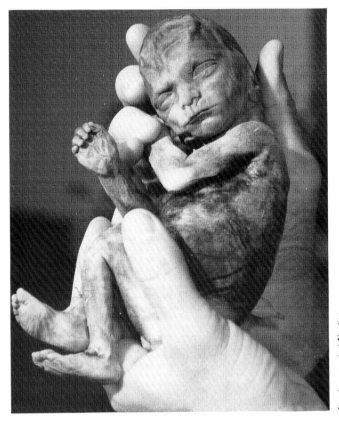

Americans against Abortion

PART SIX

ARGUMENTS AGAINST THE CHARACTER OF PROLIFERS

ARGUMENTS AGAINST THE
CHARACTER OF PROLIFERS

32. "Anti-abortionists are so cruel that they insist on showing hideous pictures of dead babies."

32a. What is hideous is not the pictures themselves, but the reality they depict.

Pictures of aborted babies are not invented by prolifers. Anyone who thinks they are is simply ignorant of the medical facts about the development of the unborn and the nature of abortion procedures. The pictures are authentic. What people object to is their content. No one wants to look at dead babies.

When a prolife candidate ran television ads showing actual aborted babies, people were outraged. A reporter on the "CBS Evening News" declared the abortion debate had reached a "new low in tastelessness." There was no outrage that babies were being killed, only that someone had the audacity to show they were being killed. This was a classic case of "shooting the messenger"—taking vengeance on the one who points out an evil as if he were responsible for doing it.

What is it that makes a picture beautiful or hideous? Not the picture itself but what is *in* the picture. The pictures document that babies are being killed. Proabortionists are against the pictures of killed babies. Prolifers are against the killing of the babies in the pictures.

The question we should ask is not "Why are these people showing these pictures?" but "Why would anyone defend the legitimacy of what is shown in these pictures?" When a prochoice person looks at the pictures and says, "This is sick, it's horrible," the prolifer responds, "Exactly. That's why we are opposed to doing such a horribly sick thing to a baby."

A radio talk show host expressed outrage that this book is "filled" with "horrible " pictures of aborted babies. (In fact, it contains three pictures of live preborn babies, three of miscarried babies, and only two of aborted babies.) I asked her "Why are you angry at me? Who do you think killed these babies? Me?" Her reply was revealing—"No, I guess it was the doctor." In other words, it was someone holding the host's own pro-choice position who did the killing she described as "horrible."

32b. Pictures challenge our denial of the horrors of abortion. If something is too horrible to look at, perhaps it is too horrible to condone.

Some prolifers choose to show pictures of the developing child and rarely or never show pictures of aborted babies. Others believe that the pictures of aborted babies are essential to wake up society to the reality of butchered children. The holocaust was something so evil that words alone could not describe it. The descriptions of Nazi death camps had long been fed to western newspapers. But it was the pictures of slaughtered people that communicated the reality of what was happening. Most of us would neither understand nor believe the extent of the holocaust were it not for the pictures.

The solution to the holocaust was not to ban the disgusting pictures of the death camps. The only solution was to end the killing. Similarly, the solution to our current situation is not to get rid of the pictures of dead babies. The solution is to end what is making the babies dead—abortion. Like the holocaust, abortion is an evil so great that words fall short of describing it. Prolife people hope that showing pictures of aborted babies will help end the killing.

Gregg Cunningham, director of the Center for Bio-ethical Reform, argues for the vital need to show pictures of aborted babies: "Pictures state the hideous truth so forcefully that lies and deception are robbed of their power to distort reality. Words alone will never change the way a person feels about abortion when they are in denial; and most Americans are deeply in denial over this issue."[1]

32c. Nothing could be more relevant to the discussion of something than that which shows what it really is.

I was on a television program where prochoice and prolife advocates were discussing abortion. After we'd been talking a few minutes, one of the prolifers tried to illustrate his point by showing a picture of an aborted baby. As soon as he did, there were audible gasps, people started waving their arms, and the prochoice activist next to me cried out, "God, don't let them show that." The cameras turned quickly away, and there was momentary panic and confusion in the studio.

Had the issue not been so serious, the response would have been humorous. The picture was no more gruesome than pictures of holocaust victims that appear in countless documentaries. And it was just as authentic. It simply showed what abortion is, and what is left of the unborn baby afterward. What could be a more relevant piece of evidence when discussing abortion than a picture of an abortion?

Anyone who has participated in debates about abortion knows that the prochoice side typically insists that the prolife side not be allowed the choice of showing pictures of aborted babies. This attempt at censorship is never reciprocated—prolife advocates invite their opponents to present their best case, and only ask that they be allowed to do the same. When one side in a debate insists on not allowing the other side to present critical evidence, what does it suggest about their interest in the truth, or in letting the audience choose for themselves? What does it suggest about the weakness of their position?

Banning such pictures from the abortion debate is like banning x-rays of smoke-damaged lungs from the smoking debate, or saying we cannot show pictures of harpooned whales when discussing animal rights. If the fetus is simply a lump of tissue, then fine—let the public see the pictures of the lump of tissue. Let them be treated like adults and allowed to choose for themselves what they believe. If this is not a baby, what could be the harm in looking at the pictures? The truth will surely serve the position that is true.

The success of the prochoice position is dependent on the public's denial that abortion kills children. The pictures are a devastating challenge to this denial. Yet the denial itself has become an accepted part of not just public opinion, but medical practice. Consider this advice in a national publication for obstetricians and gynecologists:

> Sonography in connection with induced abortion may have psychological hazards. Seeing a blown-up, moving image of the embryo she is carrying can be distressing to a woman who is about to undergo an abortion, Dr. Dorfman noted. She stressed that the screen should be turned away from the patient.[2]

The doctor's job is to not allow the woman to see the truth, thereby perpetuating the mental fiction that this is not a baby. This is the extent of our social commitment to denial. This denial is so extreme and widespread that the prolife movement has no choice but to continue to point to the pictures of unborn babies, both dead and alive, even though those in the deepest denial will be outraged.

32d. It is the prochoice position, not the prolife position, that is cruel.

The prochoice position has made it open season on the unborn, and the result has been cruelty beyond imagination. The saline abortion, which is agonizingly painful to the child and emotionally devastating to the mother, was originally developed in the concentration camps of Nazi Germany.[3] That alone should tell us something. (See photograph #5 at the center of this book.)

Live fetuses have been subjected to grisly experiments—bodies have been dissected, chests sliced open to observe heart action, heads cut off for bizarre purposes.[4] In Arizona, the E.R. Squibb Drug Company offered $10,000 to fourteen pregnant women if they would take a certain drug before having abortions and let their baby's blood be tested after they were killed.[5] Babies have been conceived and aborted for the purpose of using their cells to treat adults with diabetes, Alzheimer's, and Parkinson's disease.[6]

Though nine out of ten Americans support a ban on abortion for purposes of choosing a preferred gender, Planned Parenthood and other prochoice groups favor keeping sex selection abortions legal.[7] How can anyone defend such cruelty to young females?

Gianna Jessen's biological mother had a saline abortion in a southern California abortion clinic. Gianna was severely burned and traumatized, but managed to survive.[8] Babies surviving abortions—estimated at more than five hundred a year—are typically suffocated, drowned, or left to die of exposure. But someone had mercy on Gianna and smuggled her out to a nearby hospital. Her medical records read, "Saline Abortion Survivor."

Gianna was adopted by a caring prolife family. As a result of her abortion trauma she suffers from celebral palsy. She is now a vivacious teenager and a gifted singer. She is also an articulate prolife spokesperson, who speaks with an authority like that of survivors of the Nazi holocaust. Gianna Jessen has been affected by both sides in the abortion debate. Ask *her* which side is the cruel one.

Aborted babies are dumped into plastic bags for disposal, yet it is fashionable to be more concerned whether the plastic sacks are recyclable than to be concerned about the lives of the babies. The killing of

100,000 dolphins is an "ecological holocaust" while the killing of fifteen times that many babies every year is an accepted way of life.

Isn't it ironic that those who endorse this killing label those who oppose it as "cruel"?

33. "Prolifers don't care about women, and they don't care about babies once they're born."

A publication of the National Abortion Rights Action League states, "The 'prolife' concerns of abortion foes are only for fetal lives, not the lives of women or unwanted babies."[1]

33a. Prolifers are actively involved in caring for women in crisis pregnancies and difficult child-raising situations.

A "Dear Abby" letter, signed "Hates Hypocrites," angrily challenges people opposing abortion: "Why aren't you volunteering to baby-sit a child born to a single mother so she can work? Why haven't you opened your door to a pregnant teenager whose parents have kicked her out when she took your advice and decided not to have an abortion?" The writer rails against prolifers, calling them hypocrites. Abby responds, "I couldn't have said it better."[2]

This approach has two basic flaws. First, it is possible to point out an injustice even when one does not provide the solution. People could say slavery was wrong even if they did not open their homes to a slave. A man can say it is wrong for his neighbor to beat his wife, even if he isn't in a position to give her a home.

I wholeheartedly agree, however, that people who point out injustices should seek to be part of the solution. This raises the second and most important flaw in the argument—no evidence whatsoever is offered for the damning assumption made by the writer and by Abby. Who says prolifers are not doing the things they are assumed not to be doing? The truth is, they are!

In virtually every part of the United States there are abortion alternative centers that provide free pregnancy tests, free counseling, and free material and human resources to pregnant women. There are more prolife help-giving centers, well over three thousand of them, than there are prolife education and political action centers.[3] Though their services cost them a great deal of money—as opposed to making them a great deal of money—there are more abortion alternative centers in the United States than there are abortion clinics.[4]

Since these clinics draw business away from abortion clinics, they have come under fire from the prochoice movement and its representatives in the media.[5] When a U.S. House committee, chaired by Oregon's Ron Wyden, investigated so-called "fake" abortion clinics, they did not allow a single prolife representative from any of the centers in question to testify. Had they done so, they would have found that the Crisis Pregnancy Centers require that their clinics advertise themselves as offering "Abortion Alternatives," and train their workers to give accurate medical information.[6]

Having served on the board of an abortion alternative organization with two local centers, I have seen firsthand the provision of free prenatal care, free clothing, baby clothes, furnishings, and other help to needy women. Prolife families give free room and board as well as love and support to women who need it. Often prolife doctors volunteer no-cost medical help, and prolife lawyers donate legal aid to help with adoptions, when this is the woman's choice. When women choose to keep their children, single mother support groups and childcare are offered. Like tens of thousands of prolife families, my family opened our home to a pregnant teenage girl and helped her financially and legally.

I believe prolifers can and should do more and more to help women in crisis pregnancies. But what they are doing already is considerable. It amounts to one of the largest and most effective volunteer efforts in our nation's history. While there are hypocrites in any group, to label prolifers in general as hypocrites is unfair and unsupported by the facts.

33b. Prolifers are actively involved in caring for "unwanted" children and the other "disposable people" in society.

I was on a radio talk show when one irate caller asked, "Once you people 'save the lives of the unborn,' where are you for the next eighteen years?" I said, "At this very moment, one of my friends is picking up his eighteenth adopted child, a hard-to-place handicapped minority. Three of his other adopted children have Down's syndrome." I told of many prolife families waiting to adopt, and many others involved in foster care with "drug babies" and other children with special needs. The claim that prolife people don't help with unwanted children makes inflammatory rhetoric, but it is simply false.

Many prolifers are also on the cutting edge of care for the poor, elderly, and handicapped. There are hundreds of organizations across the country that specialize in helping such people. The organization I am part of is committed not only to meeting spiritual needs, but to feeding the hungry and providing education and resources for the poor. Helping women and children who are victims of abortion is only one aspect of our people-helping focus.

33c. It is "abortion providers" who do not provide support for women choosing anything but abortion.

When you hear abortion providers talk about the help they offer women, ask them: "If a fifteen-year-old girl comes into your clinic with no money, no one to help her, no home to go to, and no desire to have an abortion, what services does your facility provide for her?"[7] The answer is always the same—none. Abortion advocates don't offer help. They offer only abortion, and then only to those who can pay their price.

34. "The anti-abortionists are a bunch of men telling women what to do."

34a. More women than men oppose abortion.

A 1989 poll conducted by the University of Cincinnati revealed that 59 percent of women opposed abortion, while only 46 percent of men opposed it.[1] A 1989 *New York Times* poll found that 67 percent of women agreed that America "continues to need a strong women's movement to push for changes that benefit women."[2] Significantly, about half of this same group of women favored stricter limitations on abortions.

Opposition to Abortion By Gender
OHIO, Statewide Poll
University of Cincinnati, 1989

Women 59%

Men 46%

0 10 20 30 40 50 60
Percent Opposed to Abortion

191

A 1991 Gallup Poll asked, "At what point in the pregnancy do you personally feel that the unborn child's right to be born outweighs the woman's right to choose whether she wants to have a child?" 52.6 percent of women and 47.3 percent of men answered "conception." Only 5.5 percent of women compared to 9.6 percent of men answered "birth."[3] More women than men affirmed the rights of unborn children.

According to the polls, "the most pro-abortion category in the United States (and also in other nations) is white males between the ages of twenty and forty-five."[4] More specifically, "the group that is most consistently prochoice is actually single men."[5]

34b. The great majority of prolife workers are women.

The largest prolife affiliation in America is National Right to Life. Nearly two-thirds of Right to Life's members are women.[6] Nine out of ten volunteers at Birthright, another large prolife organization, are women. The national office of Crisis Pregnancy Centers estimates that 80 to 90 percent of their workers are women. Of the Right to Life delegates elected by each of the fifty states and the District of Columbia, thirty-eight were women, and only thirteen were men.[7]

At the prolife gatherings I have attended, typically there are many more women than men, often twice as many. My experience is confirmed by the past president of National Right to Life, who says, "Look at who is at prolife rallies. You will find the composition of the crowd is consistently better than 2 to 1 women, with a heavy sprinkling of young people and some children."[8]

34c. If men are disqualified from the abortion issue, they should be disqualified on both sides.

It is common for men to pressure women into abortion. The vast majority of doctors who perform abortions are men, as are most prochoice congressmen. Why do prochoice advocates continuously quote from Dr. Alan Guttmacher and other male authorities? Why do they embrace the judgment of the all-male Supreme Court that legalized abortion in 1973? And why do prochoice groups donate sizable campaign funds to male legislators who endorse abortion? If men should be eliminated from the abortion debate, shouldn't they be eliminated from both sides?

34d. Men are entitled to take a position on abortion.

Abolitionist Samuel May once said to feminist Susan B. Anthony that because she was single she had no business talking about the institution of marriage. Anthony pointed out that the same logic demanded May should quit speaking about slavery since he had never been a slave.[9] Should stock brokers and investors be the only ones allowed to discuss stock market ethics? Should debates about war be restricted to those in the military?

Abortion is a human issue, not a gender issue. Facts, logic, reason, and compassion have no anatomy. Whether they are espoused by men or women is no more relevant than whether they are espoused by black or white. The point is whether the arguments are accurate, not the gender of those advancing them. To believe otherwise is simply sexism.

34e. Of women who have had abortions, far more are prolife activists than prochoice activists.

The arguments against male involvement in prolife activities are often based on the idea that only those who have had abortions can know firsthand how important it is to have abortion rights. Leaving men completely out of the picture, then, which movement has more women who have had abortions—the prochoice movement or the prolife movement?

An article in Planned Parenthood's *Family Planning Perspectives* gives the results of sociologist Donald Granberg's study of the nation's two largest groups supporting and opposing abortion.[10] Of National Right to Life's female membership of 7.5 million members, about 245,000 have had abortions. Of NARAL's 125,000 women about 39,000 have had abortions.[11] While the percentage of women who have had abortions in NARAL is, as you would expect, much higher than in National Right to Life, it is not the percentages but the total numbers that tell the story. Planned Parenthood's figures suggest that *women who have had abortions are six times more likely to be prolife activists than prochoice activists.*

35. "Anti-abortionists talk about the sanctity of human life, yet they favor capital punishment."

A prochoice newspaper claims, "Almost all legislators who oppose abortion rights also support the death penalty. One might ask if they think people who are convicted of murder are no longer human."[1]

35a. Not all prolifers favor capital punishment.

Prolifers are a diverse constituency with a wide variety of personal and political convictions. In fact, many prolife leaders oppose capital punishment.[2]

35b. Capital punishment is rooted in a respect for innocent human life.

History's earliest argument for capital punishment is found in the Bible (Genesis 9:5-6). Capital punishment was to be imposed in cases of premeditated murder. The rationale is simple—innocent human life is so highly valued that if a person deliberately takes such a life, he forfeits his own right to live. Justice demands that the murderer receives the ultimate punishment.

Capital punishment is prolife in that it affirms the value of innocent human lives. Furthermore, it assures protection for the lives of other innocent people. Those who claim capital punishment is not a deterrent to crime forget that those who are executed for murder do not reenter society to murder again.

35c. There is a vast difference between punishing a convicted murderer and an innocent child.

It is twisted logic to say if one believes innocent children should not be put to death, he is a hypocrite to believe a convicted murderer should be put to death. Unlike the murderer, the child has committed no crime, no jury has found him guilty, and he is not being executed by the state. He is innocent and is being put to death by a private and subjective decision.

The real inconsistency lies with many prochoice advocates. They oppose the death penalty for men who rape, torture, and murder women and children, yet support the killing of innocent unborn children.

Capital punishment and abortion are radically different issues. That these differences are not obvious to many prochoice advocates raises the question of whether they are thinking clearly about moral issues.

36. "Anti-abortion fanatics break the law, are violent, and bomb abortion clinics."

36a. Media coverage of prolife civil disobedience often bears little resemblance to what actually happens.

The pro-abortion bias of the media is well documented, but has never been more blatant than in its reports of prolife rescues. The media's opposition to the prolife position, coupled with extreme resentment at any appearance of interference with someone's free choice, has resulted in subjective and selective reporting.

After observing the peaceful behavior of the participants in a prolife rescue, my daughters were shocked to read the account in the next day's newspaper that described the rescue as "violent." They had a clear view of the events and had not seen anything remotely violent. The newspaper was full of other inaccuracies as well, leading my then ten-year-old to ask through tears, "Daddy, how can they lie like that?" Unfortunately, most Americans have never seen a rescue firsthand, and are wholly dependent on the media for their impressions.

A classic example of such media distortions is the coverage of the Wichita rescues in the summer of 1991.[1] After ignoring the situation for the first week, the media consistently distorted the nature of the events. They spoke of "violence," while those present said there was no violence. They said the protesters were unwelcome by the citizens of Wichita, not mentioning that some local hotels, restaurants, and other businesses provided free or low-cost services for these protesters because they believed in what they were doing. They falsely stated that most of the protesters were from out of town, when the majority were from Wichita itself.

The Associated Press printed a story picked up by many newspapers, including *USA Today*, which said, "Prosecutors are weighing charges against a man, 36, suspected of beating his three kids with a board because they refused to wear red ribbons in support of abortion foes."[2] Yet the district attorney's office in Wichita—which was never contacted for confirmation—says this report was "erroneous."[3] But the 6.6 million readers of *USA Today*, outraged that anyone would do such a thing, will never know that in fact no one did.

Newspapers around the world printed another Associated Press report quoting a proabortion spokesperson: "Who could have ever assumed that people would push 2-year-old children in front of moving vehicles? To use children like that is just so appalling." It would have been appalling, but it never happened—this report was also totally false.[4] Furthermore, AP failed to mention that the woman who made this claim was an employee of the abortionist whose clinic the protesters were surrounding. When asked why he didn't check to see if the charge was true, the reporter said he was under a deadline and didn't have time.[5] Of course, there was no retraction, and literally millions of people—including many Christians—still believe what was reported.

Some news sources did not even report a rally of thirty thousand people, mostly Wichitans, who gathered to support the prolife efforts. Thousands of peaceful protesters were arrested, again most of them locals. The protesters had the support of many community leaders. Even the governor of Kansas, Joan Finney, said, "It is the character and courage of our state which is at risk. We shall not achieve the ideals for which this state is founded as long as Kansas turns its back on the powerless, the helpless, the unborn."[6] Most Americans didn't hear this quote, but instead heard from proabortion advocates, selected according to the political tastes of reporters.

While media coverage of the 1992 rescues in Buffalo, New York, was not as dramatically biased, it still left many inaccurate and misleading impressions. One of these was the continuously repeated footage of a man in a business suit angrily yelling at and shoving prochoice demonstrators. This man was called a "prolife activist" when in fact he was a passer-by trying to walk down a blocked sidewalk. He had no connection with the rescuers, but millions of Americans were left with a very different impression.

In any case, the great majority of prolife groups do not practice civil disobedience. Furthermore, there is honest disagreement among prolifers as to both the legitimacy and effectiveness of civil disobedience to save the lives of unborn children. Those groups that do practice civil disobedience have strict codes of conduct, and they require a commitment to peaceful nonviolence before they allow anyone to participate.[7]

36b. Rescuing should not be condemned without understanding the reasons behind it.

Rescuing is a united action in which people peacefully place themselves in front of the entrances of an abortion clinic. The primary purpose of this civil disobedience is to keep the clinic closed for the day, and to thereby save the lives of unborn children. A secondary purpose is to make the statement to society that the unborn are human beings deserving the same protection afforded born people.

Of course, mothers denied entrance may reschedule an appointment, at the same clinic or a different one. But the rescue buys time for the unborn child. He does not die today, or at least not this hour. There is a good chance the child will not die at all, since the mother will now have opportunity to read the literature given to her by sidewalk counselors when she approached the clinic. There are any number of other reasons the child's mother might decide not to have an abortion, including the realization that people believed in the value of her child so much they were willing to go to jail.[8] Regardless of the reasons, Planned Parenthood estimates that 20 percent of women who miss their initial appointment for an abortion end up not getting an abortion at all.

Those who participate in rescues cite many biblical references that advocate saving innocent people from imminent harm.[9] They also cite numerous examples from the Bible, church history, and secular history where civil disobedience was necessary to save lives and draw attention to social evils.[10] These people believe that just as it would be right to violate a no-swimming sign to save a drowning child or to violate a trespass law to rescue someone from a burning building, it is also right to break a trespass law for the higher purpose of saving a child about to die and a woman about to kill her child.

36c. Peaceful civil disobedience is consistent with the belief that the unborn are human beings.

Some people believe there is an inherent contradiction in saying that unborn babies are human beings, yet saying one should never be willing to break the law to save their lives. Prochoice columnist B. D. Colen describes a scenario in which the reader is a Pole living near Auschwitz in 1943. He asks, "Are you morally obligated to save what lives you can? Of course you are." Though Colen does not believe abortion is murder, he goes on to say,

How is the person who considers abortion to be murder any different from the Pole who knew what was going on at Auschwitz? If the Pole was morally obligated to attempt to save lives, isn't the person who opposes abortion under the same obligation? . . .

No, the question being asked about Operation Rescue shouldn't be, "Why are these people doing this?" Rather, it should be, "Why has it taken them so long to get to this point? Where have they been?"[11]

Most rescuers have been given fines and jail sentences, and many have been sued. Occasionally, however, a court of law has allowed them to present the scientific and moral evidence and has recognized the legitimacy of their life-saving activity. Missouri Judge George R. Gerhard came to this conclusion:

The overwhelming credible evidence in this case is that life begins at conception. . . . The Court finds that the credible evidence in these cases established justification for the defendants' actions. Their violations of the ordinances involved here were necessary as emergency measures to avoid the imminent private injuries of death and maiming of unborn children. . . . The Court therefore finds the defendants . . . not guilty of the charges against them.[12]

36d. Prolife protests have been remarkably nonviolent, and even when there has been violence it has usually been committed by clinic employees and escorts.

Of the thousands of rescues conducted in this country since 1987, the large majority have occurred without any violence. Most police have been gentle, and some have even supported and joined groups of rescuers.[13] Unfortunately, in some parts of the country police have used martial arts weapons and mace against peaceful and nonresistant rescuers. In our own area, militant prochoice activists have yelled obscenities, and pushed and shoved peaceful prolifers, who with few exceptions have not retaliated. One local abortion clinic owner took a baseball bat and, as witnesses looked on, assaulted a woman who was standing peacefully outside a clinic door.

The "Coalition against Operation Rescue" has published a guide for how to make rescuers look bad. *Clinic Defense: A Model* proudly points to the success of one of its many recommended tactics: "There are innumerable instances of clinic defenders neutralizing male ORs [Operation Rescuers] by shouting, 'Get your hands off me, don't you dare touch me,' all the while they are tugging or pushing OR out of line."[14]

The amount of violence has been very small, and most hostile acts have been inflicted on rescuers rather than by them. This stands in sharp contrast to many other protests for different causes. Nuclear protests, animal rights protests, anti-war protests, and homosexual protests have all involved destruction of property, yet none of these protesters has been given the lengthy jail sentences given prolife rescuers. Those arrested for participating in rescues far outnumber those arrested in the civil rights movement.[15] Yet the rescue movement has had far less violence and property damage than the civil rights movement.

36e. Abortion clinic bombing and violence are rare, and are neither done nor endorsed by prolife organizations.

The vast majority of prolife groups oppose abortion clinic bombings and violence. The wide variety of peaceful prolife efforts offers constructive alternatives that minimize such actions. In a number of cases the persons behind abortion clinic bombings have not been prolife advocates but angry men whose girlfriends or wives have gotten an abortion. The number of abortion clinic bombings tied to prolife activists is extremely small. Though a 1991 television episode of "Law and Order" fictitiously portrayed a prolife leader masterminding an abortion clinic bombing that killed a woman and a child, I have been unable to find a single case of this sort where anyone has been injured.

The 1993 killing of a Florida abortionist was portrayed by the media as if it were typical prolife behavior, when the truly amazing fact was it constituted the first attempt of its kind in the twenty year history of legal abortion. (It was followed by a nonfatal shooting five months later.) The prolife movement has been considerably less violent than the civil rights movement, yet most people immediately see the illegitimacy of trying to discredit that movement because of the violence of some.

In its 1992 report, The National Abortion Federation (NAF) stated that in the six years 1985 to 1990, there were a total of ten actual abortion clinic bombings and thirty-three arsons.[16] This amounts to a total of seven such incidents per year—hardly the *hundreds* of cases one might expect from the media coverage. The NAF might be expected to overstate these numbers, but clearly it would not understate them.

The few cases where prolifers *have* bombed abortion clinics do not change the issue of whether abortion is killing children at those clinics. Nor does it discredit the peaceful efforts of 99.99 percent of prolifers. To blame the prolife movement for such isolated events is like discrediting the anti-slavery movement because some zealous abolitionists burned the crops of the slave-owners. Or, it would be like blaming all prochoice people for the personal threats received by some prolife advocates.

Finally, arson and other property destruction for insurance fraud and other self-serving purposes does occur. The most effective way for abortion clinics to gain public sympathy, and to damage the reputation of prolifers, is to portray themselves as the victims of prolife violence. A Concord, California, abortion clinic was burned to the ground, and local prolifers were blamed. Later the truth came out that a pro-abortion neighbor set the fire to discredit the prolifers he opposed.[17] I spoke with the police detective in charge of the arson investigation of an abortion clinic in our area. His official conclusion was that the fire was set by the abortion clinic owner. Nevertheless, the fire is still blamed on prolifers.

37. "The anti-abortionists distort the facts and resort to emotionalism to deceive the public."

37a. The facts themselves make abortion an emotional issue.

Every photograph of an aborted child, every testimony of women devastated by post-abortion stress syndrome, every story of women being lied to and exploited by the abortion industry is emotional. No wonder, since all the facts point one direction—abortion kills children. Prolifers do not make this an emotional issue; it *is* an emotional issue. How could the killing of children be anything else?

37b. It is not the prolife position but the prochoice position that relies on emotionalism more than truth and logic.

University of Nevada-Las Vegas philosophy professor Francis Beckwith is trained in the discipline of logic. He argues persuasively that the prochoice position is filled with logical flaws. In contrast, he finds prolife logic far more compelling and consistent with the facts.[1] Prochoice advocates compensate for their lack of factual foundations by appealing to the emotions through horror stories of back-alley abortions and pregnancies due to rape.

37c. The prolife position is based on documented facts and empirical evidence, which many prochoice advocates ignore or distort.

Though there are occasional and unfortunate exceptions, prolife organizations typically disseminate documented scientific information, often obtained from secular research and sources that are not prolife. In contrast, many prochoice groups routinely ignore the scientific facts and do not tell the public what they privately know to be true.

For instance, in 1961, Dr. Alan Guttmacher, director of Planned Parenthood, wrote that when "fertilization has taken place; a baby has been conceived."[2] A 1963 Planned Parenthood publication stated, "An abortion kills the life of a baby after it has begun."[3] What Planned Parenthood knew three decades ago has been repeatedly proven since. Yet Planned Parenthood and other prochoice groups do not share this information with women because it does not serve their social agenda.

Prochoice advocates frequently misuse research and statistics. A Planned Parenthood "Fact Sheet" says, without qualification, "90 percent of Americans think abortion should be available under some or all circumstances."[4] Though it is technically true, this statement is completely misleading. Only one-fourth of Americans actually "seldom disapprove" of abortion whereas three-fourths either "often disapprove" or "consistently disapprove."[5] Only 17 percent consider themselves "strongly prochoice," whereas 26 percent call themselves "strongly prolife."[6] By including in their 90 percent statistic those who believe abortion is acceptable to save a mother's life—which includes the vast majority of prolifers—Planned Parenthood misleads people into thinking it represents a point of view most Americans agree with.

Physician and novelist Walker Percy wrote:

> The onset of individual life is not a dogma of church, but a fact of science. How much more convenient if we lived in the thirteenth century when no one knew anything about microbiology, and arguments about the onset of life were legitimate. Nowadays, it is not some misguided ecclesiastics who are trying to suppress an embarrassing scientific fact. It is the secular juridical-journalistic establishment.[7]

A Fund for the Feminist Majority video asks: "Are we concerned about a one-inch tissue or a dead woman?"[8] Of course, the "tissue" is a perfectly formed human being, and the consequence of letting that human being live is not a "dead woman." It is blatantly deceptive to portray the issue of abortion as a forced choice between removing tissue or killing women. This appeal to the emotions is effective, provided the audience does not realize it is simply not true.

37d. The prochoice movement consistently caricatures and misrepresents prolifers and their agenda.

A prochoice video refers to prolife information and activity in these terms: *hysteria, propaganda, immoral, almost obscene, medical McCarthyism,* and *domestic terrorism.* Prolifers are described as "anti-choice," and are said to be "often opposed to sexuality in general." The video says, "The anti-choice people really don't care about people, and they really don't care about children."[9] Planned Parenthood claims:

> The anti-abortion leaders really have a larger purpose. They oppose most ideas and programs which can help women achieve equality and freedom. They also oppose programs which protect the health and well-being of women and their children. . . . "Life" is not what they're fighting for. What they want is a return to the days when a woman had few choices in controlling her future.[10]

A NARAL publication says prolifers have a "vindictive, self-righteous attitude" which "stems from a belief that sex is bad and must be punished."[11]

Instead of dealing with facts, reason, and logic, prochoice material often resorts to highly charged emotional arguments without substance, misrepresenting the prolife position and attacking the character of prolifers.

38. "Anti-abortion groups hide behind a profamily facade, while groups such as Planned Parenthood are truly profamily because they assist in family planning."

38a. The prochoice movement's imposition of "family planning" on teenagers has substantially contributed to the actual cause of teen pregnancy.

Though you would never know it from prochoice literature, the cause of unwanted pregnancies is *not* the absence of birth control. It is the presence of teenage sexual activity. Planned Parenthood has had a profound influence on the young people of America for two decades, yet the rate of teen pregnancy has skyrocketed in that time. Why? Largely because of the philosophy stated by former Planned Parenthood president Faye Wattleton: "We are not going to be an organization promoting celibacy or chastity."[1]

By their massive distribution of birth control and its advocacy of abortion as a "solution" to unwanted pregnancy, Planned Parenthood and other prochoice organizations have removed the traditional (and still valid) reasons for teenagers not to have sex. Consequently, the number of teenagers having sex has risen dramatically, resulting not only in increased pregnancies and sexually transmitted diseases, but in emotional and psychological scars.

Historically, Planned Parenthood has believed it is naive to expect fifteen-year-olds to abstain from sex. This is no different than saying teenagers cannot be taught to abstain from drugs. I suspect if Planned Parenthood were put in charge of children's traffic safety, it would devote its efforts to teaching children the art of dodging cars, rather than teaching them to stay off the freeway in the first place. (The AIDS crisis has finally forced the term *abstinence* into Planned Parenthood's vocabulary. However, no moral foundation is laid, and discussions quickly move to how to use condoms.)

38b. Through its opposition to parental notification and consent, Planned Parenthood consistently undermines the value and authority of the family.

When Planned Parenthood comes to school classrooms, it typically passes out birth control samples and instructs students in how each is used. It tells students where the local clinic is located, its phone number, and hours of operation. Children are continuously reassured their parents will never know. After thorough investigation, one magazine claims "parental non-involvement is the cornerstone of PPFA's youth marketing strategy."[2]

In many states it is not legal for a girl to get her ears pierced, nor to go on a school field trip, without parental consent. Yet in these same states junior high and high school girls are taken for abortions without their parents knowledge, much less their consent. Girls who cannot even be given an aspirin by the school nurse unless the nurse first gets permission from her parents, can be driven from the school by the same nurse to an abortion clinic without the parents ever being notified. In some areas Planned Parenthood actually provides an "abortion bus" to pick up students from local schools.[3]

It is no wonder that a 1990 poll by NBC News and the *Wall Street Journal* indicated three-fourths of Americans favor a law requiring parental notification of abortion.[4] Prior to 1981 teen pregnancy had skyrocketed in Minnesota, but after a parental notification law went into effect, teen pregnancies and teen abortions declined dramatically.[5] If Planned Parenthood's real goal is to reduce teen pregnancy, it would support such laws. But despite the undeniable reduction of teen pregnancies by Minnesota's law, Planned Parenthood vehemently opposes that law and all similar laws.[6]

How can this contradiction be explained? According to Planned Parenthood's own statistics, mandatory parental involvement provisions result in a 24 percent to 85 percent reduction in the teen caseloads of family planning clinics.[7] This means huge numbers of family planning employees would lose their jobs. Furthermore, every pregnancy test paid for by tax money brings in $57.51 to Planned Parenthood, as opposed to an average of $16.36 for those who pay for themselves.[8] As America's largest abortion provider, Planned Parenthood has become financially dependent on teen pregnancies and abortion. When teen pregnancies and abortions decrease so does Planned Parenthood's cash flow and its ability to maintain its expensive programs and personnel.

Prochoice groups oppose not only parental consent legislation, but in Oregon they managed to defeat a bill that simply required that parents be *notified* of their child's abortion, even if they didn't consent to it. The whole situation defies belief. This very moment hundreds of parents across America are not even aware their daughters are in pain, bleeding, and emotionally distraught, because they had an abortion within the last few days. These parents don't know to look for such signs or to get immediate medical care if complications occur.

Distraught teenage girls often think, "My parents would disown me if they knew I was pregnant." Usually they are wrong. The majority of parents love their children and are in the best position to give them help and counsel. Yet by their opposition to parental consent laws, prochoice advocates teach girls they cannot trust their parents (who know and love them), while they *can* trust the abortion and family planning clinics (who neither know nor love them).

Students at a California high school were told, "At Planned Parenthood you can also get birth control without the consent or knowledge of your parents. So, if you are 14, 15 or 16 and you come to Planned Parenthood, we won't tell your parents you've been there. *We swear we won't tell your parents*."[9] A 1986 piece in the *Dallas Observer* read, "If your parents are stupid enough to deny you access to birth control and you are under 18 you can get it on your own without parental permission. Call Planned Parenthood."

Is it possible that parents are not as stupid as some people think— that they understand that providing birth control encourages sexual activity and they wish to teach abstinence instead? Is it possible that a girl's parents love her even more than the abortion clinics that will take her $300 and never see her again?

38c. As demonstrated in the case of Becky Bell, the prochoice movement is willing to distort and exploit family tragedies to promote its agenda.

The most widely publicized prochoice case study in history is Becky Bell, a seventeen-year-old Indiana teenager who died in 1988. According to prochoice advocates her death was the fault of a state law requiring her to get parental consent for an abortion. As *Ms.* magazine put it, "She Died Because of a Law."[10]

Prochoice groups have placed both of Becky's parents on their payrolls, and have flown them around the country for political rallies and television interviews. They have been extremely effective in helping defeat parental consent legislation in states where polls show people actually favor it.

Major newspapers and magazines, using the language of prochoice press releases, contradict each other in their accounts of what actually happened to Becky Bell. Some say she had a botched abortion surgery, others that she took a "home remedy" abortion. None have bothered to investigate her actual cause of death.[11]

Becky Bell's autopsy report describes the tissue lining her uterus as "smooth and glistening," with no infection, discoloration, or any other indications of an induced abortion.[12] The doctor who performed the autopsy states that Becky died of pneumonia. He also says there had been a *spontaneous* abortion (a miscarriage) as opposed to an *induced* abortion. After he put *abortion* on the cover of the autopsy report, someone else added the word *septic* in front of it. This doctor stated flatly, "There is absolutely no evidence whatever of an induced abortion," and that Becky Bell's parents never talked to him about the autopsy or cause of death.[13]

John Curry, former head of the Tissue Bank at Bethesda Naval Hospital, says the pathology report clearly indicates massive infection in the lungs, but no infection whatsoever in or even near the uterus.[14] He maintains the pneumonia was "unlikely to originate from a contaminated abortion procedure." He also says Becky's death could have been prevented by treatment of her pneumonia within the first six days. Dr. Bernard Nathanson studied Becky Bell's autopsy and concluded definitively, "Rebecca Bell did not die from a septic illegal abortion: there is not one shred of credible evidence to support this preposterous claim."[15]

Suppose, however, that Becky did die from an abortion. What would have happened if the Indiana parental consent law had been followed and the Bells had been told their daughter was pregnant and wanted an abortion? First, they could have expressed their support for having the child or giving him up for adoption. They could have warned her of the physical and psychological dangers of abortion. But even if they would have agreed to an abortion, they would have been alert to her recent surgery and would have taken her to a doctor when they first saw how ill she was days before her death.[16] The media failed to point out that Becky Bell desperately needed her parents' help in making decisions about her health and welfare. Her boyfriend was a drug supplier with a tendency toward violence, and she had recently been hospitalized for substance abuse. The coroner's report says that only days before she got sick she had been at a party where drugs were being used, and that she "claimed that someone had put 'speed' in her drink."[17]

Columnist Cal Thomas states, "The medical cause of Becky Bell's death may have been pneumonia, but the underlying cause remains unclear. One thing is clear: her death was *not* due to Indiana's parental consent law."[18]

38d. The prochoice movement and the media ignore family tragedies that do not support the prochoice agenda.

There may be past or future examples of someone who does suffer or die because she chooses to get an illegal abortion rather than to consult her parents. But what prochoice advocates do not point out is that many more girls (not to mention babies) suffer as a result of the lack of parental notification laws.

> In all the years parental notification and consent bills have been on the books, Becky's case is the only one that pro-abortionists have been able to find which—if misrepresented thoroughly enough—could lend even a semblance of credibility to their side of the debate. By contrast teenage girls have died and been crippled precisely *because* they were not required to involve their parents or because others maneuvered to get around telling the parents.[19]

Less than six months after Becky Bell's death, Erica Richardson, a Maryland sixteen-year-old, died from a legal abortion.[20] Only a few local newspapers covered her death. Erica underwent an abortion without her parents' knowledge or consent, since neither is required in Maryland. Had she been required to talk with her parents they could have helped her make a more informed and careful decision. Had they done so, Erica Richardson would likely be alive today.

Most of the country knows the name of Becky Bell, whose death was unrelated to her state's parental consent law. Almost no one knows the names of girls such as Erica Richardson, who probably would not have died if their states required that parents be consulted or at least informed of their children's abortions.

It is mystifying that a movement can describe itself as profamily when it fights against the rights of parents to know that their child is undergoing a major surgery with significant physical and emotional risks—a surgery that will, among other things, kill their own grandchild.

SUMMARY ARGUMENT

39. "The last two decades of abortion rights have helped make our society a better place to live."

39a. Abortion has left terrible holes in our society.

Reader's Digest tells a heart-warming story involving a young Italian woman named Catuzza, living in New York. Back in the 1950s, Catuzza let an eleven-year-old neighbor boy and his three-year-old brother Joey touch her stomach when her unborn baby was kicking. Some thirty-five years later Joey was dying, until his life was saved by a skilled and dedicated physician. After recognizing the doctor's last name, Joey's older brother put the pieces together: "Only then did the realization hit me. The unborn baby who had kicked inside Catuzza all those years before on Irving Street had grown up to be the doctor who saved my brother's life."[1]

How different the story might have been if abortion had been legal in New York when Catuzza was pregnant. Her son would have had at least a one-in-three chance of being killed before he was born. How many life-saving "connections" like that of Joey and Catuzza's son have failed to materialize because of legalized abortion?

The classic Jimmy Stewart movie, *It's a Wonderful Life*, captures this same mystery of connections. When George Bailey's life unravels, he wishes he had never been born. As he stands on a bridge contemplating suicide, an angel is sent by God to tell George how important his life has been. The angel shows George how the world would have been a much worse place without him. Then he says, "Strange, isn't it? Every man's life touches so many other lives, and when he isn't around he leaves an awful hole to fill, doesn't he? . . . You see what a mistake it would be to throw it away?"[2]

Nearly thirty million "awful holes" have been created by legal abortion in this country. Every twenty seconds a preborn child is killed in America. That is 4,400 a day, every day of the year, every year of the decade. The number is too great for us to possibly envision. Those who have stood before the national Vietnam Memorial with its 58,132 names may be helped by a comparison. Every two weeks, year in and year out, there is an aborted child for each and every name on that memorial. How many miles would a memorial stretch if every aborted child were listed?

The total American casualties in all wars in our nation's history approaches 1.5 million people. This is slightly less than the number of children killed *annually* in the war against our offspring. Since 1991, high school graduating classes have been missing up to a third of the members they would have had if they had not been killed by abortion.

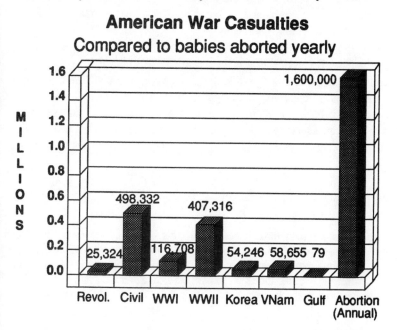

American War Casualties
Compared to babies aborted yearly

39b. Abortion has made us a nation of schizophrenics about our children.

On the one hand, we value children as our greatest national resource. We are appalled at the dramatic rise in child abuse, and the lack of care given many children. In the early 1990s the major newsmagazines devoted whole issues to the plight of children in America. A 1991 *Mother Jones* cover story, "America's Dirty Little Secret: We Hate Kids," called for a new commitment to the value of children's lives.[3] A feature article in *Parade* pleaded, "Save our Babies."[4] It decried America's mortality rate of 9.1 infant deaths per 1000 live births.

Yet our infant mortality rate is actually about thirty-two times the official figure, due to abortion. Not one of the articles makes the obvious connection between how we treat our unborn children and how we treat them when they are just a little older. Several of the articles emphasize the importance of prenatal care. None point out that the greatest violation of prenatal care is to kill the baby.

Our hospitals live daily in a state of extreme schizophrenia. Doctors and nurses feverishly attempt to save the life of a twenty-two week "fetus" born prematurely, while in the very next room a child at twenty-four weeks is deliberately and legally killed. Some states require a medical team to back up late-term abortions in case the child survives. One medical team is trying to destroy the life, but if the job is botched and the child somehow survives, the other team takes over and tries to save his life.

An editorial in the *Oregonian*, a strongly prochoice newspaper, was titled, "Slaughtering Our Babies." It concerns an infant killed by a stray bullet in a drug-gang war. The editorial asks:

> What hope is there for a community that slaughters its young? What in heaven's name is wrong with us? . . . No community—no civilized and caring community, at least—can allow this kind of slaughter to go by without comment. . . . Portlanders . . . must make clear again and again that this kind of activity is absolutely unacceptable and that they will help to choke it out in this city.[5]

Yet the same community and the same newspaper is indifferent to the vicious slaughter of infants that occurs daily in its four abortion clinics. More than indifferent, the newspaper and many in the community applaud and defend the right to butcher thousands of infants annually, each just as human, just as alive, and just as valuable as the single infant the editorial laments. What else but a combination of blindness and schizophrenia can explain how we can abhor the death of one infant, while tolerating and even embracing the deaths of thousands of infants?

One prolife woman has taken photographs of aborted babies in abortion clinic dumpsters. Twice the photo developing lab has reported her to the police, who began a homicide investigation. When she explained the child was killed at an abortion clinic, the investigation was called off. Whether the woman or the clinic killed the child, in both cases a child was killed. *What's the difference?* To any rational person, there is no difference.

39c. Abortion is a modern holocaust in which we are accomplices.

The unspeakable evil of child-killing has left a cloud over our country. We have immunized ourselves to this evil. Dr. Bernard Nathanson says:

> The abortion holocaust is beyond the ordinary discourse of morality and rational condemnation. It is not enough to pronounce it absolutely evil. . . . The abortion tragedy is a new event, severed from connections with traditional presuppositions of history, psychology, politics, and morality. It extends beyond the deliberations of reason, beyond the discernment of moral judgment, beyond meaning itself. . . . This is an evil torn free of its moorings in reason and causality, an ordinary secular corruption raised to unimaginable powers of magnification and limitless extremity.[6]

39d. Abortion is taking us a direction from which we might never return.

A NARAL publication states, "There is no evidence that respect for life has diminished or that legal abortion leads to killing of any persons."[7] On the contrary, there are unmistakable signs everywhere that abortion has desensitized us to the value of human life.

It is hard to believe less than three decades have passed since the New Jersey Supreme Court issued a decision that protected handicapped preborns. This decision was hailed by almost everyone at the time as the only conclusion a decent society could come to. It stated, "We are not talking here about the breeding of cattle. It may be easier or less expensive for the father to have terminated the life of his child, but these alleged deficits cannot stand against the preciousness of a single human life."[8] Now over half of such children are routinely killed and some have advocated legal requirements forcing the other half to be killed as well.[9]

After a seventeen-year-old Florida girl smothered her newborn daughter, a judge sentenced her to two years in prison and to psychological counseling and birth control instruction.[10] Of course, the sentence for killing someone perceived as "a real person" would have been much more severe. As one social analyst points out, "A two-year sentence for the willful murder of an infant demonstrates beyond any shadow of doubt that the life of a child does not have the same value as the life of an adult."[11]

University of Chicago biologist Dr. Leon Kass says, with the direction of modern science and medicine, "we are already witnessing the erosion of our idea of man as something splendid or divine, as a creature with freedom and dignity. And clearly, if we come to see ourselves as meat, then meat we shall become."[12]

Abortion sets us on a dangerous brink. We may come to our senses and back away from the slippery slope, or we may continue down it until we completely lose control. As one feminist group points out, if unborn children are not safe, no one is safe:

> If we take any living member of the species homo sapiens and put them outside the realm of legal protection, we undercut the case against discrimination for everyone else. The basis for equal treatment under the law is that being a member of the species is sufficient to be a member of the human community, without consideration for race, gender, disability, age, stage of development, state of dependency, place of residence or amount of property ownership. Abortion dynamites the foundation of feminism, and poisons the well against civil rights for African Americans, the elderly, the disabled, and others.[13]

39e. Abortion has ushered in the brave new world of human pesticides.

What lies ahead in the war against our children? The "abortion pill," RU- 486, first developed in France, induces an abortion without surgery. Other similar "breakthroughs" that are sure to come will make abortion appear cleaner and less disturbing. But they will do nothing to change reality. Children will be killed with greater ease and efficiency, but *children will still be killed*. Abortion pills will not change the grisly reality of abortion any more than the Nazi's more efficient and sanitary killing procedures changed the reality of the holocaust.

Not only children, but women will suffer from the new abortion drugs. RU- 486 still has considerable medical risks.[14] Researcher George

Grant documents the drug's serious and sometimes deadly side-effects.[15] Secular magazines ranging from the *American Druggist* to *Wall Street Journal* to *Vogue* have pointed out that RU- 486 is a powerful steroid that causes heavy bleeding and other dangerous side effects.[16] Even the prochoice American Medical Association acknowledges that RU- 486 has been proven neither safe nor effective.[17] RU- 486 has been sharply criticized by three prochoice feminists, including a professor of Women's Studies and Medical Ethics at the University of Massachusetts.[18] The three claim that women are being treated as "guinea pigs" in experiments with this dangerous drug.

Despite all this, prochoice groups have portrayed RU- 486 as a "wonder drug." Even if it remains illegal, they have promised to import or produce it. They claim RU- 486 will solve not only the problem of unwanted pregnancy, but may also cure breast cancer and AIDS. Ignoring its dangers to women, the Fund for the Feminist Majority (FFM) is waging an all out campaign to legalize RU- 486. One donor contributed ten million dollars to the FFM for this purpose.[19]

Even if a "safe" child-killing drug is developed, this will not minimize the tragedy at all. There is no "clean" way to kill innocent children, and there is no way that child-killing can leave any society unscarred. Abortion pills are nothing less than chemical warfare against our own species. They are, quite literally, human pesticides.

A nation determines its future by how it treats its children. We hold in our hands not only the fate of the unborn, but the fate of our nation. Will we remove our children as we would remove a wart? Will we take a medication to relieve ourselves of our children, as we would take an antacid to relieve ourselves of a sour stomach? The abortion pill is one more test for America—perhaps one last test—of how inhuman we are willing to become.

FINAL APPEALS

An Appeal to Women Considering Abortion

Don't succumb to the pressure to kill your baby. The testimony of one woman who gave into that pressure echoes the feelings of hundreds of thousands of women, and says much more than I can:

> My family would not support my decision to keep my baby. My boyfriend said he would give me no emotional or financial help whatsoever. All the people that mattered told me to abort. When I said I didn't want to, they started listing reasons why I should. They said it would be detrimental to my career, and my health, and that I would have no social life and no future with me. Could I actually keep it alone. I started feeling like maybe I was crazy to want to keep it.
>
> I finally told everyone that I would have the abortion just to get them off my back. But inside I still didn't want to have the abortion. Unfortunately, when the abortion day came I shut off my inside feelings. I was scared to not do it because of how my family and boyfriend felt. I'm *so* angry at myself for giving in to the pressure of others. I just felt so alone in my feelings to have my baby.[1]

Every pregnant woman has an inner voice telling her not to abort her child, that she will regret this decision the rest of her life. Don't let the loud voices of society drown out this small voice. Listen to it. It's your conscience, and it's telling you the truth.

There are people who will help you. Look up "Abortion Alternatives" in the Yellow Pages and call for help. Or call one of the toll free hotlines for women in crisis pregnancies (under the first listing in Appendix D). Instead of finding people who will kill your baby for a fee, you'll find people who will understand and help for free. If you don't know how to find help in your area, contact our organization listed on the last page of this book, and we will gladly assist you at no cost.

An Appeal to the Abortion and Family Planning Clinics

I appeal to the clinics to take me up on a sincere offer. I promise to help them find an abortion alternative center in their area that will allow a clinic employee or volunteer to present to each client the best case for

215

abortion. The client will then weigh the information given by the abortion alternative center against that given by the abortion clinic, and make her own decision. All that is required is that the abortion or Planned Parenthood clinic do the same thing—allow one employee or volunteer from an abortion alternative center to present to each client the facts about fetal development, visual aids showing what abortion is, psychological and physical risks of abortion, and the availability of abortion alternatives. The woman—not the counselors from either side—will make her own choice.

Isn't that what the prochoice movement says it wants—women informed and free to choose? Isn't that a fair arrangement? I know lots of abortion alternative centers that would gladly agree. I have yet to hear of an abortion clinic or Planned Parenthood clinic that would. I invite any abortion clinic to take me up on the offer.

An Appeal to the Media

For too long journalists have rehearsed prochoice rhetoric rather than engage in objective reporting. Any journalist with integrity should be offended at the words of a former proabortion leader who confesses the key to his group's success in misleading the public was its ability to manipulate the media: "We fed a line of deceit, of dishonesty, of fabrication of statistics and figures. We coddled, and caressed, and stroked the press."[2] It should further distress you to hear one of your own, a respected columnist, say:

> If the pro-abortionists were not in control of the press, I am convinced that not only would the debate on abortion be over by now (have we really even had a national debate?), but the prolife side would be victorious because we would have seen the pictures every night on television of what is taking place behind the doors of the abortion clinics and hospitals.[3]

It should offend journalists, who of all people most abhor censorship, to learn that *in four cases the book you are reading was censored.* When I tried to obtain rights to use scientific photographs of unborn children, and was willing to pay the going rate for such usage, I was denied the use of them because this book takes a position against abortion. These are objective, scientific materials that were withheld from the readers of this book because they clearly demonstrate the humanity of the unborn.

Furthermore, both Chrysler and Volvo refused permission to reproduce two of their advertisements (from which I quoted in Answer 8e) simply because this was a prolife book. I've been told that Volvo has been under pressure from prochoice advocates because they used an actual ultrasound image of an unborn child in their ad. There is only one word for this—*censorship*.

But censorship has become routine in the abortion debate. For instance, a Bellingham, Washington, library has a display case for publicly contributed educational exhibits, which stay up for thirty days. One citizen set up an attractive exhibit using a series of plastic models and *Life* magazine photos. These showed—with scientific accuracy—the development of an unborn child from conception to birth. Because it was sending a prolife message (the message the facts send), the library director ordered the display taken down. Only the threat of legal action against the city kept it up.[4] Where is the media outcry when such attempts at censorship surface?

I appeal to all journalists who hate censorship to muster the courage to stop censoring the facts about abortion themselves, and to speak out boldly against those who do. I appeal to you to do exposés of the abortion industry with the same fervor you would apply to uncovering unethical practices in the White House. I appeal to you to tell the public that abortion clinics are immune to the informed consent, health, and safety requirements placed upon all legitimate hospitals.

I appeal to you to show the pictures of aborted babies the same way you showed the pictures of children killed in Viet Nam. I appeal to you to present the prolife position as it actually is, as presented in sources such as this book, not as it is caricatured by prochoice advocates. Stop being ministers of propaganda for the politically correct position. Present the American public with the facts, and let them make up their own minds.

An Appeal to Physicians

Dr. Bernard Nathanson accuses the medical community of "a willful and conscious disregard of the massive and still-growing data identifying the prenatal person as a living, valuable, and fully protectable human being."[5] He goes on to level these indictments against most of his fellow physicians:

I accuse them of abandoning the canons and principles which lent legitimacy to their organizations, and caving in to the trendy political fashion of the moment. I accuse them of a heinous abuse of their professional trust in failing to protect this unborn patient in their charge. I accuse them of voluntary collaboration in an unprecedented surgical holocaust against these mute and defenseless victims, and I accuse all physician members of these organizations who fail to speak up against this unspeakable crime of complicity in that crime. History will not forgive them.[6]

I appeal to physicians to exonerate themselves by refusing to turn a deaf ear when they hear politically correct but scientifically absurd pro-choice claims such as, "It's just a blob of tissue." You know better, or if you don't you should. Integrity demands that you correct the unscientific propaganda being served up to the public to make abortion palatable.

When you hear objections to showing pictures of aborted babies, integrity demands that you stand up and say, "Like it or not, these are real pictures of what happens in an abortion. Those who support abortion must face the fact that it dismembers unborn babies, stops beating hearts, and stops measurable human brain waves. This is not prolife rhetoric. It is established scientific fact."

I know it is unpopular for physicians to speak out against the practices of other physicians, but such loyalty is misplaced when it comes to the killing of human beings. The whole medical profession lies under a shadow of dishonor and guilt for endorsing the practices of those who make their living killing unborn children. I appeal to all prolife doctors and nurses to state clearly your position among your colleagues and medical associations, and to stand firmly on it. I appeal to you to band together as local groups and to take out full-page advertisements in local newspapers and make your position clear and unmistakable. I appeal to you to actively participate in prolife activities, to serve on the boards of prolife organizations, even if doing so subjects you to abuse from the politically correct elements of your profession. I appeal to you to remember your oaths and your commitment to human life and welfare.

I appeal to physicians sitting on the fence to get off it once and for all. The only way to come out of the abortion holocaust clean is to separate yourself from the practice of child killing. You must refuse to acknowledge it as part of the medical profession, regardless of its current legal status. It is time to refuse not only to do abortions, but to refuse to practice medicine with or make referrals to those who do. Do not allow yourself to be remembered as we now remember those who collaborated with the Nazi doctors and were accomplices to their atrocities.

An Appeal to Representatives and Legislators

All those in political office must be painfully aware of the contempt with which many regard you. You are seen as people without integrity or moral courage, as chameleons who kowtow to special interest groups, as spineless bureaucrats more concerned about reelection than the welfare of people. *Show the public they are wrong about you.* Be different. Don't make your goal to keep your job but to do your job. History condemns politicians who defended slavery because it was unpopular to oppose it. Don't let history condemn you for defending what all people will some-day recognize to have been the killing of innocent children.

If you put popularity over morality, at least do so with common sense. Realize that only 9.2 percent of Americans will withhold their vote from a prolife candidate with whom they largely agree in other areas, but 15.7 percent of Americans will withhold their vote from a candidate purely because he takes a prochoice position, even if they agree with him in other areas.[7] "Hardcore" prolifers outnumber their prochoice counter-parts over three times among Republicans, but also outnumber them among Democrats and Independents.[8] Poll after poll indicates that legis-lators favoring such measures as parental consent, informed consent, and restriction of all convenience abortions *have the overwhelming support of most Americans.* Though you should take the prolife position for scien-tific and moral reasons, not political ones, realize that in the majority of cases, holding consistently to the prolife position will gain you more votes than it will lose.

An Appeal to Those Undecided on Abortion

Ironically, people who are not sure whether they should be prochoice or prolife often end up talking and voting as if they are prochoice. The benefit of their doubt goes to choice rather than life.

If we are standing gun in hand, looking at movement in a bush, we must assume the movement is being made by a person, not a nonperson. Assuming it is a nonperson will motivate us to shoot, whereas assuming it's a person will motivate us not to shoot. What is good for hunter safety is good for social ethics. When we're unsure, let's not do something that could kill an innocent person.

The burden of proof is on the prochoice movement. If you have read this book I hope you agree that the evidence of the humanity of the unborn and the reasons against abortion are overwhelming. But even if you don't agree, if you have no more than a reasonable doubt about this matter, surely the benefit of your doubt should go to human life. You should oppose abortion in conversation and at the ballot box. If you don't, then you're shooting into the moving bush and one day, after it's too late, you'll be sorry you did.

An Appeal to Prochoice Christians

I appeal to you to come to grips with the impossibility of being pro-choice about abortion without undermining the essence of what it means to be a Christian. A Christian can no more be prochoice about killing children before they are born than he can be prochoice about kidnaping or killing two-year-olds.

To endorse or even to be "neutral" about killing innocent children created in God's image is unthinkable in the Scriptures, was unthinkable to Christians in church history, and should be unthinkable to Christians today. (See Appendix B, "Abortion in the Bible and Church History.") True Christians do not mindlessly parrot whatever society happens to be saying. They go back to the Scriptures to see what God says, and they believe it even if it is unpopular. They realize that one day they will stand before the Audience of One, and in that day *God's* position on abortion will be the standard by which all others are judged.

An Appeal to Conservative Christians

A 1990 Oregon ballot measure proposed that convenience abortions be made illegal, and that abortion be allowed only in the cases of rape, incest, and risk to the life of the mother. Though prolifers would want a measure to go even further, this one would have protected the lives of 98 percent of the babies dying in our state. Yet an exit poll found that among those identifying themselves as "fundamentalist Protestants," a full 40 percent *voted against* this measure.[9] Furthermore, on the same ballot, one out of four "fundamentalist Protestants" voted against a measure requiring parental *notification* (not even consent) when minors get abortions.[10] Needless to say, with that showing from the church, both ballot measures failed. (Surprisingly, Catholic voters polled were even more proabortion.)

The church's weak and half-hearted beliefs about abortion come to the surface when Christians face the hardship of a crisis pregnancy. Crisis Pregnancy Center counselors confirm that many Christian girls seriously consider getting abortions, and that many have been encouraged to do so by parents who profess to be Christians. One out of six women getting an abortion identifies herself as a "born again Christian."[11] The church is killing its own children at the rate of a quarter of a million per year. Our pews are filled with single girls and boys, young couples, parents, grand-parents, sympathetic friends, and even pastors who, through their counsel or lack of counsel, have innocent blood on their hands.

Prolife Christians have believed too long that our primary job is to convince the world of what we already know to be true about the unborn. In fact, *the church has failed to educate its own people about abortion.* If the church is to stop the killing in society, it must start by stopping the killing in its own midst. "For it is time for judgment to begin with the family of God" (1 Peter 4:17). If the church does not stand up for the unborn, surely the world never will.

An Appeal to Pastors and Church Leaders

Church leaders must take responsibility for the sad state of the church just described. A bulletin insert or thirty-minute sermon once a year on Sanctity of Human Life Sunday is not nearly enough. We are dealing in our churches with people whose minds have been conformed to the world. It is our job to help transform the church's thinking according to God's Word (Romans 12:1-2). We must address the pervasive pro-choice arguments that daily bombard Christians. (This book could be used with other resources as a text or training manual for this purpose.)

We must not hold back from speaking the truth just because there is no consensus about abortion in our church. It is our job, given to us by God, to teach and minister in such a way as to create that consensus. But if consensus never comes—and it may come only with great difficulty—our job is still to teach the truth.

Pastors should resist the temptation to decide for their people not to see pictures that show the reality of what abortion is. No one should be forced to view such pictures, but neither should others be deprived of the opportunity. By not showing actual pictures of abortion we keep people from emotionally experiencing the children's humanity and the horrors of abortion. By sparing our churches some short-term discomfort, we leave them liable to consider abortion when they, their family, or friends face an unwanted pregnancy. (Forcing such visuals on those who do not choose to see them creates anger, resentment, and resistance. We should carefully prepare our audience. The "Hard Truth" video is ideal—it has a musical background without narration and is only seven minutes long, allowing people to look away or close their eyes without having to leave or call attention to themselves.[12])

We must teach what the Bible says in no uncertain terms. (See Appendix B.) We must make use of the many fine prolife resources to educate our people and to equip them to educate the community. (See Appendix D.) We must participate in prolife strategies, programs, and activities that allow our people to do something for women and children being exploited by abortion. (See Appendix C.) And, knowing that when we address this subject many women who have had abortions will be touched, we must offer forgiveness and emotional support. (See Appendix A.)

We must not stay away from this subject for fear of "laying a guilt trip" on women in our churches who have had abortions. On the contrary, we must address it for their sake. There can be no healing without forgiveness, no forgiveness without confession and repentance, and no confession and repentance until abortion is clearly seen to be sin. If we don't speak out, our people will continue to suffer—and continue to kill their babies—without knowing the forgiveness and healing of Christ. The sorrow that comes in facing the reality of abortion is not to be avoided—it is a "godly sorrow" that leads to forgiveness and "leaves no regret" (2 Corinthians 7:10). Without it, there can be no healing and wholeness.

We must not be deceived into thinking that we need only wait for spiritual revival to come and solve the abortion problem. It is our responsibility to draw near to God by dealing with our sin and guilt, so that he is free to come near and bless us. Revival is likely not to precede but to follow our coming to terms with child-killing:

Come near to God and he will come near to you. Wash your hands, you sinners, and purify your hearts, you double-minded. Grieve, mourn and wail. Change your laughter to mourning and your joy to gloom. Humble yourselves before the Lord, and he will lift you up (James 4:8-10).

We must be alert to the demonic forces behind child-killing. Abortion is Satan's attempt to kill God in effigy by destroying the little ones created in God's image. We are not dealing here with "one more social issue," but a unique and focused evil in which Satan has deeply vested interests. We are dealing with a force of darkness that will bitterly resist every effort to combat it, and which requires earnest and sustained prayer and alertness to the spiritual battle.

Finally, we must realize that we will be held accountable, both in this life and in eternity, for our failure to deal with this issue. We must take the strongest possible measures to stop the killing, to minister to our hurting women, and to make a difference in our community. The desire to be popular and avoid people's disapproval is a common reason for church leaders to hold back in prolife efforts. But for every reason we have we must be ready to answer a question on the last day: "Was that reason more important than the lives of all those children?"

Martin Luther addressed the pastor's role in facing the greatest evil of his day:

> If I profess with the loudest voice and clearest exposition every portion of the truth of God except precisely that point which the world and the devil are at that moment attacking, I am not confessing Christ. Where the battle rages, there the loyalty of the soldier is proven, and to be steady on all the battle fronts besides is mere flight and disgrace if he flinches at that point.

An Appeal to Prolife Churches Afraid of Being Distracted from the "Main Thing"

There are many hindrances to establishing a prolife emphasis in the church. One is the deeply held conviction of some that prolife work distracts us from the main thing. To those who say the job of the church is evangelism, I would point out that prolife activities open great doors for evangelism. Students who do a speech on abortion have follow-up conversations that can lead to sharing the gospel. Those who work at Crisis Pregnancy Centers have regular built-in opportunities to share Christ they would otherwise not have. Those who pass out literature at abortion clinics regularly share the love of Christ. People who open their homes to pregnant women can demonstrate a love that is more than words, then follow with the words of the gospel. My own family had the joy of seeing a pregnant young woman accept Christ while living with us.

Many, both church leaders and members, still insist it isn't the job of the church to get involved in prolife activities. But what *is* the job of the church? I appeal to you to come to grips with the fact that loving God cannot be separated from loving our neighbor (Matthew 22:34-40). To a man who wished to define "neighbor" in a way that excluded certain groups of needy people, Christ presented the Good Samaritan as a model for our behavior (Luke 10:25-37). He went out of his way to help the man lying in the ditch. In contrast, the religious hypocrites looked the other way because they had more "spiritual" things to do.

In Matthew 25:31-46 Christ makes a distinction of eternal significance based not merely on what people believe and preach, but on what they have *done* for the weak and needy. Can anyone read this passage and still believe that intervening for the needy is some peripheral issue that distracts the church from its main business? On the contrary, it is part and parcel of what the church is to be and do. It is at the heart of our main business.

In his Great Commission Jesus didn't tell us only to evangelize. He told us to be "teaching them to obey everything I have commanded you" (Matthew 28:20). Jesus commanded us to be compassionate and to take sacrificial action for the weak and needy. If we fail to do this—and if we fail by our words and example to teach others to do this—*then we fail to fulfill the Great Commission.* We show the world and the church that our words about the gospel are only that—words.

Finally, I appeal to you to look to the example of some of the most evangelistically oriented Christians in history. John Wesley actively opposed slavery and encouraged mine workers to unite in order to resist the inhuman treatment by their employers. Evangelist Charles Finney had a major role in the illegal Underground Railroad, saving the lives of many blacks, while under criticism from fellow Christians. D. L. Moody opened homes for underprivileged girls, rescuing them from hopelessness and exploitation. Charles Spurgeon built seventeen homes to help care for elderly women, and a large school to provide education for hundreds of children. Spurgeon and his church built homes for orphans in London, rescuing them from starvation and vice on the streets. Amy Carmichael intervened for the sexually exploited girls of India, rescuing them from prostitution in the temples. She built them homes, a school, and a hospital.

We remember all of these Christians for their evangelism, but forget their commitment to intervention for the weak, needy, and exploited. Perhaps they were effective in evangelism because, unlike many other Christians of their day—and this day—*they lived out the gospel they preached.* I appeal to churches today to do the same. Otherwise we may be prolife by belief, but prochoice by default.

An Appeal to Active Prolifers

Those of us already involved in prolife work need to be challenged to reexamine both our attitudes and our efforts. We must resist the turf-consciousness that inhibits cooperative action and therefore contributes to the very killing we are trying to stop. We must stop needless duplication of efforts in the same communities, and learn from the experience and expertise of others. We must let go of our volunteers and donors and not fear losing them to other groups working for the same cause. We must set aside some of our personal agendas and realize we can accomplish a great deal more if it doesn't matter who gets the credit.

We must realize there are a variety of legitimate prolife activities. The Army, Air Force, Navy, Marines and their special forces all have their role in winning a war, but without strategy and cooperation they would end up wasting resources and getting caught in each others' cross-fire. Likewise, there is an important place for abortion alternative centers, prolife education, literature distribution, sidewalk counseling, picketing, rescuing, boycotts, political action, Life Chain, and many other activities. But each of these is to serve the whole, not as "the" prolife effort but one working in concert with the others. If one of us wins, we all win; if one loses, we all lose. Without mutual respect and cooperation, prolife organizations will get caught in each other's cross-fire, and we will end up fighting the wrong side.

We must work not only harder but smarter, ever broadening the base of prolife activists, not just burning out a few. All our efforts need to be harnessed as part of a strategic long-term plan to save the most children and women from abortion. At the heart of this must be the mobilization of whole churches, not just individual Christians. *Only the churches can provide the numbers and resources needed to win the battle for children's lives.* Churches must be helped to form prolife task forces to educate and mobilize their own people and make community impact. (There are resources available for pastors, churches, and prolife groups wishing to develop a long-term prolife strategy.[13])

A Concluding Appeal from William Wilberforce

Abortion will not go away; it will long outlast *Roe v. Wade*. The changing of laws is important, but laws do not automatically change minds or hearts. States that prohibit abortion will be next to states with liberal abortion laws, which will become havens for abortion clinics. Abortion pills and do-it-yourself abortion kits may become increasingly popular. Those who think that changes in the Supreme Court have left us on the verge of an abortion-free America are sadly mistaken. Many lives can be saved through judicial reform and legislative action, and for that we should rejoice. But our work is just beginning, and the jobs of personal intervention, education, and political action will continue for decades to come, requiring great perseverance.

Shortly after his conversion to Christ in 1784, British parliamentarian William Wilberforce began his battle for the black man's freedom. Relentlessly, year after year—in the face of apathy, scorn, and all the opposition the slave industry could offer—this one man reintroduced to Parliament the motion for the abolition of slavery. Rejected again and again, Wilberforce was encouraged by only a few, among them John Wesley and John Newton, former slaveship captain and writer of "Amazing Grace."

Stating "we are all guilty" for tolerating the evil of slavery, Wilberforce said, "Never, never will we desist till we . . . extinguish every trace of this bloody traffic, of which our posterity, looking back to the history of these enlightened times will scarce believe that it has been suffered to exist so long a disgrace and dishonor to this country."[14]

Because his colleagues often refused to pay attention to his words about the realities of slavery, Wilberforce would pull heavy chains from under his chair in Parliament and drape them over himself to symbolize the inhumanity of slavery. His fellow parliamentarians, who were prochoice about slavery, would roll their eyes, mock him, and call him a fool. But it is Wilberforce, not they, who is remembered—by God and men—as the one who stood for justice and mercy.

Year after year, while both non-Christians and Christians denied or ignored reality, Wilberforce suffered sleepless nights, plagued by dreams of the suffering black man. Finally, in 1807, against incredible odds, Wilberforce saw the slave trade outlawed. Even then, he had to fight eighteen more years for the emancipation of existing slaves. Wilberforce died in 1833—three days after the Bill for the Abolition of Slavery passed its second reading in the House of Commons, bringing slavery in England to its final end.

Wilberforce did not enjoy opposing slavery. And though my sacrifices do not begin to compare to Wilberforce's, I for one do not enjoy opposing abortion. It is draining, time consuming, and at times discouraging; it subjects me to frequent criticism. My life would be much easier, much more pleasant, if I could pretend that babies aren't dying. But I cannot. Much as I wish it were otherwise, *abortion kills children.*

Every prochoice argument requires that we pretend, that we play mind games, that we forget, ignore, or deny the humanity, worth, and dignity of unborn babies. The prochoice movement thrives on having a silent victim. It thrives on our ability to forget and ignore innocent victims as long as they are out of our sight. Tell a lie often enough and people will eventually believe it and end up reciting it. This is the story of the prochoice deception in America.

Not all of us are Wilberforces. But had England been filled with people of conviction who would have done what they could for the suffering slaves, Wilberforce's job would have been much easier and untold suffering could have been prevented. Isn't it time for all those who know the truth about abortion to speak up for those who cannot speak for themselves? And not only to speak up, but to show a better way, the way of love. May we reach out with truth and compassion to mothers feeling the pressure to abort. And may we show a morally disintegrating society the better way of mercy and justice for innocent children.

APPENDICES

APPENDIX A

FINDING FORGIVENESS AFTER AN ABORTION

There are two victims in an abortion—one dead, one damaged. If you have been damaged by an abortion, this appendix is written for you.

It is a mistake to try to eliminate feelings of guilt without dealing with the root cause of guilt. No matter how often someone may say to you, "You have nothing to feel guilty about," your guilt feelings will remain because you know better. Only by a denial of reality can you avoid guilt feelings, but such a denial is unhealthy. It sets you up for an emotional collapse whenever something reminds you of the child you once carried. You need a permanent solution to your guilt problem, a solution based on reality, not denial or pretense.

Because the Bible offers such a solution to your guilt problem, I will quote from it, citing specific biblical books, chapters, and verses. This way you may look up these verses in a Bible and think about them on your own.

Because of Christ's death on our behalf, forgiveness is available to all.

The word *gospel* means "good news." The good news is that God loves you and desires to forgive you for your abortion, whether or not you knew what you were doing when you had it. But before the good news can be appreciated we must know the bad news. The bad news is there is true moral guilt, and all of us are guilty of many moral offenses against God, of which abortion is only one. "All have sinned and fall short of the glory of God" (Romans 3:23).

Sin is falling short of God's holy standards. Sin separates us from a relationship with God (Isaiah 59:2). Sin deceives us and makes us think that wrong is right and right is wrong (Proverbs 14:12). The Bible says, "The wages of sin is death, but the gift of God is eternal life in Christ Jesus our Lord" (Romans 6:23).

Jesus Christ is the Son of God who loved us so much that he became a member of the human race to deliver us from our sin problem (John 3:16). He came to identify with us in our humanity and our weakness, but did so without being tainted by our sin, self-deception, and moral failings (Hebrews 2:17-18; 4:15-16). Jesus died on the cross as the only one worthy to pay the penalty demanded by the holiness of God for our sins (2 Corinthians 5:21). Being God, and being all-powerful, he rose from the grave, defeating sin and conquering death (1 Corinthians 15:3-4, 54-57).

When Christ died on the cross for us, he said, "It is finished" (John 19:30). The Greek word translated "it is finished" was commonly written across certificates of debt when they were canceled. It meant "paid in full." Christ died so that the certificate of debt consisting of all our sins could once and for all be marked, "paid in full."

The Bible is full of offers of forgiveness for every sin.

Because of the work of Jesus Christ on the cross on our behalf, God freely offers us pardon and forgiveness. Here are just a few of those offers:

He does not treat us as our sins deserve
   or repay us according to our iniquities.
For as high as the heavens are above the earth,
   so great is his love for those who fear him;
as far as the east is from the west,
   so far has he removed our transgressions from us.
As a father has compassion on his children,
   so the LORD has compassion on those who fear him;
for he knows how we are formed,
   he remembers that we are dust (Psalm 103:10-14).

Who is a God like you,
   who pardons sin and forgives the transgression
   of the remnant of his inheritance?
You do not stay angry forever
   but delight to show mercy.
You will again have compassion on us;
   you will tread our sins underfoot
   and hurl all our iniquities into the depths of the sea (Micah 7:18-19).

He who conceals his sins does not prosper,
   but whoever confesses and renounces them finds mercy (Proverbs 28:13).

If we confess our sins, he is faithful and just and will forgive us our sins and purify us from all unrighteousness (1 John 1:9).

Therefore, there is now no condemnation for those who are in Christ Jesus (Romans 8:1).

Forgiveness is a gift that must be received to take effect.

The Bible teaches that Christ died for every person, without exception (1 John 2:2). He offers the gift of forgiveness, salvation, and eternal life to everyone: "Whoever is thirsty, let him come; and whoever wishes, let him take the free gift of the water of life" (Revelation 22:17).

There is no righteous deed we can do that will earn us salvation (Titus 3:5). We come to Christ empty handed. Salvation is described as a gift—"For it is by grace you have been saved, through faith—and this not from yourselves, it is the gift of God—not by works, so that no one can boast" (Ephesians 2:8-9). This gift cannot be worked for, earned, or achieved. It is not dependent on our merit or effort but solely on Christ's generosity and sacrifice on our behalf.

Like any gift, the gift of forgiveness can be offered to you, but it is not yours until you choose to receive it. There are cases where convicted criminals have been offered pardon by governors, but have actually rejected their pardons. Courts have determined that a pardon is valid only if the prisoner is willing to accept it. Likewise, Christ offers each of us the gift of forgiveness and eternal life, but just because the offer is made does not automatically make it ours. In order to have it, we must choose to accept it.

You may feel, "But I don't deserve forgiveness after all I've done." That's exactly right. None of us deserves forgiveness. If we deserved it, we wouldn't need it. That's the point of grace. Christ got what we deserved on the cross, so we could get what we don't deserve—forgiveness, a clean slate, a fresh start. Once forgiven we can look forward to spending eternity in heaven with Christ and our spiritual family (John 14:1-3; Revelation 20:11-22:6). And once forgiven, you can look forward to being reunited in heaven with all your loved ones covered by the blood of Christ, including the child you lost through abortion (1 Thessalonians 4:13-18).

Because of forgiveness we need not dwell any longer on our past sins.

God does not want you to go through life punishing yourself for your abortion or for any other wrong you have done. Jesus said to a woman who had lived an immoral lifestyle, "Your sins are forgiven. Your faith has saved you; go in peace" (Luke 7:47-50). Jesus was surrounded by women who were rejected by society, but who found compassion, forgiveness, and hope in his love.

No matter what you have done, no sin is beyond the reach of God's grace. God has seen us at our worst and still loves us. The apostle Paul was a murderer—he had participated in the killing of Christians. He called himself the "worst of sinners" (1 Timothy 1:15-16). Yet God not only forgave him, he elevated Paul to leadership in the church. *There are no limits to the forgiving grace of God.*

Having trusted God to forgive us, we must resist the temptation to wallow in our guilt, for we are no longer guilty. Accepting God's grace does not mean pretending we didn't do something wrong, but realizing that even though we did, we are now fully forgiven. Christ asks us to accept his atonement, not to repeat it.

Many women who have had abortions can identify with King David's description of the anguish that plagued him long after the sinful deed was done:

When I kept silent [about sin],
  my bones wasted away
  through my groaning all day long.
For day and night
  your hand was heavy upon me;
my strength was sapped
  as in the heat of summer.
Then I acknowledged my sin to you
  and did not cover up my iniquity.
I said, "I will confess my transgressions to the LORD"—
and you forgave the guilt of my sin (Psalm 32:3-5).

You may feel immediately cleansed when you confess your sins, or you may need some help working through some of the things you've experienced. Either way, *you are forgiven*. You should try to forget what lies behind you and move on to a positive future made possible by Christ (Philippians 3:13-14). Whenever we start feeling "unforgiven," it's time to go back to all those verses from the Bible and remind ourselves of the reality of our forgiveness.

Forgiveness for the past should be followed by right choices in the present.

Many women who have had abortions carry understandable bitterness toward men who used and abused them, toward parents who were insensitive to their situation, and toward those who misled them or pressured them into a choice that resulted in the death of their child. God expects us to take the forgiveness he has given us and extend it to others (Matthew 6:14-15). Among other things, this frees us from the terrible burden of resentment and bitterness. The warm light of forgiveness—both Christ's toward us and ours toward others—brightens the dark corners of our lives and gives us a whole new joy in living.

One of the most important things you need to do is become part of a therapeutic community, a family of Christians called a "church." You may feel self-conscious around Christians because of your past. You shouldn't. A true Christ-centered church is not a showcase for saints but a hospital for sinners. You will not be judged and condemned for a sin Christ has forgiven. The people you are joining are just as human, just as imperfect, just as needy as you are. Most people in the church aren't self-righteous, and those who are should be pitied because they don't understand God's grace.

There will be others in the church who have also had abortions. A good church will teach the truths of the Bible, and will also provide love, acceptance, help, and support for you. If you are looking for such a church in your area, but cannot find one, contact the author's organization at the address on the last page of this book and we will gladly help you.

One very healthy thing you can do for others and yourself is to reach out to women in crisis pregnancies. God can use your experience to equip you to help others and to share with them the love and guidance he has given you. My wife and I have a number of good friends who've had abortions. Through their prolife efforts they have given to many other women the help they wish someone had given them when they were pregnant. This has not only saved children from dying, and mothers from the pain and guilt of abortion, but also has helped bring healing to them. It can do the same for you.

Appendix B

Abortion in the Bible and Church History

There is a small but influential circle of prochoice advocates who claim to base their beliefs on the Bible. They maintain that "nowhere does the Bible prohibit abortion."[1] Yet the Bible clearly prohibits the killing of innocent people (Exodus 20:13). All that is necessary to prove a biblical prohibition of abortion is to demonstrate that the Bible considers the unborn to be human beings.

Personhood in the Bible

A number of ancient societies opposed abortion,[2] but the ancient Hebrew society had the clearest reasons for doing so because of its foundations in the Scriptures. The Bible teaches that men and women are made in the image of God (Genesis 1:27). Mankind was the climax of God's creation, with an intrinsic worth far greater than that of the animal kingdom placed under his care. Throughout the Scriptures, personhood is never measured by age, stage of development, or mental, physical, or social skills. Personhood is endowed by God at the moment of creation, when there was not a human being before but there is one now. That moment of creation can be nothing other than the moment of conception (see Arguments 1 through 8).

The Hebrew word used in the Old Testament to refer to the unborn (Exodus 21:22-25) is *yeled*, a word that "generally indicates young children, but may refer to teens or even young adults."[3] The Hebrews did not have or need a separate word for unborn children. They were just like any other children, only younger. In the Bible there are references to born children and unborn children, but there is no such thing as a potential, incipient, or "almost" child.

Job graphically described the way God created him before he was born (Job 10:8-12). The person in the womb was not some*thing* that might become Job, but some*one* who was Job, just a younger version of the same man. To Isaiah God says, "This is what the LORD says—he who made you, who formed you in the womb" (Isaiah 44:2). What each person is—not merely what he might become—was present in his mother's womb.

Psalm 139:13-16 paints a graphic picture of the intimate involvement of God with a preborn person. God created David's "inmost being," not at birth but before birth. David says to his Creator, "You knit me together in my mother's womb." Each person, regardless of his parentage or handicap, has not been manufactured on a cosmic assembly line, but has been personally knitted together by God in the womb. All the days of his life have been planned out by God before any have come to be (Psalm 139:16).

As a member of the human race that has rejected God, each person sinned "in Adam," and is therefore a sinner from his very beginning (Romans 5:12-19). David says, "Surely I was sinful at birth." Then he goes back even further, back before birth to the actual beginning of his life, saying he was "sinful from the time my mother conceived me" (Psalm 51:5). *Each person has a sinful nature from the point of conception.* Who but an actual person can have a sinful nature? Rocks and trees and animals and human organs do not have moral natures, good or bad. Morality can be ascribed only to a person. That there is a sin nature at the point of conception demonstrates there is a person present who is capable of having such a nature.

Jacob was given prominence over his twin Esau "though not yet born" (Romans 9:11). When Rebekah was pregnant with Jacob and Esau, Scripture says, "The *babies* jostled each other within her" (Genesis 25:22). The unborn are regarded as "babies" in the full sense of the term. God tells Jeremiah, "I knew you in the womb" (Jeremiah 1:5). He could not know Jeremiah in his mother's womb unless Jeremiah, the person, was present in his mother's womb. The Creator is involved in an intimate knowing relationship not only with born people but with unborn people.

In Luke 1:41,44 there are references to the unborn John the Baptist, who was at the end of his second trimester in the womb. The word translated "baby" in these verses is the Greek word *brephos*. It is the same word used for the already-born baby Jesus (Luke 2:12,16) and for the babies brought to Jesus to receive his blessing (Luke

18:15-17). It is also the same word used in Acts 7:19 for the newborn babies killed by Pharaoh. To the writers of the New Testament, like the Old, whether born or unborn a baby is simply a baby. It appears the preborn John the Baptist responded to the presence of the preborn Jesus in his mother Mary, when Jesus was probably no more than ten days beyond his conception (Luke 1:41).

The angel Gabriel told Mary that she would be "with child and give birth to a son" (Luke 1:31). In the first century, and in every century, to be pregnant is to be *with child*—not that which might become a child. The Scriptures teach the psychosomatic unity of the whole person, body, soul, and spirit (1 Thessalonians 5:23). Wherever there is a genetically distinct living human being, there is a living soul and spirit.

The Status of the Unborn

One scholar states, "Looking at Old Testament law from a proper cultural and historical context, it is evident that the life of the unborn is put on the same par as a person outside the womb."[4] When understood as a reference to miscarriage, Exodus 21:22-25 is sometimes used as evidence that the unborn is subhuman. But a proper understanding of the passage shows the reference is not to a miscarriage but to a premature birth, and that the "injury" referred to, which is to be compensated for like all other injuries, applies to the child as well as to his mother. This means that, "far from justifying permissive abortion, it in fact grants the unborn child a status in the eyes of the law equal to the mother's."[5]

Meredith Cline observes, "The most significant thing about abortion legislation in Biblical law is that there is none. It was so unthinkable that an Israelite woman should desire an abortion that there was no need to mention this offense in the criminal code."[6] All that was necessary to prohibit an abortion was the command, "You shall not murder" (Exodus 20:13). Every Israelite knew that the preborn child was indeed a child. Therefore, miscarriage was always viewed as the loss of a child, and abortion as the killing of a child.

Child Sacrifice

Child sacrifice is condemned throughout Scripture. Only the most degraded societies tolerated such evil, and the worst of these defended and celebrated it as if it were a virtue. Ancient dumping grounds have been found filled with the bones of hundreds of dismembered infants. This is strikingly similar to discoveries of thousands of dead babies discarded by modern abortion clinics. One ancient Near East scholar refers to infant sacrifice as "the Canaanite counterpart to abortion."[7] Unlike the pagan sacrifices, however, with abortion, child-killing need no longer be postponed till birth.

Scripture condemns the shedding of innocent blood (Deuteronomy 19:10; Proverbs 6:17; Isaiah 1:15; Jeremiah 22:17). While the killing of all innocent human beings is detestable, the Bible regards the killing of children as particularly heinous (Leviticus 18:21; 20:1-5; Deuteronomy 12:31). The prophets of Israel were outraged at the sacrifice of children by some of the Jews. They warned it would result in the devastating judgment of God on their society (Jeremiah 7:30-34; Ezekiel 16:20-21, 36-38; 20:31; compare 2 Kings 21:2-6 and Jeremiah 15:3-4).

Abortion and Church History

Christians throughout church history have affirmed with a united voice the humanity of the preborn child.[8] The second-century *Epistle of Barnabas* speaks of "killers of the child, who abort the mold of God." It treats the unborn child as any other human "neighbor" by saying, "You shall love your neighbor more than your own life. You shall not slay a child by abortion. You shall not kill that which has already been generated" (*Epistle of Barnabas* 19.5).

The Didache, a second-century catechism for young converts, states, "Do not murder a child by abortion or kill a new-born infant" (*Didache* 2.2). Clement of Alexandria maintained that "those who use abortifacient medicines to hide their fornication cause not only the outright murder of the fetus, but of the whole human race as well" (*Paedogus*, 2:10.96.1).

Defending Christians before Marcus Aurelius in A.D. 177, Athenagoras argued, "What reason would we have to commit murder when we say that women who induce abortions are murderers, and will have to give account of it to God? . . . The fetus in the womb is a living being and therefore the object of God's care" (*A Plea for the Christians*, 35.6.)

Tertullian said, "It does not matter whether you take away a life that is born, or destroy one that is coming to the birth. In both instances, destruction is murder" (*Apology*, 9.4). Basil the Great affirmed, "Those who give abortifacients for the destruction of a child conceived in the womb are murderers themselves, along with those receiving the poisons" (*Canons*, 188.2). Jerome called abortion "the murder of an unborn child" (*Letter to Eustochium*, 22.13). Augustine warned against the terrible crime of "the murder of an unborn child" (*On Marriage*, 1.17.15). Origen, Cyprian, and Chrysostom were among the many other prominent theologians and church leaders who condemned abortion as the killing of children. New Testament scholar Bruce Metzger comments, "It is really remarkable how uniform and how pronounced was the early Christian opposition to abortion."[9]

Throughout the centuries, Roman Catholic leaders have consistently upheld the sanctity of human life. Likewise, Protestant reformer John Calvin followed both the Scriptures and the historical position of the church when he affirmed:

> The fetus, though enclosed in the womb of its mother, is already a human being and it is a most monstrous crime to rob it of the life which it has not yet begun to enjoy. If it seems more horrible to kill a man in his own house than in a field, because a man's house is his place of most secure refuge, it ought surely to be deemed more atrocious to destroy a fetus in the womb before it has come to light.[10]

Modern theologians with a strong biblical orientation agree that abortion is the killing of a child. Dietrich Bonhoeffer, who lost his life standing up against the murder of the innocent in Germany, argued that abortion is "nothing but murder."[11] Karl Barth stated, "The unborn child is from the very first a child . . . it is a man and not a thing, not a mere part of the mother's body. . . . Those who live by mercy will always be disposed to practice mercy, especially to a human being which is so dependent on the mercy of others as the unborn child."[12]

In the last few decades it has become popular for certain theologians and ministers to be proabortion. The Religious Coalition for Abortion Rights, for instance, has adopted the motto, "Prayerfully Pro-Choice," and is pointed to by prochoice advocates as proof that conscientious Christians can be prochoice. Yet the arguments set forth by such advocates are shallow, inconsistent, and violate the most basic principles of biblical interpretation. Their arguments are clearly read in to the biblical texts rather than derived from them.[13]

The "Christian" prochoice position is nothing more than an accommodation to modern secular beliefs, and flies in the face of the Bible and the historical position of the church. If the church is to be the church, it must challenge and guide the morality of society, not mirror it.

Conclusion: The Bible and the Children

Even if church history were unclear on the matter, the Bible is very clear. Every child in the womb has been created by God, and he has laid out a plan for that child's life. Furthermore, Christ loves that child and proved it by becoming like him—he spent nine months in a mother's womb. Finally, Christ died for that child, showing how precious he considers him to be.

Christ's disciples failed to understand how valuable children were to him, and they rebuked those who tried to bring them near him (Luke 18:15-17). But Jesus called the children to him and said, "Let the little children come to me, and do not hinder them, for the kingdom of God belongs to such as these." He did not consider attention to children a distraction from his kingdom business, but an integral part of it.

The biblical view of children is that they are a blessing and gift from the Lord (Psalm 127:3-5). Society is treating children more and more as liabilities. We must learn to see them as God does—"He defends the cause of the fatherless and the widow, and loves the alien, giving him food and clothing" (Deuteronomy 10:18). Furthermore, we must act toward them as God commands us to act:

> Defend the cause of the weak and fatherless;
>   maintain the rights of the poor and oppressed.
> Rescue the weak and needy;
>   deliver them from the hand of the wicked (Psalm 82:3-4).

As we intervene on behalf of his littlest children, let us realize it is Christ himself for whom we intervene (Matthew 25:40).

APPENDIX C

FIFTY WAYS TO HELP UNBORN BABIES AND THEIR MOTHERS

Direct Personal Involvement

1. Open your home to a pregnant girl. Help her financially, emotionally, and spiritually.

2. Open your home to an "unwanted" child for foster care or adoption.

3. Volunteer time with organizations helping pregnant women, newborns, drug babies, orphans, the handicapped, elderly, street people, and others in need. Personal care is the most basic prolife activity.

4. Establish a pregnancy counseling and abortion alternative service that offers free pregnancy tests, counseling, and support. You can often get the very first listing in the Yellow Pages as "Abortion Alternatives," which precedes "Abortion Services." (For help getting started, see "Abortion Alternatives and Support For Women" in Appendix D, "Prolife Resources.")

5. Donate materials, office equipment, furniture, baby clothes, professional services, and money to Crisis Pregnancy Centers, Birthright, Bethany Christian Services, and other prolife groups.

6. Teach your children and other young people how to say no to premarital sex. Teenage sexual abstinence is not only psychologically healthy, it is the only sure way to prevent teen pregnancies. (Josh McDowell's *Why Wait?* and *How to Teach Your Child to Say "No" to Sexual Pressures,* and James Dobson's *Preparing for Adolescence* are helpful resources. See also the prochastity curricula listed in Appendix D.)

Educating Yourself and Others

7. Become thoroughly informed about the abortion issue. Many fine books, tapes, and videos are available, as well as excellent (and usually free) prolife newsletters. (See Appendix D.) Know the facts so you can rehearse in advance the best responses to the prochoice arguments. Be prepared so no opportunities are missed.

8. Talk to your friends, neighbors, and coworkers about the abortion issue. Challenge them to rethink their assumptions, and to be careful not to buy into an illogical or morally untenable position. Give them a copy of this book, with some pages marked for their attention. (Refer women who have had abortions to Appendix A, "Finding Forgiveness after an Abortion.") Use this book to read and discuss in a class or small group.

9. Volunteer your services as a prolife speaker for schools and church groups. Use the arguments laid out in this book as your presentation outline. Approach a church or Christian school and offer to teach a course in "Prolife Logic and Action."

10. Call in and speak up on talk shows, and ask for equal time on television and radio stations that present the prochoice position. They often welcome a variety of positions. To say nothing is to endorse what is often an unchallenged prochoice bandwagon.

11. Students: Write papers, make speeches, and start a campus prolife group. See "Organizing a Student Prolife Organization" under "Books on Prolife Strategies" in Appendix D.

12. Display attractive prolife posters and information at your office or shop. You may lose a little business, and gain a little. But the truth will be served, and some innocent human lives will be saved.

Literature, Visuals, and Advertising

13. Order and distribute prolife literature. Have it displayed or available at your place of business. Leave it on your coffee table. Distribute literature door to door to influence opinion. An attractive piece left on each porch on a Saturday morning will be read by many. In some areas "every home" distribution has radically changed community sentiments about abortion. (See Appendix D for a list of the best literature.)

14. Donate prolife books and magazine subscriptions to public and school libraries. They are usually well-stocked with prochoice literature—point out that you just want to provide a little balance and make sure the other position isn't censored.

15. Use a pre-made prolife slide presentation, assemble your own, or buy a video tape, and offer to show it in schools, churches, to your neighbors and government representatives. (See Appendix D.)

16. Wear prolife symbols, "precious feet" pins, buttons, and shirts. These often stimulate conversations. Use prolife bumperstickers or lawn signs. Place prolife stickers on letters—more than a dozen people see the average piece of mail. (See Appendix D.)

17. Place newspaper ads, bench ads, and billboard posters. Attractive pre-made ads and beautiful full-size billboard posters are available. (See Appendix D.)

Letter-Writing

18. Write letters to the editor. Be courteous, concise, accurate, and memorable. Quote brief references cited in this book. Some local newspapers have a policy of printing every letter to the editor. *The opportunity for influence is enormous.* Letters to the editor in a major national magazine may be read by a million people.

19. Compile a list of names, addresses, and phone numbers of politicians, newspapers, television stations, hospitals, and others in your area that people can contact to express their prolife views. Distribute them widely.

20. Select the most strategic measures and issues and host a prolife letter-writing party. People can help each other compose informed and succinct letters to the right people and places. Since legislators and others assume there are a hundred others who feel the same way for every one that writes, there is considerable impact from each letter.

21. Write letters of encouragement to the sometimes tired and discouraged prolife activists.

Personal Conversation

22. Refuse any indirect or business support of abortion clinics, and explain your refusal. Boycott proabortion companies, landlords of abortion clinics, and businesses that share space with abortion clinics and abortion-promoters such as Planned Parenthood. Explain your reasons nicely, and they will often take you seriously.

23. Contact physicians and hospitals that perform abortions—and insurance companies that cover them—and express your convictions. Be polite but firm, stating that you, your family, and your business cannot in good conscience patronize those who contribute to the killing of innocent children. *Does your own physician perform abortions?* Ask him—you may be surprised to discover he does. If so, tell him you must reluctantly change doctors. Is your doctor prolife? Encourage him to take a public stand and participate in local prolife events. Share this book with him and ask his opinion of it.

24. Talk to journalists about your concern that they accurately represent the prolife side in their reporting. Many have never heard an accurate presentation of the prolife position. Until we present it to them, how can we expect them to be fair? Highlight sections of this book for their interest. Many will read what you provide, and some may use the material in future articles.

25. Talk to teachers, especially junior high, high school, and college teachers. Express your desire that they understand and be able to represent the prolife position rather than ignore or distort it. Whatever a teacher believes is multiplied a hundred times over in his students and those they in turn influence. Give them a copy of this or other prolife books or videos. (See Appendix D.)

Political Action

26. Write to representatives and others in government at local, state, and national levels. Be respectful, legible, straightforward, brief, and nondefensive. Enclose attractive prolife literature. The more personal your letter the better. Pre-printed postcards are not as effective.

27. Personally phone or set up a meeting with your representatives to share your views on abortion. Groups of three are most effective. If possible include a prolife doctor or other professional. Be careful how you come across—show them prolifers are intelligent and rational.

28. Draft, circulate, and sign petitions for prolife ballot measures, school board members, and so on.

29. Run for political office, school board, or precinct chairman. Or stand by other prolife candidates with your time and money. The only way there will be long-term legal restrictions on abortion is if our state legislatures have a prolife majority. Churches and prolife groups should identify and support character-qualified, knowledgeable, and skilled candidates.

30. Help a bright young prolifer through law school. Challenge him or her to set a goal of becoming a judge. The legal and judicial arenas, as well as the medical and political, desperately need intelligent and skilled prolifers.

Prolife Events

31. Picket abortion clinics, hospitals, and physicians who perform abortions. Write a brochure or fact sheet documenting their performance of abortions. When abortions are only part of their practice they are much more inclined to eliminate them to preserve their reputation in the community. But until they are exposed they usually won't stop.

32. Make prolife signs for yourself and others. Make them large and attractive, with concise messages. "Abortion Kills Babies." "Adoption, not Abortion." "Every Child Is Wanted by Someone." "Give Your Baby a Chance to Choose." "Please Let Your Baby Live." "Equal Rights for Unborn Women." "She's a Baby, not a Blob." "We Care—Talk to Us." "We'll help financially if you'll let your baby live."

33. Organize or participate in a "Life Chain," where hundreds or thousands of prolifers stand on public sidewalks and display signs supporting the unborn and opposing abortion. This is an extremely effective means of mobilizing prolifers and making a clear statement for the children. Many who begin with Life Chain will solidify a prolife commitment and get involved in future prolife activities. (See "Life Chain" under "Prolife Event and Action Organizations," in Appendix D.)

34. Join prolife rallies and marches to galvanize prolife efforts. Have walk-a-thons and other projects to earn money for prolife groups. Get your children involved. They'll love it, and it's great education as well as family activity.

35. Attend prochoice rallies as a counter-demonstrator. Be peaceful. The quiet presence of your group and your signs will make others think and lead to conversations with passersby.

36. Participate in "rescues" through peaceful nonviolent civil disobedience at the doorways of abortion clinics. Or do the legal sidewalk counseling, singing, or praying in conjunction with rescues.

Abortion Clinic Strategies

37. Research and write a brochure on your local abortion clinic, citing specific lawsuits and health code violations, which are a matter of public record. Write a leaflet or brochure asking, "What Do You Know about the Third Street Abortion Clinic?" Make it neat and attractive, perhaps with a photo of the clinic on the front. Give this brochure to women coming to the clinic, neighbors, nearby businesses, and passersby. Include information from this book on physical and psychological risks of abortion. Or use pre-made brochures specially designed for women entering abortion clinics. (See Appendix D.)

38. Collect information and initiate lawsuits against abortion clinics. Place newspaper or billboard ads asking, "Problems after an abortion?" Give a local or national phone number to call for medical, legal, or emotional help. (1-800-634-2224, the American Rights Coalition, is already set up for this purpose.) Many abortion clinics have been shut down by successful lawsuits.

39. Hand out questionnaires and legal information to women entering and leaving clinics. "Did you have a doctor-patient relationship? Did the doctor ask you for a complete medical history? Did he explain to you the possible complications of abortion? Did he show you a picture or explain to you the state of development of your unborn child?" This will encourage them to reconsider their decision, to seek other counsel, or—if the abortion is over—not to come back for another abortion, and possibly to initiate legal action against the clinic. Include the number of an alternative pregnancy center where they can get complete and accurate information the clinic won't give them.

40. Keep new abortion clinics out of your community by informing the public, writing letters to councilmembers, and contacting potential landlords and real estate agents. Abortion clinics mean loss of business and declining property values to everyone due to public sentiment and frequent demonstrations. Those who do not respond to moral reasoning often do respond to public opinion and even more to financial loss. It is usually easier to keep a clinic out of an area than to shut it down once it's there.

41. Rent space as close as possible to an abortion clinic or Planned Parenthood office and establish a pregnancy counseling clinic or prolife information center.

Influencing Your Church

42. Organize a prolife task force and target key church leaders for influence. Identify pastors and other strategic leaders and speak with them one by one. Give them literature and ask them to watch a video. Recruit prolife activists in your church who will help you formulate and implement a plan of education and mobilization. Ask your church leaders to include prolife activities and literature in the budget.

43. Set up a prolife table at church with the best prolife literature and materials. (See Appendix D.) The presence of the table itself is a vital reminder of the prolife cause.

44. Show in church services or classes prolife films and videos such as *The Abortion Providers, The Hard Truth,* and *The Eclipse of Reason.* Offer to pay the film rental yourself. (See Appendix D.)

45. Place a prolife newspaper ad, bench ad, or billboard with your church's name and phone number, offering your help to pregnant girls. (See Appendix D for pre-made ads.)

46. Take your church bus to prolife activities. Many people who won't go alone will go with a group. Some will discover an aptitude for regular prolife ministry they would otherwise never have realized.

47. Have special prolife emphasis Sundays, with special music, speakers, films, and literature. This should include, but not be limited to, the Sanctity of Human Life Sunday in mid-January. (Special bulletin inserts and materials are available from the Christian Action Council and Right to Life of Michigan, listed in Appendix D.)

48. Bring prolife issues and opportunities to the attention of your pastor, Sunday school class, Bible study, or men's, women's, or youth group. Show them one of the videos listed in Appendix D. Provide relevant newspaper clippings and other information to inform your pastor and provide him with sermon ideas and illustrations. Give him this book as a resource. Instead of expecting him to fulfill your prolife agenda, help him out by offering to be a resource and facilitator for him.

49. Start a group of sidewalk counselors from your church that go once or twice a week to talk to women outside abortion clinics. This is hard but rewarding work, and you need the camaraderie of others by your side. Some excellent sidewalk counseling materials are listed in Appendix D.

50. Pray daily for prolife ministries and victimized mothers and babies. Organize your own prayer group, perhaps combining prolife concerns with other vital needs, such as missions. Go to prolife rallies, rescues, or sidewalk counseling and focus on the ministry of prayer. If the darkness of child-killing is to be overcome with the light of truth and compassion, it will require spiritual warfare, fought with humble and consistent prayer (Ephesians 6:10-20).

Appendix D
Prolife Resources

Abortion Alternatives and Support for Women

Bethany Christian Services, 901 Eastern Ave. NE, Grand Rapids, MI 49503, (616) 459-6273.

Birthright International, 686 N. Broad Street, Woodbury, NJ 08096, (609) 848-1818.

Crisis Pregnancy Centers, Christian Action Council, 101 W. Broad Street, Suite 500, Falls Church, VA 22046, (703) 237-2100.

International Life Services, 2606 1/2 West 8th Street, Los Angeles, CA, 90057, (213) 382-2156.

Liberty Godparent Foundation, P.O. Box 27000, Lynchburg, VA 24506, (800) 542-4453.

Lighthouse, 1409 E. Meyer Boulevard, Kansas City, MO 64131, (816) 361-2233.

Nurturing Network, 910 Main Street, Suite 360, P.O. Box 2050, Boise, ID 83701, (208) 344-7200.

Pearson Foundation, 3663 Lindell Boulevard, Suite 290, St. Louis, MO 63108, (314) 652-5300.

Women Exploited by Abortion, Route 1, Box 821, Venus, TX 76084, (214) 366-3600.

The following toll-free hotlines for women in crisis pregnancies can be called from anywhere in the United States at no charge:

Auburne Center, 1-800-521-5530

Bethany Christian Services, 1-800-BETHANY

Birthright, 1-800-848-LOVE

Liberty Godparent Foundation, 1-800-542-4453

The Nurturing Network, 1-800-TNN-4MOM

Open Arms, 1-800-368-3336

One or more chapters of these groups, or their equivalents, are located in most average-sized cities across America, as well as in many smaller ones. Most states have a number of local pregnancy hotlines which offer counseling and referrals. Call the national organizations above or see your local Yellow Pages under "Abortion Alternatives," "Pregnancy Centers," or a similar listing.

A large listing of local prolife groups throughout the United States and Canada can be purchased from International Life Services, 2606 1/2 West 8th Street, Los Angeles, CA 90057, (213) 382-2156.

Adoption Resources

Bethany Christian Services, 901 Eastern Ave. N.E., Grand Rapids, MI 49503, (616) 459-6273.

Catholic Charities USA, 1319 F Street NW, Washington, DC 20004, (202) 639-8400

Holt International Children's Services, P.O. Box 2880, Eugene, OR 97402, (503) 687-2202.

Michael Fund, 400 Penn Center, Pittsburgh, PA, 15146, (315) 823-6380.

National Committee for Adoption, 1930 17th Street NW, Washington, DC 20009, (202) 328-1200. (Ask for publication list.)

Post-Abortion Support for Women

Abortion Trauma Services, 1608 13th Avenue S. #112, Birmingham, AL 35205, (205) 939-0302.

American Rights Coalition, P.O. Box 487, Chattanooga, TN 37401, (615) 698-7960. Call 1-800-634-2224 for medical, legal, and emotional help.

American Victims of Abortion, 419 7th Street N.W. Suite 402, Washington, DC 20004, (202) 626-8800.

The Elliot Institute, P.O. Box 9079, Springfield, IL 62791, (217) 546-9522.

International Life Services, 2606 1/2 West 8th Street, Los Angeles, CA 90057, (213) 382-2156.

Open Arms, P.O. Box 1056, Columbia, MO, 65205, (314) 449-7672.

Post Abortion Counseling and Education (PACE), 101 West Broad Street, Suite 500, Falls Church, VA 22046, (703) 237-2100.

Post Abortion Ministries, P.O. Box 3092, Landover Hills, MD 20784, (301) 773-4630.

Post Abortion Reconciliation & Healing (National Office), P.O. Box 07477, Milwaukee, WI 53207, (414) 483-4141. National Referral Line, 1-800-5WE-CARE.

Project Rachel, Respect Life Office, P.O. Box 2018, Milwaukee, WI 53201, (414) 769-3391.

Victims of Choice, P.O. Box 6268, Vacaville, CA 95696, (707) 448-6015.

Women Exploited by Abortion (WEBA International), Route 1 Box 821, Venus, TX 76084, (214) 366-3600.

Educational, Resource, and Legislation-Influencing Groups

Many of the organizations below have regular newsletters available on request at no or nominal charge:

Ad Hoc Committee in Defense of Life, 1187 National Press Building, Washington DC 20045, (202) 347-8686.

American Collegians for Life, P.O. Box 1112, Washington, D.C. 20013

American Life League, P.O. Box 1350, Stafford, VA 22554, (703) 659-4171.

Americans Against Abortion, Box 40, Lindale, TX 75771, (214) 963-8671.

Americans United for Life, 343 S. Dearborn Street, Suite 1804, Chicago, IL 60604, (312) 786-9494.

Athletes for Life, P.O. Box 1350, Stafford, VA 22554, (703) 659-4171.

Christian Action Council, 101 West Broad Street, Suite 500, Falls Church, VA 22046-4200, (703) 237-2100.

Christian Coalition, 825 Greenbriar Circle, Suite 202, Chesapeake, VA 23320, (804) 424-2630.

Concerned Women for America, 370 L'Enfant Promenade, SW, Suite 800, Washington, DC 20035, (202) 488-7000.

Eagle Forum, P.O. Box 618, Alton, IL 62002.

Family Research Council, 700 Thirteenth Street NW, Suite 500, Washington, DC 20005, (202) 393-2100.

Feminists for Life of America, 811 East 47th Street, Kansas City, MO 64110, (816) 753-2130.

Focus on the Family, Colorado Springs, CO 80995, (719) 531-3400. (FOF's *Citizen* magazine is an excellent source of prolife information.)

Human Development Resource Council, 3961 Holcomb Bridge Road, Suite 200, Norcross, GA 30092, (404) 447-1598.

Human Life Foundation, 150 East 35th St., New York, NY 10157.

Legacy Communications, P.O. Box 680365, Franklin, TN 37068, (615) 794-2898.

Life Advocates, 4848 Guiton, Suite 209, Houston, TX 77027.

Life Issues Institute, 1802 West Galbraith Road, Cincinatti, OH 45237, (513) 729-3600.

LifeNet, P.O. Box 185066, Fort Worth, TX 76181.

Media Associates Resource Coalition (MARC), P.O. Box 5100, Zionsville, IN 46077, (317) 873-6649. (Broadcasters, journalists, musicians, graphic artists, and communications specialists volunteering as resources to prolife efforts.)

National Committee for a Human Life Amendment, 1511 K. St., NW, Suite 335, Washington, DC 20005, (202) 393-0703.

National Right to Life Committee, Suite 500, 419 7th Street NW, Washington, DC 20004, (202) 626-8800. (Outstanding newsletter.)

National Teens for Life, 419 7th Street NW, Suite 500, Washington, DC 20004.

Pro-Life Athletes, 76 Fuller Circle, Chatham, NJ 07928, (201) 635-4027.

Right to Life League of Southern California, 50 N. Hill Avenue, #306, Pasadena, CA 91106.

Teen American Life League, P.O. Box 1350, Stafford, VA 22554, (703) 659-2586.

Prolife Minority Groups

African-American Committee, P.O. Box 1350, Stafford, VA 22554, (703) 659-4171.

Black Americans for Life, 419 7th Street NW, Suite 402, Washington, D.C. 20004.

Hispanics for Life and Human Rights, P.O. Box 9086, Torrance, CA 90501.

VIDA Humana Internacional, 7105 SW 8th Street, Suite 210, Miami, FL 33144, (305) 262-6464.

Prolife Law Firms

American Center for Law and Justice, P.O. Box 64429, Virginia Beach, VA 23467.

American Rights Coalition, P.O. Box 487, Chattanooga, TN 37401, (615) 698-7960.

Americans United for Life (Public Interest Law Firm), 343 South Dearborn St. Suite 1804, Chicago, IL 60604, (312) 786-9494.

CASE (Jay Sekelow), P.O. Box 450349, Atlanta, GA 30345, (404) 633-2444.

Free Speech Advocates, 6375 New Hope Road, New Hope, KY 40052, (502) 549-5454.

Legal Action for Women (LAW), Box 11061, Pensacola, FL 32524, (904) 474-1091.

Rutherford Institute, P.O. Box 7482, Charlottesville, VA 22906, (804) 978-3888.

Prolife Event and Action Organizations

Advocates for Life, P.O. Box 13656, Portland, OR 97213, (503) 257-7023.

Life Advocates, 17 Maple Street, Allendale, NJ 07401, (201) 934-0886.

Life Chain (National), Please Let Me Live, 3209 Colusa Highway, Yuba City, CA 95993, (916) 671-5500.

Life Dynamics, P.O. Box 185, Lewisville, TX 75067, (214) 436-3885.

March for Life, P.O. Box 90300, Washington, DC 20090, (202) 543-3377.

Operation Rescue, P.O. Box 1180, Binghamton, NY 13902.

Pro-Life Action League, 6160 N. Cicero, Chicago, IL 60646, (312) 777-2900.

Pro-Life Action Ministries, 611 S. Snelling Ave, St. Paul, MN 55116, (612) 690-2960.

Sidewalk Counselors for Life, Box 5123, Wheat Ridge, CO 80034, (303) 238-1687.

Stop Planned Parenthood (STOPP), P.O. Box 8, La Grangeville, NY 12540, (914) 473-3316.

Vital Signs Ministries, P.O. Box 3826, Omaha, NE 68103, (402) 341-8886.

Religious/ Denominational Prolife Groups

Catholics United for Life, 3050 Gap Knob Road, New Hope, KY 40052.

Christian Life Commission of the Southern Baptist Convention, 901 Commerce Street, Suite 550, Nashville, TN 37203, (615) 244-2495.

Jewish Anti-Abortion League, P.O. Box 262, Grazesend Station, Brooklyn, NY 11223, (718) 336-0053.

Lutherans for Life, 275 North Syndicate, St. Paul, MN 55104, (612) 645-5444.

National Conference of Catholic Bishops, c/o Fr. John Gouldrick C.M., 3211 4th Street NE, Washington, DC 20017, (202) 541-3070.

National Organization of Episcopalians for Life, 10523 Main Street, Suite 35, Fairfax, VA 22030, (703) 591-6635.

Orthodox Christians for Life, P.O. Box 805, Melville, NY 11747.

Presbyterians Pro-Life, P.O. Box 19290, Minneapolis, MN 55419, (612) 861-1842.

Rosary Novena for Life, P.O. Box 40213, Memphis, TN 38174, (901) 725-5937.

WELS Lutherans for Life, 2401 N. Mayfair Road, Suite 300, Milwaukee, WI 53226, (414) 774-1331.

Medical Prolife Groups

American Association of Pro-Life OB/GYNS, 4701 N. Federal Highway, Suite B-4, Ft. Lauderdale, FL 33308, (305) 771-9242.

American Association of Pro-Life Pediatricians, 11055 S. St. Louis Avenue, Chicago, IL 60655, (312) 233-8000.

Bernadell, P.O. Box 1897, Old Chelsea Station, New York, NY 10011, (212) 463-7000.

National Association of Pro-Life Nurses, P.O. Box 82, Elysian, MN 56028, (507) 267-4489.

National Doctors for Life, 11511 Tivoli Lane, St. Louis, MO 63146, (314) 567-3446.

Pharmacists for Life International, P.O. Box 130, Ingomar, PA 15127, (412) 487-8960.

Physicians for Moral Responsibility, P.O. Box 98257, Tacoma, WA 98498.

Value of Life Committee, 637 Cambridge Street, Brighton, MA 02135, (617) 787-4400.

World Federation of Doctors Who Respect Human Life, H. Serruyslaan 76, B-8400 Ostend, Belgium.

Quality Brochures for Personal or Mass Distribution

"Facts of Life," Human Development Resource Council, 3961 Holcomb Bridge Road, Suite 200, Norcross, GA 30092.

"The First Nine Months," Focus on the Family, Colorado Springs, CO, 80995, (719) 531-3400.

"They're Forgetting Someone" and "Tiny Fist" fliers and bulletin inserts, Right to Life of Michigan Educational Fund, 2340 Porter Street SW, P.O. Box 901, Grand Rapids, MI 49509, (616) 532-2300.

"Children—Things We Throw Away?" "The Questions Most People Ask about Abortion," and "Abortion Clinics: An Inside Look." All available from Last Days Ministries, Box 40, Lindale, TX 75771, (214) 963-8671.

"Facts You Should Know About Abortion," Christian Action Council, 101 W. Broad St., Suite 500, Falls Church, VA, 22046 (703) 237-2100.

"America Must Decide," Please Let Me Live, P.O. Box 10090, Bakersfield, CA 93389, (805) 397-0245. (Effective and inexpensive tabloid format.)

"If someone you know considers an abortion," Life Cycle Books, P.O. Box 420, Lewiston, NY 14092, (416) 690-5860.

"When You Were Formed in Secret/ Abortion in America"; Intercessors for America, P.O. Box 2639, Reston, VA, 22090; or National Right to Life Educational Trust, 419 7th Street NW, Washington DC, 20004.

Brochures to Use With Women Outside Abortion Clinics or Considering Abortion (in addition to some of above)

"Abortion: Your Risks," American Life Lobby, P.O. Box 1350, Stafford, VA 22554, (703) 659-4171.

"Before You Make the Decision," WEBA International, Route 1 Box 821, Venus, TX 76084, (214) 366-3600.

"Have You Been Told Everything You Need to Know About Abortion?" Open Arms, P.O. Box 19835, Indianapolis, Indiana 46219, (317) 359-9950.

"There's More You Need to Know," American Tract Society, Box 462008, Garland, TX 75046.

"Did You Know?" Hayes Publishing, 6304 Hamilton Ave., Cincinnati, OH 45224.

"Life Before Birth," Good News Publishers, 9825 W. Roosevelt Rd., Westchester, IL 60153.

"Behind These Doors," "You Have a Right to Know," "For Men Only" (for boyfriends or husbands); all three of the preceding brochures also available in Spanish. "What I Saw in the Abortion Industry" (by Carol Everett), Easton Publishing Co., P.O. Box 1064, Jefferson City, MO 65102, (314) 635-0609.

Prolife Videos and Films

"The Hard Truth," "Meet the Abortion Providers," "The Eclipse of Reason," "Parents Rights Denied" (Parental Consent Issue), "The Silent Scream," "Prolife Doctors Speak Out," "UltraSound: A Window to the Womb," "The Right to Kill," "Assignment: Life," "Your Crisis Pregnancy," "Tell the Truth" (1990 March for Life), "Champions for Life" (six members of New York Giants). For teenagers: "No Alibis" and "One in a Million." Other videos as well—ask for catalog. American Portrait Films, 503 E. 200th St.,

Euclid, OH 44119, (216) 531-8600 or 1-800-736-4567.

"Preview of a Birth," Human Development Resource Council, 3961 Holcomb Bridge Road Suite 200, Norcross, GA 30092, (404) 447-1598.

"Living Proof," Institute for the Study of Human Reproduction, 6901 Mercy Road, Omaha, NE 68106, (402) 390-6600.

"Baby Choice" and "Fight the Fight" (a Christian music video by popular recording artists), Last Days Ministries, Box 40, Lindale, TX 75771, (214) 963-8671.

"Whatever Happened to the Human Race?" with Francis Schaeffer and Dr. C. Everett Koop; five episodes, Gospel Films, Box 455, Muskegon, MI 49443, (616) 773-3361.

"The First Days of Life," For Life, Inc., Drawer 1279, Tryon, NC 28782.

"A Life Too Brief," Skyline Films, Inc., P.O. Box C 1012, New Rochelle, NY 01804.

"Question and Answers on Abortion," Dr. and Mrs. John Willke, Hayes Publishing, 6304 Hamilton Ave., Cincinnati, OH 45224. (Slide presentation also available.)

"No More Excuses Pro-Life Seminar," and "Pro-Life Boot Camp Video Series," with Gregg Cunningham, Center for Bioethical Reform, 3855 E La Palma Ave. Suite 126, Anaheim, CA 92807, (714) 632-7520.

Miscellaneous Literature, Slides, Cassette Tapes, and Information

American Life League, P.O. Box 1350, Stafford, VA 22554, (703) 759-4171.

Couple to Couple League, 3621 Clenmore Avenue, Cincinnati, OH, 45211.

Easton Publishing Co., P.O. Box 1064, Jefferson City, MO 65102, (314) 635-0609. (Request prolife catalog and samples.)

Focus on the Family, Colorado Springs, CO 80995, (719) 531-3400. (Cassette tapes and booklets; ask for prolife resource list.)

Frontlines Publishing, 415 Cherry SE, Grand Rapids, MI 49503,

(616) 456-6874. (Ask for samples.)

Hayes Publishing Co., 6304 Hamilton Ave., Cincinnati, OH 45224, (513) 681-7559. (Slide presentations)

Human Life International, 7845-E Airpark Road, Gaithersburg, MD, 20879, (301) 670-7884.

Last Days Ministries, Box 40, Lindale, TX 75771, (214) 963-8671.

Right to Life of Michigan, 2340 Porter Street SW, P.O. Box 901, Grand Rapids, MI 49509, (616) 532-2300.

Sun Life, Thaxton, VA 24174, (703) 586-4898.

Special Prolife Products

Large attractive photographs, posters, and billboards of intrauterine preborn babies: Right to Life of Michigan Educational Fund, 2340 Porter Street SW, P.O. Box 901, Grand Rapids, MI 49509, (616) 532-2300.

Quality pre-made newspaper advertisements, T-shirts: Last Days Ministries, Box 40, Lindale, TX 75771, (214) 963-8671.

Newspaper supplement samples: Life Issues, Box 2222, Oklahoma City, OK 73101.

"Precious Feet" pins, buttons, mailing stickers, bumper-stickers, and literature: Heritage House, P.O. Box 730, Taylor, AZ 85939, (602) 536-7592.

T-shirts, rubber stamps, bumper-stickers, etc.: Salt 'n Light, 710 N. Yale, Wichita, KS 67208, (316) 684-7258. Pro-Life Movement, 833 N. St. Mary's St., San Antonio, TX 78205, (512) 225-3437.

T-shirts: The International Youth Pro-Life Federation (IYPLF), P.O. Box 35800, STE. 262, Houston, TX 77235.

Greeting cards: Life Expressions, P.O. Box 10001, Silver Spring, MD 20914, 1-800-736-LIFE. Precious Life Cards, 714 Swarthmore Dr., Newark, DE 19711.

Bank checks with prolife message: Identity Check Printers, Box 149-D, Park Ridge, IL 60068, (312) 992-0882.

Quality polyurethane model of actual size preborn at 10 to 12 weeks: Womanity, 1700 Oak Park Blvd. Annex, Pleasant Hill, CA 94523, (415) 943-6424.

Quality models of unborn at 4, 6, 10, 14, and 18 weeks, in display box: NRL Educational Trust Fund, 419 7th St. NW, Suite 500, Washington, DC 20004 (202) 626-8809.

Prolife calendar: Choose Life Calendar, The Light House, 14098 E. Meyer Blvd., Kansas City, MO 64131.

"Pre-View of a Birth," large attractive educational booklet on human development from conception to birth: Human Development Resource Council, 3961 Holcomb Bridge Road, Suite 240A, Norcross, GA 30092, (404) 447-0759.

Books on the Abortion Issue

Ankerberg, John and John Weldon, *When Does Life Begin?* Brentwood, Tenn.: Wolgemuth & Hyatt, 1989.

Beckwith, Francis, *Politically Correct Death*. Grand Rapids, Mich.: Baker Book House, 1993.

Brennan, William, *The Abortion Holocaust*. St. Louis: Landmark Press, 1983.

Brown, Judie, Jerome LeJeune and Robert G. Marshall, *RU-486: The Human Pesticide*. Stafford, Va.: American Life League, n.d.

Davis, John J., *Abortion and the Christian*. Phillipsburg, N.J.: Presbyterian & Reformed, 1984.

Feminists for Life Debate Handbook. Kansas City, Mo.: Feminists for Life of America.

Fowler, Paul, *Abortion: Toward an Evangelical Consensus*. Portland, Ore.: Multnomah Press, 1987.

Garton, Jean, *Who Broke the Baby?* Minneapolis: Bethany House, 1979.

Hoffmeier, James, ed., *Abortion: A Christian Understanding and Response*. Grand Rapids, Mich.: Baker Book House, 1987.

Kennedy, D. James, *Abortion: Cry of Reality*. Ft. Lauderdale, Fla.: Coral Ridge Ministries, 1989.

Olasky, Marvin, *Abortion Rites: A Social History of Abortion in America*. Wheaton, Ill.: Crossway Books, 1992.

Powell, John, *Abortion: The Silent Holocaust*. Allen, Tex.: Argus, 1981.

Reagan, Ronald and C. Everett Koop, *Abortion and the Conscience of a Nation*. Nashville: Thomas Nelson, 1984.

Reardon, David, *Aborted Women: Silent No More*. Westchester, Ill.: Crossway Books, 1987.

Schaeffer, Francis and C. Everett Koop, *Whatever Happened to the Human Race?* Westchester, Ill.: Crossway Books, 1983.

Shettles, Landrum and David Rorvik, *Rites of Life: The Scientific Evidence for Life Before Birth*. Grand Rapids, Mich.: Zondervan Publishing House, 1983.

Smith, F. LaGard, *When Choice Becomes God*. Eugene, Ore.: Harvest House, 1990.

Sproul, R. C., *Abortion: A Rational Look at An Emotional Issue*. Colorado Springs: NavPress, 1990.

Swindoll, Charles, *Sanctity of Life*. Waco, Tex: Word Publishing, 1990.

Willke, John, *Abortion Questions and Answers*. Cincinnati: Hayes Publishing Co., 1988.

Young, Curt, *The Least of These*. Chicago: Moody Press, 1984.

Books on the Abortion Industry

Everett, Carol, *Blood Money: Getting Rich Off a Woman's Right to Choose.* Sisters, Ore.: Multnomah Books, 1992.

Grant, George, *Grand Illusions: The Legacy of Planned Parenthood.* Brentwood, Tenn.: Wolgemuth & Hyatt, 1988.

Grant, George, *The Quick and the Dead: RU-486 and the New Chemical Warfare Against Your Family*. Westchester, Ill.: Crossway Books, 1991.

Nathanson, Bernard, *Aborting America*. New York: Doubleday, 1979.

_____. *The Abortion Papers: Inside the Abortion Mentality*. New York: Frederick Fell, 1983.

Terry, Randall, *Accessories to Murder*. Brentwood, Tenn.: Wolgemuth & Hyatt, 1990.

Books on Prolife Action and Strategies

Alcorn, Randy, *Is Rescuing Right?* Downers Grove, Ill.: InterVarsity Press, 1990.

Belz, Mark, *Suffer the Little Children*. Westchester, Ill.: Crossway Books, 1989.

Benedict, Patrick, *Organizing a Student Pro-Life Organization*, P.O. Box 40213, Memphis, TN 38174.

Crutcher, Mark, *Firestorm: A Guerrilla Strategy for a Pro-Life America*. Lewisville, Tex.: Life Dynamics, 1992.

Engle, Stan and Fiona, *Putting Together a Newspaper Supplement*, Stafford, Va.: American Life League, 1989.

Glessner, Thomas, *Achieving an Abortion-Free America by 2001*. Portland, Ore.: Multnomah Press, 1990.

Grant, George, *Third Time Around*. Brentwood, Tenn.: Wolgemuth and Hyatt, 1991.

How to Start a Crisis Pregnancy Center, Christian Action Council, 101 W. Broad St., Suite 500, Falls Church, VA 22046, (703) 237-2100.

Marshall, Robert G., *Pro-Life Precinct Power: A Workbook*. Stafford, Va.: American Life League, 1990.

Pierson, Anne, *52 Simple Things You Can Do to Be Pro-Life*. Minneapolis: Bethany House, 1991.

Scheidler, Joseph, *Closed: 99 Ways to Stop Abortion*. Westchester, Ill.: Crossway Books, 1985.

Terry, Randall, *Operation Rescue*. Springdale, Penn.: Whitaker House, 1988.

Books for Women's Counselors and Helpers

Curro, Ellen, *Caring Enough to Help: Counseling at a Crisis Pregnancy Center*. Grand Rapids, Mich.: Baker Book House, 1990.

Freeman, Richard, *The Chicago Method of Abortion Center Street Counseling*. Pro-Life Brotherhood, 350 S. Orchard Drive, Park Forest, IL 60466.

Hill, Jeannie, *Sidewalk Counseling Workbook*. Easton Publishing Co., P.O. Box 1064, Jefferson City, MO 65102, (314) 635-0609.

Michels, Nancy, *Helping Women Recover From Abortion*. Minneapolis: Bethany House, 1988.

Monahan, Mike & Donna, *The Shepherding Family Experience* (for those opening their homes to pregnant girls). The Shepherd's Care, P.O. Box 462, Taylor, AZ 85939.

Pierson, Anne, *Mending Hearts, Mending Lives: A Guide to Extended Family Living*. Shippensburg, Penn.: Destiny Image Publishers, 1987.

Zimmerman, Martha, *Should I Keep My Baby?* Minneapolis: Bethany House, 1983.

Responding to a Woman With a Crisis Pregnancy; Struggling with a Crisis Pregnancy: Four Personal Stories; Help for Pregnant Teens. Colorado Springs: Focus on the Family.

Books on Post-Abortion Healing for Women and Their Helpers

Baker, Don, *Beyond Choice: The Abortion Story No One is Telling.* Portland, Ore.: Multnomah Press, 1985.

Cochrane, Linda, *Women in Rama: A Postabortion Bible Study.* Falls Church, Va.: Christian Action Council, 1987.

Koerbel, Pam, *Abortion's Second Victim.* Wheaton, Ill.: Victor Books, 1986.

Mannion, Michael, *Abortion and Healing.* Kansas City, Mo.: Sheed and Ward, 1986.

Peretti, Frank, *Tilly.* Westchester, Ill.: Crossway Books, 1988.

Reisser, Teri and Paul, *Help for the Post-Abortion Woman.* Grand Rapids, Mich.: Zondervan Publishing House, 1989.

Selby Terry, *The Mourning After.* Grand Rapids, Mich.: Baker Book House, 1990.

Speckhard, Anne, *Postabortion Counseling: A Manual for Christian Counselors.* Falls Church, Va.: Christian Action Council.

Trimble, Holly, *Healing Post Abortion Trauma.* Stafford, Va.: American Life League, 1989.

Winkler, Kathleen, *When the Crying Stops.* Milwaukee: Northwestern Publishing House, 1992.

Books on Adoption

Anderson, Anne Kiemel, *And With the Gift Came Laughter.* Wheaton, Ill.: Tyndale House, 1987.

Donnelly, Douglas, *A Guide to Adoption.* Colorado Springs: Focus on the Family, 1988.

National Committee on Adoption, *The Adoption Fact Book.* Washington, D.C.: NCA, 1989.

Project Share, *The Adoption Option: A Guidebook for Pregnancy Counselors.* Rockville, Md.: Project Share, 1986.

A Case for Adoption, Colorado Springs: Focus on the Family, 1991.

Prochastity Curricula and Abstinence Education

Alliance for Chastity Education, P.O. Box 1350, Stafford, VA 22554, (703) 659-4171.

Character Curriculums, Inc., 112 E. Church, Cuero, TX 77954.

Deppa Publications, P.O. Box 383, Sumter, SC 29151, (803) 775-1098.

National Association for Abstinence Education, 6201 Leesburg Pike, Suite 404, Falls Church, VA 22044, (703) 532-9459.

Project Respect, P.O. Box 97, Golf, IL 60029.

Respect Inc., P.O. Box 349, Bradley, IL 60915, (815) 932-8389.

Seton Home Study School, One Kidd Lane, Front Royal, VA 22630, (703) 636-9990.

Teen-Aid, N. 1330 Calispel, Spokane, WA 99201, (509) 328-2080.

Womanity, 1700 Oak Park Blvd., Annex, Pleasant Hill, CA 94523, (510) 943-6424.

Prolife Speakers and Trainers (contact other listed organizations as well)

Randy Alcorn, Eternal Perspective Ministries, 2229 E. Burnside #23, Gresham, OR 97030, (503) 663-6481.

Judie Brown (and others), American Life League, P.O. Box 1350, Stafford, VA 22554, (703) 659-4171.

Mark Crutcher, Life Activist Seminar, P.O. Box 185, Lewisville, TX 75067, (214) 436-3885.

Gregg Cunningham, Center for Bio-Ethical Reform, 3855 E. La Palma Avenue, Suite 126, Anaheim, CA 92807, (714) 632-7520.

Carol Everett, 17430 Campbell Road, Suite 206, Dallas, TX 75252, (214) 931-2273.

Wanda Franz (and others), National Right to Life Committee, Suite 500, 419 7th Street NW, Washington, DC 20004, (202) 626-8800.

George Grant, Legacy Communications, P.O. Box 680365, Franklin, TN 37068, (615) 794-2898.

Gianna Jessen (abortion survivor), 612 Calle Ganadero, San Clemente, CA 92672, (714) 366-0727.

Frederica Mathewes-Green, Feminists for Life of America, 811 East 47th Street, Kansas City, MO 64110, (816) 753-2130.

Dr. Beverly McMillan, 1501 N. State Street, Jackson, MS 39202, (601) 948-6634.

Dr. Bernard Nathanson, Bernadel, P.O. Box 1897, Old Chelsea Station, NY 10011.

Mark Newman, Frontline Commmunication Services, 1493 Palomar Drive, San Marcas, CA 92069, (619) 737-9684.

Joseph M. Scheidler, Pro-Life Action League, 6160 N. Cicero Avenue, Suite 600, Chicago, IL 60646, (312) 777-2900.

Randall Terry, P.O. Box 570, Windsor, NY 13865.

Cal Thomas, Los Angeles Times Syndicate, P.O. Box 17725, Washington, DC 20041, (703) 361-9440.

Kathy Walker, WEBA, Route 1 Box 821, Venus, TX 76084, (214) 366-3600.

NOTES

INTRODUCTION: WHY THIS BOOK IS NECESSARY

1. National Center for Health Statistics, Atlanta, Georgia.

2. "Abortion: Facts at a Glance" (New York: Planned Parenthood of America), 1.

3. Edward Lenoski, *Heartbeat* vol. 3, no. 4, December 1980; cited by John Willke, *Abortion Questions and Answers* (Cincinnati: Hayes Publishing Co., 1988), 140-41.

4. U.S. Department of Health and Human Services, Center for Disease Control, Abortion Surveillance Report, May 1983.

5. Alan Guttmacher Institute, "Abortion and Women's Health," 1990.

6. James Patterson and Peter Kim, *The Day America Told the Truth* (New York: Prentice Hall Press, 1991), 32.

7. *Newsweek*, 14 January 1985, 22.

8. Marvin Olasky, *The Prodigal Press* (Westchester, Ill.: Crossway Books, 1988), 116.

9. *Between the Lines*, May 1989.

10. *Washington Post*, 9 April 1989.

11. David Shaw, "Abortion Foes Say Media Bias Most Evident in Terminology," *The Oregonian*, 6 August 1990, A2.

12. John Leo, "Is the Press Straight on Abortion?" *U.S. News and World Report*, 16 July 1990, 17.

13. David Kupelian and Mark Masters, "Pro-choice 1990: Skeletons in the Closet," *New Dimensions*, October 1990, 22.

14. Shaw, "Abortion Foes."

15. Ibid.

16. Jerry Adler, "Taking Offense," *Newsweek*, 24 December 1990, 54.

PART ONE: ARGUMENTS CONCERNING LIFE, HUMANITY, AND PERSONHOOD
Argument 1

1. Polly Rothstein and Marian Williams, "Choice" (New York: Westchester Coalition for Legal Abortion, 1983), printed and distributed by The NARAL Foundation, Washington, D. C.

2. Bradley M. Patten, *Human Embryology*, 3rd ed. (New York: McGraw Hill, 1968), 43.

3. Keith L. Moore, *The Developing Human: Clinically Oriented Embryology*, 2nd ed. (Philadelphia: W.B. Saunders, 1977), 1.

4. Ibid., 12.

5. J. P. Greenhill and E. A. Friedman, *Biological Principles and Modern Practice of Obstetrics* (Philadelphia: W. B. Saunders, 1974), 17 (cf. 23).

6. Louis Fridhandler, "Gametogenesis to Implantation," *Biology of Gestation*, vol. 1, ed. N.S. Assau (New York: Academic Press, 1968), 76.

7. E. L. Potter and J. M. Craig, *Pathology of the Fetus and the Infant*, 3rd ed. (Chicago: Year Book Medical Publishers, 1975), vii.

8. Time Magazine and Rand McNally, *Atlas of the Body* (New York: Rand-McNally, 1980), 139, 144.

9. "Pregnancy," The New Encyclopedia Britannica, 15th ed., Macropedia, vol. 14 (Chicago: Encyclopedia Britannica, 1974), 968.

10. Report, Subcommittee on Separation of Powers to Senate Judiciary Committee S-158, 97th Congress, 1st Session 1981.

11. Landrum Shettles and David Rorvik, *Rites of Life: The Scientific Evidence of Life Before Birth* (Grand Rapids, Mich.: Zondervan Publishing House, 1983), 113.

12. Ashley Montague, *Life Before Birth* (New York: Signet Books, 1977), vi.

13. Bernard N. Nathanson, "Deeper Into Abortion," *New England Journal of Medicine,* 291 (1974):1189-90.

14. Bernard Nathanson, *Aborting America* (Garden City, N.Y.: Doubleday, 1979).

15. Shettles and Rorvik, *Rites of Life*, 103.

16. John C. Willke, *Abortion Questions and Answers* (Cincinnati: Hayes Publishing, 1988), 42.

17. Report, Subcommittee on Separation of Powers to Senate Judiciary Committee S-158, 97th Congress, 1st Session 1981, 7.

Argument 2

1. John G. Davis, *Abortion and the Christian* (Phillipsburg, N.J.: Presbyterian & Reformed Publishing Co., 1984), 23.

2. "Brain Dead Woman Gives Birth," *The Oregonian*, 31 July 1987.

3. From a November 1970 speech titled "The Termination of Pregnancy or the Extermination of the Fetus." Cited by Jean Garton, *Who Broke the Baby*? (Minneapolis: Bethany House Publishers, 1979), 41-42.

4. Dr. Peter Nathanielsz, cited by Sharon Begley, "Do You Hear What I Hear?" *Newsweek*, Special Summer Edition 1991, 14.

5. Mark Crutcher, "Abortion Questions They'd Rather Duck," *Focus on the Family Citizen*, 20 May 1991, 4.

Argument 3

1. Dorothea Kerslake and Donn Casey, "Abortion Induced by Means of the Uterine Aspirator," *Obstetrics and Gynecology* 30 (July 1967):37, 43.

2. Naomi Wade, "Aborted Babies Kept Alive for Bizarre Experiments," *National Examiner*, 19 August 1980, 20-21.

3. Raul Hilberg, *The Destruction of European Jews* (Chicago: Quadrangle Books, 1967), 567-68.

4. John Jefferson Davis, *Abortion and the Christian* (Phillipsburg, N.J.: Presbyterian and Reformed Publishing Co., 1984), 23. Davis cites as a source R. Houwink, *Data: Mirrors of Science* (1970), 104-90.

5. Lennart Nilsson, "Drama of Life Before Birth," *Life*, 30 April 1965.

6. Sharon Begley, "Do You Hear What I Hear?" *Newsweek*, Special Summer Edition 1991, 14.

7. "The Facts of Life" (Norcross, Ga.: Human Development Resource Council), 2.

8. These are well-established scientific facts. See, for instance, Landrum Shettles and David Rorvik, *Rites of Life: The Scientific Evidence for Life Before Birth* (Grand Rapids, Mich.: Zondervan Publishing House, l983), 41-66.

9. "Abortion: Facts at a Glance," Planned Parenthood Federation of America, 1.

10. "The Doctor's Dilemma," *Newsweek*, 17 July 1989, 25.

11. Dr. Hicks' audio tape of an unborn child's beating heart at six weeks and five days of development is available for $3.00 from Cincinnati Right to Life, 1802 W. Galbraith Road, Cincinnati, OH 45239.

12. Bernard Nathanson, *Aborting America* (New York: Doubleday, 1979).

13. Ellen Kreuger, quoted by *Winnipeg Sun*, cited in *Kansans for Life*, May 1991, 9.

14. Ibid.

15. "Abortion: For Survival," a video produced by the Fund for the Feminist Majority.

16. Leonide M. Tanner, ed., "Developing Professional Parameters: Nursing and Social Work Roles in the Care of the Induced Abortion Patient," *Clinical Obstetrics and Gynecology* 14 (December 1971):1271.

17. Paul Marx, *The Death Peddlers: War on the Unborn* (Collegeville, Minn.: St. John's University Press, 1971), 21.

18. *Feminists for Life Debate Handbook* (Kansas City, Mo.: Feminists for Life of America, n.d.), 3.

Argument 4

1. Faye Wattleton, in a debate following TNT's airing of "Abortion: For Survival," produced by the Fund for the Feminist Majority.

2. Carl Sagan and Ann Druyan, "Is It Possible to Be Pro-Life and Pro-Choice?" *Parade*, 22 April 1990, 4.

3. *The First Nine Months* (Colorado Springs.: Focus on the Family), 3.

4. *Preview of a Birth* (Norcross, Ga.: Human Development Resource Center, 1991), 4.

5. Warren Hern, "Operative Procedures and Technique," *Abortion Practice* (Boulder, Colo.: Warren Hern, n.d.), 154.

6. Dr. Thomas W. Hilgers, Dennis J. Horan and David Mall, eds., *New Perspectives on Human Abortion* (Frederick, Md.: University Publications of America Inc./Aletheia Books, 1981), 351.

7. Paul Ramsey, "Points in Deciding About Abortion," *The Morality of Abortion: Legal and Historical Perspectives*, ed. John T. Noonan (Cambridge, Mass.: Harvard University Press, 1970), 66-67.

Argument 5

1. Roland M. Nardone, "The Nexus of Biology and the Abortion Issue," *The Jurist*, Spring 1973, 154.

2. Carl Sagan and Ann Druyan, "Is It Possible to Be Pro-Life and Pro-Choice?" *Parade*, 22 April 1990, 5.

3. Joseph Fletcher, "Indicators of Humanhood: A Tentative Profile of Man," *The Hastings Center Report* 2 (November 1972), 1. Cited by Paul Fowler, *Abortion: Toward an Evangelical Consensus* (Portland, Ore.: Multnomah Press, 1987), 36.

4. Ashley Montague, *Sex, Man and Society* (New York: G. P. Putnam and Sons, 1967). Cited by Fowler, 34-35.

5. *Roe v. Wade*, 410 U.S., 1973.

6. Associated Press, cited in Christian Action Council's *Action Line*, March/April 1991.

7. Sharon Begley, "Do You Hear What I Hear?" *Newsweek*, Special Summer Edition 1991, 12.

8. Ibid.

9. T. Verney and J. Kelley, *The Secret Life of the Unborn Child* (New York: Delta Books, 1981).

10. H. B. Valman and J. F. Pearson, "What the Fetus Feels." (This is a printed article with no reference to the publication in which it appeared. Dr. Valman is consultant pediatrician at Northwick Park Hospital and Clinical Research Center in Harrow; Pearson is senior lecturer and consultant obstetrician and gynecologist at Welsh National School of Medicine in Cardiff.)

11. John Willke, *Abortion Questions and Answers*, (Cincinnati: Hayes Publishing Co., 1988), 53.

12. Begley, "Do You Hear?" 14.

13. Peter Singer, *Practical Ethics* (1979), 97. Cited by Charles E. Rice, *Fifty Questions* (New Hope, Ky.: Cashel Institute, 1986), 64-65.

14. Peter Singer, "Sanctity of Life or Quality of Life," *Pediatrics*, July 1983, 129.

15. Winston L. Duke, "The New Biology," *Reason*, August 1972.

16. Charles Hartshorne, "Concerning Abortion: An Attempt at a Rational View," *The Christian Century*, 21 January 1981, 42-45.

Argument 6

1. *Roe v. Wade*, 410 U.S. 113 (1973), 38.

2. Molly Yard, quoted in "Voices of the Abortion Debate," *New Dimensions*, October 1990, 109.

3. Kenneth L. Woodward, "The Hardest Question," *Newsweek*, 14 January 1985, 29.

4. F. LaGard Smith, *When Choice Becomes God* (Eugene, Ore.: Harvest House, 1990), 146.

Argument 8

1. Jean Staker Garton, *Who Broke the Baby?* (Minneapolis: Bethany House Publishers, 1979), 7-8.

2. Gina Kolata, "Infant Healthy after Surgery in the Womb," *The Oregonian*, 31 May 1990, A16.

3. Pat Ohlendorf-Moffat, "Surgery Before Birth," *Discover*, February 1991, 59.

4. "A New Ethic for Medicine and Society," editorial, *California Medicine* (September 1970), 68.

5. Fred Leeson, "Judge Sends Mother to Jail to Protect Unborn Child," *The Oregonian*, 9 December 1989, A1.

6. Ann McDaniel, "Home Remedy Abortions," *Newsweek*, 17 July 1989, 25.

7. Marvin Olasky, *The Prodigal Press* (Westchester, Ill.: Crossway Books, 1988), 116.

8. Barbara Cornell, "Do the Unborn Have Rights?" *Time*, Special Fall Edition 1990, 23.

9. Volvo advertisement *Time*, 29 October 1990, inside back cover.

10. Chrysler advertisement, *Time*, 15 October 1990, 28-29.

11. "The Unborn and the Born Again," editorial, *The New Republic*, 2 July 1977, 6.

12. Magda Denes, "The Question of Abortion," *Commentary* 62 (December 1976), 6.

PART TWO: ARGUMENTS CONCERNING RIGHTS AND FAIRNESS

Argument 9

1. Cited by John Leo in "The Moral Complexity of Choice," *U.S. News & World Report*, 11 December 1989, 64.

2. Ibid.

3. William Tillman, *Christian Ethics:A Primer* (Nashville: Broadman Press, 1986), 114.

4. Peter Singer and Helen Kuhse, "On Letting Handicapped Infants Die," in *The Right Thing to Do: Basic Readings in Moral Philosophy*, ed. James Rachels (New York: Random House, 1989), 146.

5. "Abortion: Facts at a Glance," Planned Parenthood Federation of America, 1.

6. Judith Jarvis Thomson, *Philosophy and Public Affairs* 1 (1971):47-66.

Argument 10

1. Mary O'Brien Drum, "Meeting in the Radical Middle," *Sojourners,* November 1980, 23.

Argument 11

1. Mary Anne Warren, "On the Moral and Legal Status of Abortion," in *The Problem of Abortion,* 2d ed., ed. Joel Feinberg (Belmont, Calif.: Wadsworth, 1984), 103.

2. *Feminists for Life Debate Handbook* (Kansas City, Mo.: Feminists for Life of America, n.d.), 16.

Argument 12

1. Randy Alcorn, *Christians in the Wake of the Sexual Revolution* (Portland, Ore.: Multnomah Press, 1985), 175-87.

2. See Robert Jay Lifton, *The Nazi Doctors: Medical Killing and the Psychology of Genocide* (New York: Basic Books, 1986).

3. Mark Baker, "Men on Abortion," *Esquire*, March 1990, 114-25.

Argument 13

1. Cited by Charmaine Yoest, "Why Is Adoption So Difficult?" *Focus on the Family Citizen*, 17 December 1990, 10.

2. "Adoption: The Forgotten Alternative," *New Dimensions*, October 1990, 32.

3. Yoest, 10.

4. Ibid.

Argument 14

1. Susan B. Anthony, *The Revolution*, 8 July 1869, 4(1):4.

2. Mattie Brinkerhoff, *The Revolution*, 9 April 1868, 1(14):215-16.

3. Elizabeth Cady Stanton, from a letter in Julia Ward Howe's journal, 16 October 1873, available at Houghton Library, Harvard University.

4. R. C. Sproul, *Abortion: A Rational Look at An Emotional Issue* (Colorado Springs: NavPress, 1990), 117-18.

5. Guy M. Condon, "You Say Choice, I Say Murder," *Christianity Today*, 24 June 1991, 22.

6. Feminists for Life of America, 811 East 47th Street, Kansas City, MO 64110.

7. Mary Ann Schaefer, quoted by Catherine and William Odell, *The First Human Right* (Toronto: Life Cycle Books, 1983), 39-40.

8. Kate Michelman, quoted in *New York Times*, 10 May 1988.

9. *Feminists for Life Debate Handbook* (Kansas City, Mo.: Feminists for Life of America, n.d.), 17.

10. Rosemary Bottcher, "Feminism: Bewitched by Abortion," in *To Rescue the Future*, ed. Dave Andrusko (New York: Life Cycle Books, 1983).

11. D. James Kennedy, *Abortion: Cry of Reality* (Lauderdale, Fla.: Coral Ridge Ministries, 1989), 13.

12. Supreme Court 476 U.S. at 762, *Thornburgh*.

13. *Feminists for Life Debate Handbook*, 7.

14. Ibid., 16.

15. Robert Stone, "Women Endangered Species in India," *The Oregonian,* 14 March 1989, B7.

16. Jo McGowan, "In India They Abort Females," *Newsweek*, 13 February 1989.

17. "Asia: Discarding Daughters," *Time*, Special Fall Edition 1990, 40.

18. *Medical World News*, 1 December 1975, 45.

19. John Leo, "Baby Boys, to Order", *U.S. News and World Report*, 9 January 1989, 59.

Argument 15

1. F. LaGard Smith, *When Choice Becomes God* (Eugene, Ore.: Harvest House, 1990), 192-93.

2. David Reardon, *Aborted Women: Silent No More* (Westchester, Ill.: Crossway Books, 1987), 10.

3. Testimonies of clinic workers in "The Abortion Providers," a video produced by Pro-Life Action League, Chicago, Ill. Confirmed by former abortion clinic owner Carol Everett, in private telephone conversation between her, Frank Peretti, and the author on 24 May 1991.

4. *Feminists for Life Debate Handbook* (Kansas City, Mo.: Feminists for Life of America, n.d), 12.

5. Ibid., 15.

6. "Abortion: Facts at a Glance," Planned Parenthood Federation of America, 1.

Argument 16

1. Roger B. Taney, cited by James C. Dobson and Gary L. Bauer, *Children at Risk* (Waco, Tex.: Word Publishing, 1990), 141.

2. Ibid.

PART THREE: ARGUMENTS CONCERNING SOCIAL ISSUES
Argument 17

1. D. James Kennedy, *Abortion: Cry of Reality* (Ft. Lauderdale, Fla.: Coral Ridge Ministries, 1989), 21.

2. The Michael Fund, 400 Penn Center, Pittsburgh, PA 15146.

3. "Adoption: the Forgotten Alternative," *New Dimensions*, October 1990, 32.

4. "Born Unwanted: Developmental Consequences for Children of Unwanted Pregnancies," Planned Parenthood Federation of America, n.d.

5. *Nine Reasons Why Abortion Is Legal* (New York: Planned Parenthood Federation of America, 1989), 6.

6. Planned Parenthood Federation of America 1990 Services Report.

Argument 18

1. Edward Lenoski, *Heartbeat*, vol. 3, no. 4, December 1980; cited by John Willke, *Abortion Questions and Answers* (Cincinnati: Hayes Publishing Co., 1988), 140-41.

2. Report of the National Center of Child Abuse and Neglect, U.S. Department of Health and Human Services, 1973-1982.

3. Ibid.

4. U.S. Department of Health and Human Services Report; National Study on Child Abuse and Neglect Reporting, The American Humane Association, 1981 and 1991; 1977 Analysis of Child Abuse and Neglect Research, U.S. Dept. of H.E.W., 1978.

5. Nancy Michels, *Helping Women Recover from Abortion* (Minneapolis: Bethany House, 1988), 168.

6. Philip G. Ney, "A Consideration of Abortion Survivors," *Child Psychiatry and Human Development* (vol. 13-3), Spring 1983, 172-73.

7. Philip G. Ney, "Relationship between Abortion and Child Abuse," *Canadian Journal of Psychiatry* (November 1979):611-12.

8. Michels, *Helping Women*, 169-70.

9. Cited by James Dobson, "Focus on the Family" radio broadcast, 21 June 1991.

Argument 19

1. *Nine Reasons Why Abortion Is Legal* (New York: Planned Parenthood Federation of America, 1989), 5.

2. "Vital Statistics," Microsoft Corporation, 1988. Sources: Alan Guttmacher Institute; U.S. Centers for Disease Control.

3. "Abortion in the United States," Alan Guttmacher Institute, n.d., 1.

4. Frederica Matthewes-Green, "Abortion and Women's Rights," *All About Issues*, March-April 1992, 13.

5. John J. Davis, *Abortion and the Christian* (Phillipsburg, N.J.: Presbyterian & Reformed Publishing Co., 1984), 68-69.

6. Due to the difficulty at the time of obtaining originals of some issues of the *Birth Control Review,* in a few of the citations in the original edition of this book I relied on secondary sources I thought to be accurate. Unfortunately, several quotations attributed to Margaret Sanger were inaccurate, or at least the citations were inaccurate. Since I have not located these statements in any original documents, I can only assume they are not authentic. I apologize for this error and have corrected it in this edition. Citations from Sanger and the *Birth Control Review* in this edition are limited to quotations from copies of original documents now in my possession.

7. Margaret Sanger, *Pivot of Civilization* (New York: Brentano's Publishers, 1922), 176.

8. Ibid., 177

9. Ibid., 112, 116.

10. Ibid., 113.

11. Ibid., 115.

12. Havelock Ellis, "The World's Racial Problem," *Birth Control Review*, October 1920, 14-16; Theodore Russell Robie, "Towards Race Betterment," *BCR*, April 1933, 93-95; Ernst Rudin, "Eugenic Sterilization: An Urgent Need," *BCR*, April 1933, 102-4.

13. C.O. McCormick, "Defective Families," *Birth Control Review*, April 1933, 98.

14. Havelock Ellis, "Birth Control and Sterilization," *Birth Control Review*, April 1933, 104.

15. Marvin Olasky, *Abortion Rites: A Social History of Abortion in America* (Wheaton, Ill.: Crossway Books, 1992), 256-57.

16. Ibid., 258.

17. Ibid., 259.

18. Ibid., 259-63.

19. Sanger, *Pivot of Civilization*, 116-17.

Argument 20

1. John Willke, *Abortion Questions and Answers* (Cincinnati: Hayes Publishing Co., 1988), 158.

2. Landrum Shettles and David Rorvik, *Rites of Life: The Scientific Evidence for Life before Birth* (Grand Rapids, Mich.: Zondervan Publishing House, 1983), 152-53; Willke, *Abortion Questions*, 232-233.

3. "Investigational Contraceptives," *Drug Newsletter*, May 1987, 34; *Contraceptive Technology Update*, January 1990, 5.

4. *Newsweek*, 30 March 1981; cited by Willke, *Abortion Questions*, 159.

5. Roy Clinebelle, *Abortions: Alarming Socioeconomic Losses* (Stafford, Va.: American Life Lobby, n.d.), 3.

6. Willke, *Abortion Questions*, 162.

7. Clinebelle, *Abortions*, 11.

8. Willke, *Abortion Questions*, 163.

9. Marilyn vos Savant, "The World," *Reader's Digest*, February 1992, 91.

10. Robert Evangelisto, *The Moral and Logical Arguments against Abortion* (Stafford, Va.: American Life League, n.d.), 1.

11. John Whitehead, *The End of Man* (Westchester, Ill.: Crossway Books, 1986), 195.

12. Bently Class, quoted by George Will, *The Pursuit of Happiness and Other Sobering Thoughts* (New York: Harper Colophon, 1978), 61.

13. "Prochoice or No Choice?" *Christianity Today*, 4 November 1988.

14. George Grant, *Grand Illusions: The Legacy of Planned Parenthood* (Brentwood, Tenn.: Wolgemuth & Hyatt, 1988), 25.

15. Leo Alexander, "Medical Science Under Dictatorship," *New England Journal of Medicine* (14 July 1989):39-47.

Argument 21

1. Martin Luther King, Jr., *Strength to Love* (New York: William Collins & World Publishing, 1963), 33.

2. Bernard Nathanson, *Aborting America* (New York: Doubleday, 1979), 40-41.

3. Daniel Callahan, "Abortion: Thinking and Experiencing," *Christianity and Crisis*, 8 January 1973, 296.

4. David C. Reardon, *Aborted Women: Silent No More* (Westchester, Ill.: Crossway Books, 1987), 333.

Argument 22

1. *The Boston Globe,* 31 March 1989.

2. Ibid.

3. *Los Angeles Times* poll, cited by Charles Colson, "A Time to Disobey?" *Focus on the Family Citizen,* June 1989, 15.

4. *New York Times* poll cited in *The Washington Times,* 28 February 1991, 1.

5. "Poll: Abortion Key for Voters," *USA Today,* 2 January 1990, 1A, 2A.

6. "Abortion Legislation Poll," *Newsweek,* 17 July 1989, 20.

7. "Abortion and Moral Beliefs: A Survey of American Opinion," conducted by the Gallup Organization, commissioned by Americans United for Life, Washington, D.C., 1991, 10.

8. Ibid., 4.

9. Ibid., 5.

10. Ibid., 9.

11. Ibid., 11.

12. Ibid.

13. Ibid., 5.

14. "Gallup Poll: America is Pro-Life," *The Washington Times,* 28 February 1991, 1.

15. "Abortion and Moral Beliefs," 1991 Gallup Poll, 13.

16. Ibid., 15.

17. Ibid., 14.

18. News Release on Gallup Poll on Abortion, Americans United for Life, 28 February 1991, 2.

19. "Abortion and Moral Beliefs," 1991 Gallup Poll, 49.

20. Ibid.

21. Ibid., 17.

22. John Willke, *Abortion Questions and Answers* (Cincinnati: Hayes Publishing Co., 1988), 19-20.

23. Ibid.

24. Bob Woodward and Scott Armstrong, *The Brethren: Inside the Supreme Court* (New York: Avon Books, 1979), 215.

25. Ibid., 276.

26. David Kaplan, "Is *Roe* Good Law?" *Newsweek,* 27 April 1992, 50.

27. *Doe* v. *Bolton,* U.S. Supreme Court, January 1973, No. 70-40, IV, 11.

28. Essentially, the Supreme Court's 1989 *Webster* decision empowered states to regulate abortion after the point of viability. In addition, the Court allowed the state of Missouri to restrict the use of public funds, facilities, and personnel for abortion.

29. Ronald Reagan, *Abortion and the Conscience of the Nation* (Nashville: Thomas Nelson, 1984), 15.

30. Ibid., 16.

Argument 23

1. "Gallup Poll: America Is Pro-Life," *The Washington Times*, 28 February 1991, 1.

2. Anne Catherine Speckhard, "The Psycho-Social Aspects of Stress Following Abortion," (Arlington, Va.: Family Systems Center, 1985), 1.

3. Marvin Olasky, "The Village's Pro-Life Voice," *Christianity Today*, 24 June 1991, 24.

4. Ibid, 24-26.

5. Bernard Nathanson, *Aborting America* (New York: Doubleday, 1979), 227.

6. Ibid.

7. Ibid.

8. George Grant, *Trial and Error* (Brentwood, Tenn.: Wolgemuth & Hyatt, 1989), 94.

9. Walker P. Whitman, *A Christian History of the American Republic: A Textbook for Secondary Schools* (Boston: Green Leaf Press, 1939, 1948), 42. Cited by Grant, *Trial and Error*, 75.

10. Harold K. Lane, *Liberty! Cry Liberty!* (Boston: Lamb and Lamb Tractarian Society, 1939), 31.

11. David Barton, *The Myth of Separation* (Aledo, Tex.: Wall Builder Press, 1991).

12. James Patterson and Peter Kim, *The Day America Told the Truth* (New York: Prentice Hall Press, 1991).

13. Ibid., 27, 34.

14. Ibid., 61, 201.

PART FOUR: ARGUMENTS CONCERNING HEALTH AND SAFETY
Argument 24

1. Alfred Kinsey, cited by John Willke, *Abortion Questions and Answers* (Cincinnati: Hayes Publishing Co., 1988), 169.

2. Mary Calderone, "Illegal Abortion as a Public Health Problem," *American Journal of Health* 50 (July 1960):949.

3. Bernard Nathanson, *Aborting America* (New York: Doubleday, 1979), 193.

4. Ibid, 42.

5. U.S. Bureau of Vital Statistics.

6. Ibid.

7. Germain Grisez, *Abortion: The Myths, the Realities, and the Arguments* (New York: Corpus Books, 1972), 70.

8. "Abortion: For Survival," a video produced by the Fund for the Feminist Majority.

9. Hani K. Atrash, MD, Theodore Cheek, MD, and Carol Hogue, PhD, "Legal Abortion Mortality and General Anesthesia" *American Journal of Obstetrics and Gynecology* (February 1988):420.

10. Michael Kaffrissen, et al., "Cluster of Abortion Deaths at a Single Facility," *Obstetrics and Gynecology* (September 1986):387.

11. "Jury Orders Abortionist to Pay $25 Million Judgment," *Life Advocate*, June 1991, 25.

12. Dawn Stover, "Cause of Death: Legal Abortion," *Life Advocate*, August 1991, 3.

13. Carol Everett, personal conversation with the author and Frank Peretti on 24 May 1991.

14. U.S. Center of Vital Statistics.

15. James A. Miller, "A Tale of Two Abortions," *Human Life International Reports*, March 1991, 1.

16. Willke, *Abortion Questions*, 99.

17. Frank E. Peretti, *Prophet* (Wheaton, Ill.: Crossway Books, 1992).

18. Dennis Cavanaugh, "Effect of Liberalized Abortion on Maternal Mortality Rates," *American Journal of Obstetrics and Gynecology* (February 1978):375.

19. Gina Kolata, "Self-Help Abortion Movement Gains Momentum," *The New York Times*, 23 October 1989, B12; Janice Perrone, "Controversial Abortion Approach," *American Medical News*, 12 January 1990, 9.

20. David C. Reardon, *Aborted Women: Silent No More* (Westchester, Ill.: Crossway Books, 1987), 301.

Argument 25

1. *American Medical Association Encyclopedia of Medicine*, ed. Charles B. Clayton (New York: Random House, 1989), 58.

2. David C. Reardon, *Aborted Women: Silent No More* (Westchester, Ill.: Crossway Books, 1987), 113.

3. Ibid.

4. Ibid., 113-14.

5. *Family Planning Perspectives*, March/April 1983, 85-86.

6. Ann Aschengrau Levin, "Ectopic Pregnancy and Prior Induced Abortion," *American Journal of Public Health* (March 1982):253.

7. U.S. Department of Health and Human Services, *Morbidity & Mortality Weekly Report*, vol. 33, no. 15, 20 April 1984.

8. Allan Osser, M.D., and Kenneth Persson, M.D., "Postabortal Pelvic Infection Associated with Chlamydia Tracomatis and the Influence of Humoral Immunity," *American Journal of Obstetrics and Gynecology* (November 1984):669-703.

9. Lars Heisterberg, M.D. et al., "Sequelae of Induced First-Trimester Abortion," *American Journal of Obstetrics and Gynecology* (July 1986):79.

10. Ronald T. Burkman, M.D., "Culture and Treatment Results in Endometritis Following Elective Abortion," *American Journal of Obstetrics and Gynecology* (July 1977):556-59.

11. M.C. Pike, "Oral Contraceptive Use and Early Abortion as Risk Factors for Breast Cancer in Young Women," *British Journal: Cancer 1981*, 72-76.

12. David A. Grimes, "Fatal Hemorrhage from Legal Abortion in the United States," *Surgery, Gynecology and Obstetrics* (November 1983):461-66.

13. Ann Anschengrau Levin, "Association of Induced Abortion with Subsequent Pregnancy Loss," *Journal of the American Medical Association* (June 1980):2495-99; Carol Madore, "A Study on the Effects of Induced Abortion on Subsequent Pregnancy Outcome," *American Journal of Obstetrics and Gynecology* (March 1981):516-21; Shari Linn, M.D., "The Relationship Between Induced Abortion and Outcome of Subsequent Pregnancies," *American Journal of Obstetrics and Gynecology* (May 1983):136-40.

14. Janet R. Daling, PhD, "Tubal Infertility in Relation to Prior Induced Abortion," *Fertility and Sterility* (March 1985):389-94.

15. Madore, "Effects of Induced Abortion," 516-21; Linn, "Outcome of Subsequent Pregnancies," 136-40.

16. Linn, "Outcome of Subsequent Pregnancies," 136-40.

17. John A. Richardson and Geoffrey Dixon, "Effects of Legal Termination on Subsequent Pregnancy," *British Medical Journal* (1976): 1303-4.

18. Jeffrey M. Barrett, M.D., "Induced Abortion: A Risk Factor for Placental Previa," *American Journal of Obstetrics and Gynecology* (December 1981):769.

19. Reardon, *Aborted Women*, 106.

20. Thomas W. Hilgers and Dennis J. Horan, *Abortion and Social Justice* (Thaxton, Va.: Sun Life, 1980), 58, 77.

21. Stephen L. Corson, M.D., "Clinical Perspectives: Morbidity and Morality from Second-Trimester Abortions," *The Journal of Reproductive Medicine* (July 1985):505-14.

22. Carol Everett, personal conversation with the author and Frank Peretti on 24 May 1991.

23. James A. Miller, "A Tale of Two Abortions," *Human Life International Reports*, March 1991, 2.

24. Everett, personal conversation.

25. Reardon, *Aborted Women*, 234.

26. Ibid., 106-7.

Argument 26

1. Six actual fifteen- to twenty-two-week babies, victims of saline abortions, are shown in "Baby Choice," a 1986 video available from Americans Against Abortion, Box 40, Lindale, TX 75771.

2. Dorothy F. Chappel, "A Biologist's Concern for Mother and Child," in *Abortion: A Christian Understanding and Response*, ed. James K. Hoffmeier (Grand Rapids, Mich.: Baker Book House, 1987), 163.

3. Curt Young, *The Least of These* (Chicago: Moody Press, 1984), 96.

4. Chappel, "A Biologist's Concern," 161.

5. Carol Everett, personal conversation with the author and Frank Peretti on 24 May 1991.

6. Mark Baker, "Men on Abortion," *Esquire*, March 1990, 120.

7. James Patterson and Peter Kim, *The Day America Told the Truth* (New York: Prentice Hall Press, 1991), 33.

8. David C. Reardon, *Silent No More* (Westchester, Ill.: Crossway Books, 1987), 229.

9. Warren Hern and Billie Corrigan, "What About Us? Staff Reactions to the D & E Procedure," paper presented to the Association of Planned Parenthood Physicians, 26 October 1978, 7

10. Ibid., 1, 4, 5, 6.

11. Magda Denes, *In Necessity and Sorrow: Life and Death in an Abortion Hospital*: (New York: Basic Books, 1976), 50, 58-61.

12. Ibid., 222-23.

13. Bernard Nathanson, *Aborting America* (New York: Doubleday, 1979).

14. Everett, personal conversation.

15. *National Review*, 18 November 1991, 14.

16. "The Abortion Providers," a 1989 video available from Pro-Life Action League, 6160 N. Cicero, Chicago, IL 60646.

17. Ibid.

18. Ibid.

19. Letter to President Reagan, cited by John Willke, *Abortion Questions and Answers* (Cincinnati: Hayes Publishing Co., 1988), 64-65.

20. Willke, *Abortion Questions*, 68.

21. "The Silent Scream," available from American Portrait Films, 503 E. 200th Street, Euclid, OH 44119, (216) 531-8600.

22. Ibid.

Argument 27

1. Mark Baker, "Men on Abortion," *Esquire*, March 1990, 125.

2. "Tearing Down the Wall," *LifeSupport*, Spring/Summer 1991, 1-3.

3. David C. Reardon, *Aborted Women: Silent No More* (Westchester, Ill.: Crossway Books, 1987), 129.

4. Martina Mahler, "Abortion: The Pain No one Talks About," *Women's World*, 24 September 1991, 6.

5. "Tearing Down the Wall," 3.

6. American Psychiatric Association, *Diagnostic and Statistical Manual of Mental Disorders*, revised ed. (1987), 250.

7. Nancy Michels, *Helping Women Recover From Abortion* (Minneapolis: Bethany House, 1988), 35-36.

8. Vincent M. Rue, et al., *A Report on the Psychological Aftermath of Abortion*, 15 September 1987, 7. Submitted to the Surgeon General by the National Right to Life Committee.

9. "Exclusive Interview: U.S. Surgeon General C. Everett Koop," *Rutherford Journal* (Spring 1989):31.

10. Ibid.

11. Catherine A. Barnard, PhD, "Stress Reactions in Women Related to Induced Abortion," Association for Interdisciplinary Research in Values and Social Change (AIRVSC) *Newsletter*, Winter 1991, 1-3.

12. James L. Rogers, "Psychological Consequences of Abortion," an adaptation of a technical study presented to the American Psychological Association and the American Public Health Association, in *Abortion: A Christian Understanding and Response*, ed. James K. Hoffmeier (Grand Rapids, Mich.: Baker Book House, 1987), 186.

13. Ibid, 187.

14. Reardon, *Aborted Women*, 119.

15. John Leo, "Moral Complexity of Choice," *U.S. News and World Report*, 11 December 1989, 64.

16. "Psychological Sequelae of Therapeutic Abortion," editorial, *British Medical Journal* (May 1976):1239.

17. J. R. Ashton, "The Psychological Outcome of Induced Abortion," *British Journal of Obstetrics and Gynecology* (December 1980):1115-22.

18. Ibid.

19. "Report on the Committee on the Operation of the Abortion Law," Ottawa, Canada, 1977, 20-21.

20. Ibid.

21. Reardon, *Aborted Women*, 116.

22. "C. Everett Koop," 31.

23. *Los Angeles Times*, 19 March 1989.

24. Judith S. Wallerstein, "Psychosocial Sequelae of Therapeutic Abortion in Young Unmarried Women," *Archives of General Psychiatry* 27 (December 1972); Carl Tishler, PhD, "Adolescent Suicide Attempts Following Elective Abortion: A Special Case of Anniversary Reaction," *Pediatrics* 68 (November 1981):670-71.

25. Tishler, "Adolescent Suicide."

26. Reardon, *Aborted Women*, 250.

27. Ibid.

28. "Abortion, Inc.," David Kupelian and Jo Ann Gasper, *New Dimensions*, October 1991, 16.

29. Ibid., 14.

30. Ibid., 23.

31. Anne Catherine Speckhard, PhD, "The Psycho-Social Aspects of Stress Following Abortion" (Arlington, Va.: Family Systems Center, 1985), 1.

32. Reardon, *Aborted Women*, 134.

Argument 28

1. "Abortion: Facts at a Glance," Planned Parenthood Federation of America, n.d., 2

2. *The Miami Herald*, 17 September 1989.

3. "Governor Closes 10% of Florida's Clinics," *The Abortion Injury Report*, American Right Coalition, May 1990, 1.

4. *The Chicago Sun Times*, 12 November 1978; cited by Marvin Olasky, *The Prodigal Press* (Westchester, Ill.: Crossway Books, 1988), 134.

5. Pamela Zekman and Pamela Warrick, "The Abortion Profiteers," *Chicago Sun Times*, special reprint 3 December 1978 (original publication 12 November 1978), 15.

6. Ibid., 11-15.

7. David C. Reardon, *Aborted Women: Silent No More* (Westchester, Ill.: Crossway Books, 1987), 245.

8. John Willke, *Abortion Questions and Answers* (Cincinnati: Hayes Publishing Co., 1988), 79.

9. Carol Everett, personal conversation with the author and Frank Peretti on 24 May 1991.

10. Willke, *Abortion Questions*, 79.

11. Curt Young, *The Least of These* (Chicago: Moody Press, 1984), 30.

12. LeBeth Myers, *Women Around the Globe: International Status Report* (London: Guyon Social Resource Center, 1986), 137.

13. Willke, *Abortion Questions*, 186.

14. Ibid.

15. "Pro-Choice 1990: Skeletons in the Closet," *New Dimensions*, October 1990, 31.

16. Ibid.

17. Carol Everett, *Blood Money* (Sisters, Ore.: Multnomah Books, 1992).

18. "Pro-Choice 1990", 27.

19. "Meet the Abortion Providers," video produced by Pro-Life Action League, Chicago, Illinois, 1989.

20. "Pro-Choice 1990," 27.

21. Everett, personal conversation.

22. "Meet the Abortion Providers."

23. Ibid.

24. Warren M. Hern, MD and Billie Corrigan, RN, "What about Us? Staff Reactions to the D & E Procedure" (Boulder, Colo.: Boulder Abortion Clinic), presented to the Association of Planned Parenthood Physicians, 26 October 1978, 7-8.

25. Ann Tilson,"Exposé on Abortion in Wichita," *Kansans for Life*, May 1991, 10.

26. Robert Jay Lifton, *The Nazi Doctors* (New York: Basic Books, 1986), 337-83.

27. *National Review*, 2 March 1992, 12.

28. *World Medical Association Bulletin* 1 (April 1949), 22.

29. *World Medical Association Bulletin* 2 (January 1950), 6-34.

30. American Medical Association statement on abortion, *Medical Holocausts* vol. 1 (Houston: Nordland Publishing International, n.d.), 28-30.

PART FIVE: ARGUMENTS CONCERNING THE HARD CASES
Argument 29

1. Alan F. Guttmacher, "Abortion—Yesterday, Today and Tomorrow," in *The Case for Legalized Abortion Now* (Berkeley, Calif.: Diablo Press, 1967).

2. Landrum Shettles and David Rorvik, *Rites of Life* (Grand Rapids, Mich.: Zondervan Publishing House, 1983), 129.

3. Mimi Hall, "Even When a Life Saved, Abortion a Divisive Issue," *USA Today*, 26 July 1991, 2A.

Argument 30

1. David C. Reardon, *Aborted Women: Silent No More* (Westchester, Ill.: Crossway Books, 1987), 172.

2. "Abortion in the United States," *Facts in Brief*, Alan Guttmacher Institute, n.d.

3. Susan Kitching, *The London Sunday Times*, 11 February 1990.

4. Thomas Hilgers, Dennis Horan, and David Mall, *New Perspectives on Human Abortion* (Frederick, Md.: University Publications of America, 1981), 54.

5. Reardon, *Aborted Women*, 173.

6. Hymie Gordon, "Amniocentesis," *Primum Non Nocere*, September 1980, 4-6.

7. Ibid.

8. C. Everett Koop and Francis Schaeffer, *Whatever Happened to the Human Race?* (Westchester, Ill.: Crossway Books, 1979), 36.

9. John Willke, *Abortion Questions and Answers* (Cincinnati: Hayes Publishing Co., 1988), 211.

10. C. Everett Koop, "The Slide to Auschwitz," in Ronald Reagan, *Abortion and the Conscience of the Nation* (Nashville: Thomas Nelson, 1984), 45-46.

11. Curtis Young, *The Least of These* (Chicago: Moody Press, 1983), 118.

12. W. Peacock, "Active Voluntary Euthanasia," *Issues in Law and Medicine*, 1987. Cited by Willke, *Abortion Questions*, 212.

13. Story told by Jerome LeJeune, cited by Willke, *Abortion Questions*, 211.

14. J. Lloyd and K. Laurence, "Response to Termination of Pregnancy for Genetic Reasons," *Zeitschrift fur Kinderchirurgie* 38, suppl. 2 (1983):98-99.

15. B. Blumberg et al., "The Psychological Sequelae of Abortion Performed for Genetic Indication," *American Journal of Obstetrics and Gynecology* 2 (1975):215-24.

16. R. Furlong and R. Black, "Pregnancy Termination for Genetic Indications: The Impact on Families," *Social Work Health Care* 10 (1984):17-34.

17. Philip Ney, "A Consideration of Abortion Survivors," *Child Psychiatry in Human Development* 13 (1983):168-79.

18. *Feminists for Life Debate Handbook* (Kansas City, Mo.: Feminists for Life of America, n.d.), 18.

Argument 31

1. Jean Staker Garton, *Who Broke the Baby?* (Minneapolis: Bethany House, 1979), 76.

2. "Abortion: Facts at a Glance," Planned Parenthood Federation of America, n.d., 1

3. John C. Willke, *Abortion Questions and Answers* (Cincinnati: Hayes Publishing, 1988), 146-50.

4. John F. Hillabrand, "Dealing with a Rape Case," *Heartbeat*, March 1975, 250.

5. Sue Reily, "Life Uneasy for Woman at Center of Abortion Ruling," *Oregonian*, 9 May 1989, A2.

6. Garton, *Who Broke the Baby?* 77.

7. *Feminists for Life Debate Handbook* (Kansas City, Mo.: Feminists for Life of America, n.d.), 14.

Final Thoughts on the Hard Cases

1. U.S. Department of Health & Human Services, Centers for Disease Control, *Abortion Surveillance Report*, May 1983.

PART SIX: ARGUMENTS AGAINST THE CHARACTER OF PROLIFERS
Argument 32

1. Gregg Cunningham, *Hard Truth User's Guide* (Cleveland: American Portrait Films, 1991), 5-6, 19.

2. "Negative Psychological Impact of Sonography in Abortion," *Ob. Gyn. News*, 15-28 February 1986.

3. Thomas Hilgers and Dennis Horan, eds., *Abortion and Social Justice* (New York: Sheed and Ward, 1972), 292.

4. John Willke, *Abortion Questions and Answers* (Cincinnati: Hayes Publishing Co., 1988), 200-202.

5. Ibid, 203; R. Collins, *Arizona Republic*, 26 March 1981.

6. Thomas Glessner, *Achieving an Abortion-Free America by 2001* (Portland, Ore.: Multnomah Press, 1990), 39.

7. *Abortion "As Birth Control" and Abortion for Gender Selection*, Fact Sheet (New York: Planned Parenthood Federation of America, n.d.), 3.

8. Tom Ehart, "She Was an Aborted Baby . . . and Lived," *Brio*, April 1992, 14-17.

Argument 33

1. Polly Rothstein and Marian Williams, "Choice" (New York: Westchester Coalition for Legal Abortion, 1983), printed and distributed by The NARAL Foundation, Washington, D.C.

2. Abigail Van Buren, "Questions for the Foes of Abortion," *Universal Press Syndicate*, n.d.

3. John Willke, "The Real Woman's Movement," *National Right to Life News*, 14 December 1989, 3.

4. Guy Condon, "You Say Choice, I Say Murder," *Christianity Today*, 24 June 1991, 23.

5. Several news programs have attempted to discredit abortion alternative centers as "phony abortion clinics" that deceive women and give them inaccurate medical information. Out of thousands of such clinics they were able to find a few that could be presented unfavorably. However, even if their portrayal was accurate, this would not discredit the 99 percent of clinics that provide accurate information and loving assistance to women. Many more women have come forward to say that it is abortion clinics, not abortion alternative centers, that have misled them and disseminated inaccurate medical information (see Part 4: Arguments Concerning Health and Safety). Unfortunately, it does not serve the "politically correct" posture of the television networks to do exposés of abortion clinics.

6. "Pro-lifers Shut Out of Hearing," *The Life Advocate*, November 1991, 8.

7. Mark Crutcher, "Abortion Questions They'd Rather Duck," *Focus on the Family Citizen*, 20 May 1991, 2.

Argument 34

1. John Willke, "The Real Woman's Movement," *National Right to Life News*, 14 December 1989, 3.

2. *Feminists for Life Debate Handbook* (Kansas City, Mo.: Feminists for Life of America, n.d.), 21.

3. "Abortion and Moral Beliefs: A Survey of American Opinion," conducted by the Gallup Organization, 1991, 4-7.

4. Willke, "Woman's Movement," 3.

5. Guy Condon, "You Say Choice, I Say Murder", *Christianity Today*, 24 June 1991, 23.

6. David C. Reardon, *Aborted Women: Silent No More* (Westchester, Ill.: Crossway Books, 1987), 71.

7. Willke, "Woman's Movement," 3.

8. Ibid.

9. Clifton Fadimar, ed., *The Little, Brown Book of Anecdotes* (Little, Brown & Co.: Boston, 1985), 18.

10. Donald Granberg, "The Abortion Activists," *Family Planning Perspectives*, July-August 1981, 157-63.

11. Reardon, *Aborted Women*, 70-71.

Argument 35

1. Polly Rothstein and Marian Williams, "Choice" (New York: Westchester Coalition for Legal Abortion, 1983), printed and distributed by The NARAL Foundation, Washington, D.C.

2. John Willke, *Abortion Questions and Answers* (Cincinnati: Hayes Publishing Co., 1988), 180.

Argument 36

1. James T. Burtchaell, "Media's Blind (and Biased) Eye," *The Oregonian*, 15 September 1991, BI-B3.

2. *USA Today*, 22 August 1991.

3. Michael Ebert, "Violence! Mayhem! or How the Media Blew It," *Focus on the Family Citizen*, 18 November 1991, 7.

4. Ibid., 6.

5. Ibid.

6. Ibid, B1

7. Randy Alcorn, *Is Rescuing Right?* (Downers Grove, Ill.: InterVarsity Press, 1990), 169.

8. Ibid., 150-51.

9. Ibid., 84-99.

10. Ibid., 40-56, 100-122.

11. B. D. Colen, "The Anti-Abortion High Ground," *New York Newsday*, 8 November 1988.

12. St. Louis Circuit Court, St. Louis County, Mo., 16 August 1989.

13. Alcorn, *Is Rescuing Right?* 163-64.

14. K.L. Billingsley, "The J Street Five," *National Review*, 16 December 1991, 25.

15. Alcorn, *Is Rescuing Right?* 9.

16. National Abortion Federation, "Incidents of Violence and Disruption against Abortion Providers," Washington, DC: NAF, 1992.

17. David Moore, "Vandals Hit Jakobowski's Clinic," *The Life Advocate*, November 1991, 16-17.

Argument 37

1. Francis Beckwith, "Answering the Arguments for Abortion Rights," *Christian Research Journal*, four-part analysis (Fall 1990, Winter 1991, Spring 1991, Summer 1991).

2. Landrum Shettles and David Rorvik, *Rites of Life* (Grand Rapids, Mich.: Zondervan Publishing House, 1983), 112-13.

3. "Plan Your Children for Health and Happiness" (New York: Planned Parenthood—World Population, 1963), 1.

4. "Abortion" Fact Sheet, Planned Parenthood of Chicago, 2.

5. "Abortion and Moral Beliefs: A Survey of American Opinion," conducted by the Gallup Organization, 1991, 4-5.

6. Ibid.

7. George Will, "The Case of the Unborn Patient" in *The Pursuit of Virtue and Other Tory Notions* (New York: Touchstone, 1982), 109.

8. "Abortion: For Survival," a video produced by the Fund for the Feminist Majority.

9. Ibid.

10. "Nine Reasons Why Abortions Are Legal" (New York: Planned Parenthood Federation of America, 1989), 8-9.

11. Polly Rothstein and Marian Williams, "Choice" (New York: Westchester Coalition for Legal Abortion, 1983), printed and distributed by The NARAL Foundation, Washington, D.C.

Argument 38

1. *Los Angeles Times*, 17 October 1986.

2. "Abortion, Inc.," David Kupelian and Jo Ann Gasper, *New Dimensions*, October 1991, 18.

3. Ibid.

4. Ibid.

5. Ibid., 19.

6. Ibid.

7. *Issues in Brief* 4:3, March 1984, Alan Guttmacher Institute.

8. Robert Ruff, "An Ingenious System for Milking Tax Payers," *New Dimensions*, October 1991, 17.

9. Transcript of Planned Parenthood presentation, 21 April 1986, Ramona High School, Riverside, Calif.

10. Rochelle Sharpe, "She Died Because of a Law," *Ms.*, July/August 1990, 80-81.

11. Frederica Mathewes-Green, "The Becky Bell Tragedy," *Sisterlife*, Fall 1990, 1.

12. Bernard Nathanson, "In Memoriam," *Bernadell Technical Bulletin*, November 1990, 4.

13. James A. Miller, "A Tale of Two Abortions," *Human Life International Reports*, March 1991, 1.

14. Cal Thomas, "New Combatants Join Parental Consent Fight," *The Milwaukee Journal*, 9 August 1990.

15. Nathanson, "In Memoriam," 4.

16. "Exploiting the Bells' Tragic Situation," *National Right to Life News*, 16 August 1990, 14.

17. Thomas, "New Combatants."

18. Ibid.

19. "Bell's Tragic Situation," 14.

20. Miller, "Two Abortions," 11.

Summary Argument
Argument 39

1. Antoinette Bosco, "Touch of Life," *Reader's Digest*, July 1991, 125-26.

2. James Dobson and Gary Bauer, *Children at Risk* (Waco, Tex.: Word Books, 1990), 151.

3. *Mother Jones*, May-June 1991, 31ff.

4. Donald Robinson, "Save Our Babies," *Parade Magazine*, 30 June 1991, 8.

5. "Slaughtering Other Babies," *The Sunday Oregonian*, 18 August 1991, B8.

6. Bernard Nathanson, "Pro-Choice 1990," *New Dimensions*, October 1990, 38.

7. Polly Rothstein and Marian Williams, "Choice" (New York: Westchester Coalition for Legal Abortion, 1983), printed and distributed by The NARAL Foundation, Washington, D.C., 5.

8. 49 N. J. 22, 227A.2d 689 (1967); cited by Cal Thomas, *Uncommon Sense* (Brentwood, Tenn.: Wolgemuth & Hyatt, 1990), 6.

9. George Will, *The Pursuit of Happiness and Other Sobering Thoughts* (New York: Harper Colophon, 1978), 61.

10. Herbert London, "Legalized Abortions and Infanticide," *New Dimensions*, June 1991, 71.

11. Ibid.

12. Will, *Pursuit of Happiness*, 62-63.

13. *Feminists for Life Debate Handbook* (Kansas City, Mo.: Feminists for Life of America, n.d.), 9.

14. Judie Brown, Jerome LeJeune, and Robert G. Marshall, *RU-486: The Human Pesticide* (Stafford, Va.: American Life League, n.d.).

15. George Grant, *The Quick and the Dead: RU 486 and the New Chemical Warfare Against Your Family* (Westchester, Ill.: Crossway Books, 1991).

16. Richard D. Glasow, "RU 486's Dangers Begin to Surface in Media" *National Right to Life News*, 13 August 1991, 6.

17. Charlotte Allen, "Safe and Easy? Not RU-486," *Focus on the Family Citizen*, 16 September 1991, 14-15.

18. Janice Raymond, Renate Klein, and Lynette J. Dumble, *RU 486: Misconceptions, Myths and Morals* (Cambridge: Massachusetts Institute of Technology, 1991).

19. Mary Voboril, "The Abortion Pill," *The Miami Herald*, 13 October 1991, 1J, 4J.

Final Appeals

1. David C. Reardon, *Aborted Women: Silent No More* (Westchester, Ill.: Crossway Books, 1987), 31.

2. Bernard Nathanson, keynote address, National Right to Life Convention, Anaheim, Calif., 26 June 1980.

3. Cal Thomas, *Uncommon Sense* (Brentwood, Tenn.: Wolgemuth & Hyatt, 1990), 7.

4. "News Briefs," *Action*, newsletter of the Rutherford Institute, October 1991, 7.

5. Bernard Nathanson, *The Abortion Papers* (New York: Frederick Fell, 1983), 170.

6. Ibid.

7. "Abortion and Moral Beliefs: A Survey of American Opinion," conducted by the Gallup Organization, 1991, 17.

8. Ibid.

9. *Eugene* (Ore.) *Register Guard*, 7 November 1990.

10. Ibid.

11. "Abortion in the United States," *Facts in Brief* (New York: The Alan Guttmacher Institute, n.d.), 1.

12. The "Hard Truth" video is available from American Portrait Films, 1695 W. Crescent Avenue, Suite 500, Anaheim, CA 92801, 1-800-726-LIVE.

13. Gregg Cunningham of the Center for Bioethical Reform offers an excellent one-day seminar and printed materials concerning the development of such a strategy for churches and prolife groups. He can be contacted at 1003 N. Magnolia, Suite 87, Anaheim, CA 92801; (714) 632-7520. Also, Eternal Perspective Ministries has a "Life Team" program tailored to churches. For information on how to organize and present prolife presentations in your area, write EPM, 2229 E. Burnside #23, Gresham, OR 97030. Or you can call EPM's "Life Team" coordinator, Ron Norquist, at (503) 667-3013.

14. Charles Colson, *Kingdoms in Conflict* (Grand Rapids, Mich.: Zondervan Publishing House, 1988), 102.

Appendix B

1. Virginia Ramey Mollenkott, "Reproductive Choice: Basic to Justice for Women," *Christian Scholar's Review*, March 1988, 291.

2. James Hoffmeier, *Abortion: A Christian Understanding* (Grand Rapids, Mich.: Baker Book House, 1987), 46, 50; Eugene Quay, "Abortion: Medical and Legal Foundations," *Georgetown Law Review* (1967):395, 420; Meredith G. Kline, *"Lex Talionis* and the Human Fetus," *Journal of the Evangelical Theological Society* (September 1977):200-201.

3. Lawrence O. Richards, *Expository Dictionary of Bible Words* (Grand Rapids, Mich.: Zondervan Publishing House, 1985), 156-157.

4. James Hoffmeier, ed., *Abortion: A Christian Understanding and Response* (Grand Rapids, Mich.: Baker Book House, 1987), 62.

5. John Jefferson Davis, *Abortion and the Christian* (Phillipsburg, N.J.: Presbyterian and Reformed, 1984), 52.

6. Kline, *"Lex Talionis,"* 193.

7. Hoffmeier, *Abortion,* 53.

8. See George Grant *Grand Illusions: The Legacy of Planned Parenthood* (Brentwood, Tenn.: Wolgemuth & Hyatt, 1988), 190-191.

9. Michael Gorman, *Abortion and the Early Church* (Downers Grove, Ill.: InterVarsity Press, 1982), 9.

10. John Calvin, *Commentary on Pentateuch,* cited in *Crisis Pregnancy Center Volunteer Training Manual* (Washington, D.C.: Christian Action Council, 1984), 7.

11. Dietrich Bonhoeffer, *Ethics* (New York: Macmillan, 1955), 131.

12. Karl Barth, *Church Dogmatics,* vol. 3, ed. Geoffrey Bromiley (Edinburgh: T & T Clark, 1961), 415, 418.

13. An excellent refutation of the various "Christian" prochoice arguments is made by philosophy professor Francis Beckwith in "A Critical Appraisal of Theological Arguments for Abortion Rights," *Bibliotheca Sacra* (July-Sept. 1991):337-355.

INDEX

ABOUT THE AUTHOR

Randy Alcorn has been involved in a wide range of prolife activities, including assistance to women victimized by abortion, prolife education, Crisis Pregnancy Centers, Life Chain, and peaceful intervention at abortion clinics. He is the founder and director of Eternal Perspective Ministries (EPM), a nonprofit organization dedicated to Christ-like intervention for the unreached, unfed, unborn, and other "unpeople" in dire need of advocacy and help.

Alcorn has written seven other books, including *Money, Possessions and Eternity, Deadline* and *Dominion*. He is a popular conference and seminar speaker both nationally and internationally. Randy and Nanci and their two daughters, Karina and Angela, live in Gresham, Oregon.

Inquiries concerning literature, newsletter, tapes, and speaking engagements may be directed to:

> Eternal Perspective Ministries
> 2229 East Burnside #23
> Gresham, Oregon 97030
> (503) 663-6481

You can send e-mail to ralcorn@epm.org or visit EPM's web site at http://www.epm.org/~ralcorn.